Cora Wilson Stewart and Kentucky's Moonlight Schools

Cora Wilson Stewart and Kentucky's Moonlight Schools

Fighting for Literacy in America

YVONNE HONEYCUTT BALDWIN

THE UNIVERSITY PRESS OF KENTUCKY

Publication of this volume was made possible in part by
a grant from the National Endowment for the Humanities.

Scholarly publisher for the Commonwealth,
serving Bellarmine University, Berea College, Centre
College of Kentucky, Eastern Kentucky University,
The Filson Historical Society, Georgetown College,
Kentucky Historical Society, Kentucky State University,
Morehead State University, Murray State University,
Northern Kentucky University, Transylvania University,
University of Kentucky, University of Louisville,
and Western Kentucky University.

Editorial and Sales Offices: The University Press of Kentucky
663 South Limestone Street, Lexington, Kentucky 40508–4008
www.kentuckypress.com

10 09 08 07 06   5 4 3 2 1

Photographs courtesy of University of Kentucky Special Collections and Archives.

Library of Congress Cataloging-in-Publication Data
Baldwin, Yvonne Honeycutt, 1947-
    Cora Wilson Stewart and Kentucky's moonlight schools : fighting for
literacy in America / Yvonne Honeycutt Baldwin.
        p.   cm.
    Includes bibliographical references and index.
    ISBN-13: 978-0-8131-2378-3 (alk. paper)
    ISBN-10: 0-8131-2378-X (alk. paper)
    1. Stewart, Cora Wilson, 1875–1958. 2. Educators—Kentucky—Biography.
3. Literacy—Kentucky—History—20th century. 4. Adult education—Kentucky—
History—20th century. I. Title.
  LA2317.S826B35 2006
  370.92—dc22   2005030638

This book is printed on acid-free recycled paper meeting
the requirements of the American National Standard
for Permanence in Paper for Printed Library Materials.

Manufactured in the United States of America.

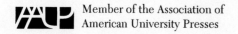 Member of the Association of
American University Presses

For my mother, Maudie Holloway Honeycutt,
a woman of courage, wisdom, and determination.
Words are not enough.

Contents

Photographs follow page 132

Preface

This book analyzes the life and work of Cora Wilson Stewart, a Progressive Era reformer who sought to eliminate adult illiteracy in a single generation, a goal she believed would also improve the quality of life in rural America. It illustrates both the strengths and the limitations of a grassroots movement, examines the politicization of the literacy crusade, and suggests that women's activism and the woman vote had important effects on male political culture. Prior to suffrage, Stewart's appeals for government aid evoked chivalrous attempts to "support" the reform agenda, generally with rhetoric and token legislation; however, after passage of the Nineteenth Amendment, male politicians granted Stewart only limited and conditional participation in politics and used both legislative maneuvering and access to the public purse to guard their own favored position in the polity.

This study attempts to capture the enigmatic southern progressive and feminist whose historic persona lingers in the shadows of relatively narrow analyses that judge her work based on the numbers of illiterates taught or the degree to which her crusade actually reduced illiteracy.[1] In the hope that both subjects will benefit from it, my work also seeks to establish Cora Wilson Stewart and the literacy campaign within the larger context of Progressive Era reform, a topic that defies precise definition and reflects broad interpretational debate among historians.[2]

Part of Stewart's importance as a historical figure lies in her attempt, like many progressives and most progressive women educators, to humanize the functions of developing education and social welfare bureaucracies even as they sought to strengthen them. Like many others set to this task, she failed, at least in the short run. Nevertheless, many of the critical elements of her philosophy and approach are embedded in current literacy and adult education policy and practice, which suggests that her vision for a literate public was insightful and even prophetic. However, her insistence on voluntary service and reliance on the "each one teach one" method not only gave legislators at all levels a convenient excuse to underfund the literacy initiative but also allowed educators who sought to limit teaching to credentialed and university-trained professionals to cast her as an antiprogressive holdover from a bygone day, a tactic they frequently used against women educators who rejected the corporate model of bureaucratization and centralization. Stewart as a historical figure, then, has suffered in a gendered double bind of time and circumstance, caught in her own life between tradition and modernism in a transitional age, and, in historical analysis, trapped by her legend and her "failure" to achieve her stated goal.

My conclusions are informed by interpretations that place Kentucky in the South and acknowledge its mountain counties as part of the social and physical construct known as Appalachia. I see Stewart as a southern reformer who embraced class-based ideals of uplift and progress that accepted, to some degree, the hierarchy of race and culture. What she did not accept was their permanence or inevitability. She believed in self-improvement as a means of eliminating such hierarchies, and she used education and the profession of teaching to blur those lines in her own life and to empower those who learned to read and write in her Moonlight Schools for adult illiterates.

I have taken a thematic approach in dealing with Stewart's networking, her attempts to secure state and federal support for adult literacy through legislation and appropriations, and her efforts to reshape and redirect the work of state and national education bureaucracies through campaigns at the local, state, national, and international level. I have, however, used the chronology of her life and work to organize these themes.

Whenever possible, I have used the language of the literacy movement itself. I chose to do this because it illustrates the rhetoric of faith, uplift, and progress that characterized much of Progressive Era reform, and because such rhetoric proved essential in garnering public and private support for multidimensional initiatives like the illiteracy crusade. The language of the time also gives voice to the movement's spirit and intent. Just as important, the original language enhances the understanding of public discourse in both politics and the education profession. Because I used oral histories to examine the legacy and memories of Cora Wilson Stewart, it seemed appropriate to treat her diaries, published and unpublished manuscripts, and even the newspaper clippings and magazine articles that she kept as a form of oral history or memoir. This approach connects the reader more intimately with Stewart and her times and provides a deeper understanding of how Kentuckians and Americans nearly a century ago attempted to deal with a social problem that continues to defy solution in our own time.

Introduction

Creating "Miss Cora"

Cora Wilson was born in 1875 in rural eastern Kentucky. The daughter of a schoolteacher and a physician, she grew up in fairly modest circumstances. In an era when education and economic or social status largely defined what a woman could and could not do, Cora attended normal school rather than a finishing school, and instead of completing a university degree, she took a job in a one-room school. Dictated by economic necessity and the realities of her life and family circumstances, these decisions later may have limited her ability to bring about change within her chosen profession, but they shaped Cora's choice of her life's work and guided her vision of the role of education in society.

Cora was born to parents who expected each of their children to "be somebody," and her whole life and body of work can be seen as an act of self-creation. From the age of four or five, when she declared her intention to be a teacher, through a career that lasted more than thirty years, Cora strove for perfection and accomplishment. Fifteen years younger than social reformer Jane Addams and eighteen years younger than muckraking author and journalist Ida Tarbell, her greatest heroes, Cora Wilson was part of a generation of reformers whose campaigns for woman suffrage and other reform issues broadened the public sphere and the horizons of women across the nation. Although she embraced the "new woman" ideal, she retained many traditional values. Schooled to selflessness and Christian service, she grew up thinking she had a mission in life, and once her vision of it emerged, she pursued it zealously.

In fact, once she recognized the extent of rural illiteracy, campaigning against it seemed the only moral thing to do. Other progressives throughout the South were waging war on the hookworm and the boll weevil, reforming women in northern and eastern cities were seeking to eliminate child labor, settlement house workers were attacking the social problems of immigrants, and others were campaigning for woman suffrage or temperance. Women of Stewart's generation took up a variety of causes, and although decades passed before historians acknowledged them, a large body of literature now documents their contributions to the Progressive Era and to American political culture.[1]

Stewart's native state of Kentucky was also home to the rural settlement school movement, which brought schooling to mountain children at Troublesome Creek's Hindman Settlement School and later saw others established at Pine Mountain and Caney Creek. Although a number of important differences exist between Stewart and the group locals often referred to as "fotched on" women, the outsiders who brought education to the mountains of southeastern Kentucky, they were remarkably similar in their approach, their views of the mountain people, and their shared faith in the ability of education to change lives.[2] They generally relied on the same groups of volunteers, employed the same rhetoric, and sought funding from the same philanthropic and charitable organizations. They could have learned much from one another, but little professional or personal interaction took place between Stewart and the settlement workers.[3]

Like her counterparts in mountain settlement school work, Cora Wilson Stewart possessed strong ambition and zealously promoted both the literacy cause and her role in it. During her thirty-year career, Cora enjoyed a measure of fame, some moments of high accomplishment and personal satisfaction, and a few moments of defeat and frustration. She embellished the former and attempted to minimize or even hide the latter, making her a historical enigma, a woman difficult to analyze and virtually impossible to categorize. She has been criticized for self-promotion and overstating the importance of the Moonlight Schools and her role in them, and ultimately her proclivity for self-promotion and her conscious effort to seek the limelight injured both her reputation with contemporaries and her historical legacy.[4]

Although some have questioned the efficacy of her crusade, Cora Wilson Stewart largely escaped the charges of cultural imperialism leveled at Katherine Pettit and May Stone for their work at the Hindman Settlement School, perhaps because she was a native of the region she sought to uplift.[5]

For the most part, Stewart has been romanticized as a hero whose selfless dedication to the Moonlight School movement made her a legend in her own time.

Stewart enjoyed the recognition, awards, and public accolades she won, took great pride in her leadership of the literacy movement, and even maintained fairly detailed records of her life and work. An avid writer, she kept a number of "diaries" that, at first glance, promise a wealth of information.[6] But careful reading of these handwritten records suggests that the author sought to create her own image and perhaps even her own history.

A few clues about her personality emerge from the scraps of paper and small notebooks in which she recorded her thoughts and experiences. She made lists of books to read, vocabulary words to master, and physical attributes and spiritual attitudes to assume. Her musings reveal a devout woman, deeply introspective, given to meditation and study, but they also reveal a stubborn streak and single-minded dedication to her cause. Stewart's correspondence reflects an innate ability to remain focused and dedicated to the task at hand despite occasional physical illness and fairly constant emotional stress. It also highlights remarkable organizational skill, insightful understanding of the male-dominated political process, and a personal charisma that attracted and held a devoted cadre of like-minded women and men. The records she left also reveal personal ambition and pride, traits that Cora Wilson Stewart did not want to see in herself and did not admire in others. When she ultimately recognized these traits, reflection led her to look back on her public and private life with more regret than she should have felt, for without them it is likely her crusade would have faltered in its infancy.

Cora's self-creation took a lifetime. Always a strong and resolute woman, she maintained her faith and independence until death at the age of eighty-three. Writing to her niece Marion McCrea, after having lost her eyesight, she dictated and a typist transcribed: "I never felt defeated or disparing [sic]. I set to work to make my adjustments, and to live my life with the use of the other senses and capabilities which I have. . . . If this affliction as to sight had to come to anybody in your generation or mine, I am glad it came to me, for I can take it, and can work despite it. I can even say of some who have sight, to quote John Milton, 'I would rather have my blindness than yours.'"[7]

As she looked back on her life, she wondered how history would treat her work and swelled with pride when the University of Kentucky expressed an interest in acquiring her papers. At age eighty she pieced together the collection that serves as the primary record of her life and the Moonlight School campaigns. With a ten-dollar gift from her niece Marion, she began the task of locating the missing pieces. "Who can say that we will not get the papers together for the [University of Kentucky]?" she wrote, detailing her attempts to locate "the important record" that included correspondence and copies of her books.[8]

Her personal correspondence is an important piece of the puzzle and reflects a strong devotion to her family. It shows that although she remained childless after the death of her son, she nurtured and encouraged the off-spring of her brothers and sisters through cards, letters, and visits. They reciprocated by encouraging and assisting her in her work and making a place for her in their homes whenever she needed rejuvenation and rest.[9] The correspondence is also important for what it does not say. Full of concern for those she cared about, she offered advice freely and urged high achievement, diligence, and hard work. But she rarely spoke of herself unless it was to rebuke some well-meaning brother who had tried once too often to give advice.

She was very close to her siblings, but Cora traveled frequently and often spent holidays and her own birthdays alone. Perhaps solitude inspired reflection because she habitually took up the pen on New Year's Eve and on her 17 January birthday, recording some of the year's events and setting goals for the year ahead. These notes and diaries provide insight into her personality, goals, dreams, and ambitions, but they are little more than pieces of a larger puzzle. Often self-promoting, her personal records raise the question of whether she revealed the truth about herself or whether she simply created an image for public consumption. Both Cora's presentation of herself in her diaries and other less biased accounts of her work also illustrate her commitment to self-improvement as a lifelong process. Although this is not an uncommon trait in middle-class Americans of any generation, it is important because it governed her thinking about herself and her work and ultimately shaped her approach to reform.

A devout and spiritual woman, Stewart cultivated a public image that was not only shaped by contemporary constructions of ideal behavior for women in public life but was also inspired by an ideal of service learned from her mother. Selflessness and commitment supposedly characterized women who chose such a life. Many of her contemporaries judged public women by the standard of Jane Addams, whom Stewart selected as a role model, calling her a "model in graciousness." She also idealized Ida Tarbell, whom she considered the greatest woman of her time.[10]

Historian Allen Davis postulates that the American public had need of a female saint, and that Jane Addams filled that role. Because people wanted to believe in that idealized image, she appeared to be a self-sacrificing spiritual leader, a kind of sage and priestess who dedicated her life to solving the human problems of an industrial society. Addams became "Saint Jane." The world reinterpreted her as a traditional woman and accepted her as the feminine conscience of the nation, thus blunting the edge of her criticism of American society. Although she rebelled against the stereotypical view of women as submissive, gentle, and compliant, she did not take a public stand against the stereotypes. It is clear that Addams helped create the public image of herself as a self-sacrificing saint rather than emphasizing her administrative skills and her ability to compete in a man's world.[11]

The same is true of Cora Wilson Stewart. Like Addams, Stewart enjoyed the support of loyal constituents, some of whom held traditional ideas about women and some who sought, through club work or teaching, to expand those narrow visions. And, as it did for Addams, the press assisted in Stewart's self-creation. She authored many of the early news releases herself, but soon journalists across the nation were telling the story of the Moonlight Schools. The leader of a romantic cause, a gracious and appealing woman, and an articulate and stirring public speaker, she made good copy. Perhaps with an eye toward posterity, Cora saved hundreds of newspaper and magazine clippings.

The correspondence, clippings, diaries, and documents open a window on Cora Wilson Stewart's public life, and her manuscript collection represents a remarkable public archive.[12] Nevertheless, her private life remains obscure. She assiduously guarded that part of herself, and therefore the papers she left reflect only what she chose to reveal. They do not mention important personal moments such as her marriages, divorces, or the birth and death of her only child. Documentation of these events is scant, and details must be patched together from family correspondence, obituaries, court records, and newspaper articles. Relatives remember her fondly and offer valuable insight into her family life and upbringing, but most of them were young when they knew their "Aunt Cora," and she did not share the details of her personal life with them. Numerous popular articles and retrospectives cloud the reality of her life, colored as they are by time, distance, and legend.[13]

Cora Wilson Stewart gained fame as the "Moonlight Lady" and attained almost legendary status in the eastern Kentucky of her birth. Her lengthy list of accomplishments includes two important firsts: she was the first woman elected superintendent of schools in Rowan County, and the first woman to serve as president of the Kentucky Education Association. She went on to head illiteracy commissions for the National Education Association (NEA) and the General Federation of Women's Clubs (GFWC) and presided over a number of national and international organizations to combat illiteracy. She accomplished much, but the record tells us little about what inspired her. What forces shaped her personal identity and life's work? How did she sustain her dedication and enthusiasm for the cause of illiteracy amid personal crises and vexing financial circumstances? To what extent was she shaped by the tradition of the southern lady and the times in which she lived? In an era when women could not vote, how did she negotiate the contested terrain of male politics and emerge with legislative support for her reform initiatives? Some of the answers to these and other questions lie in her early years in rural eastern Kentucky.

ONE

The Making of a Reformer

Born on 17 January 1875, on a small farm on the banks of Syc-amore Creek in rural Montgomery County, the sturdy, dark-eyed third child of Jeremiah Wilson and his twenty-five-year-old wife, Ann Halley Wilson, was said to be like her mother, although per-haps more headstrong.[1] Cora remembered her parents fondly, not-ing that they encouraged her love of reading and, despite modest financial circumstances, kept her supplied with books and maga-zines. Family stories describe Cora as a responsible and serious child whose mother trusted her with much of the care of her younger siblings, a responsibility she carried into adulthood.[2] Perhaps one of the most revealing clues to Cora's character is her childhood nick-name, "The General." Because she was so comfortable with orga-nizing and giving orders, Dr. Jeremiah Wilson adopted this pet name for Cora when his daughter was five or six years old. Her brothers often teased that she had been "born with her mind made up." At an early age, she declared her intention to become a teacher, like her mother. Her favorite activity was playing "school" in her backyard, where she supposedly made quite a show of dignity and efficiency, always insisting that her students call her "Miss Cora."[3] Like many legends, it is likely that these stories contain elements of the truth, and although they illustrate her calling to teaching and service as they were intended, they also reveal the degree to which even the young Cora knew her own mind.

Her mother, called Annie, was a strong and energetic woman who profoundly influenced her daughter. As a young woman, she attended public school and then secured a job as an elementary school teacher. After her father's death, she looked after his business interests and settled his estate. When she married Jeremiah Wilson, they made their home on the farm Ann had inherited. Although she had enjoyed a relatively privileged life prior to her marriage, Ann Halley quickly grew accustomed to the hard work rural life required. She became a strong partner in her marriage and supplemented the family income by teaching and assisting her husband in the operation of both a tavern and a general store. Ann served as postmistress of the small town of Percal for a time, and when her husband, a practicing physician, had to go to Louisville to meet new state requirements for a diploma at the Kentucky School of Medicine, she ran the family farm, even preparing "car loads of tan bark, peeled and sent to Louisville," to pay his expenses.[4]

Although Cora's mother shared some of the burden of family finances, child care took most of her time. Like many women of her generation, she gave birth with debilitating regularity and, like many mothers of her day, faced the incomparable sorrow of losing several children. Only seven of her twelve offspring survived to adulthood. In 1878 Cora's elder sister, five-year-old Viola, sickened and died. The loss weighed heavily on the Wilson family, and three days after burying their child, they moved to Cross Roads, now Farmers, in Rowan County.[5] There, Cora's brother Homer Lee was born in 1880. Twins, Preston Taulbee and Stella, followed two years later, and another set of twins, Cleveland and Hendricks, came in October 1884. Of the four, only Stella lived to adulthood. Another daughter, Flora, was born in the fall of 1886, and the youngest son, Glenmore Combs, in 1888.[6] By then hard work and childbirth had aged Cora's mother well beyond her nearly forty years.[7]

It is evident from her diaries and correspondence that Cora patterned herself after Ann Halley, whom she idealized as a figure of almost saintly proportions. She admired her mother's piety and devotion to God, her regular church attendance, and her "life of prayer and faith." Writing to her brother Homer the year she turned sixty-five, Cora praised her mother's energy, cheerfulness, and generosity of spirit. She recalled that "her teaching and helping to run the store . . . added much to the family income."[8] Certainly her mother's strength impressed Cora and increased her own tendency toward self-reliance. After her own marriage Cora shunned the role of stay-at-home wife and mother, focusing instead on her work.

Cora's diaries and letters indicate that the Wilsons were middle-class, hardworking, educated people who encouraged intellectual achievement and cultural awareness and valued education above all, save devotion to God. Cora, an avid reader, remembered a home filled with books, and when the family moved to Morehead, the county seat, they did so to afford the children access to a better school.[9] Located in northeastern Kentucky on the western edge of the Appalachian Mountains in the Cumberland-Allegheny Highlands, only about 32 percent of the county's land could be farmed. Corn was the main crop. Primary industries of stone, timber, and clay flourished after 1880 with the arrival of the Elizabethtown, Lexington and Big Sandy Railroad, but the timber was depleted by 1900.[10] Cora's own descriptions of her family's middle-class life, along with historic photographs and recollections of local people, show that life in Morehead, a thriving town whose economy included sawmills, spoke factories, stave mills, several saloons and hotels, and a wholesale grocery, was similar to life in small towns across the nation.[11] The photographs and descriptions differ significantly from the stereotypical representation of this part of the country as an area populated by isolated, ignorant, lawless, poverty-stricken hillbillies. Appalachian stereotypes overstated the isolation, homogeneity, and poverty of the region. Nevertheless, some of the popular press accounts contained at least a grain of truth. Roads were very poor, and schools were substandard when compared with those in the rest of the nation.[12]

Despite the shortcomings of public education in the region, Cora loved school. With her siblings, she attended a one-room country schoolhouse, later describing it as a "rather crude" facility offering classes only three months of the year. Constructed of logs, it had a dirt floor and no windowpanes.[13] In Cora's memory, the Wilsons' commitment to the education of their children set their family slightly apart from many of their neighbors, whose formal schooling was often sacrificed to the necessities of rural life. Many in eastern Kentucky had little or no education, and some believed book learning was totally devoid of practical value. Others simply valued the work their children could do at home over the education they could acquire at school. The hardships of mountain life led one young contemporary of Cora's to conclude that "such fellows as [he] were never intended to learn anything," a point of view shared by many rural mountain folk.[14]

Like many rural Appalachians, the Wilsons also possessed a strongly developed sense of tradition and place. They valued both the land and their heritage. In Cora this deeply felt sense of identification with the mountain region and its people, as they existed and as they were portrayed, shaped her ideas of self, her imagination, and the missionary rhetoric she used to promote the cause of literacy.[15] For example, when Stewart earned a humanitarian award in 1925, author Ida Clyde Clarke interviewed her for a feature in the magazine *Pictorial Review*. Cora's birth in a humble home in the mountains of Kentucky and her choice of a career in uplift formed grist for the mill of class-based benevolence rhetoric:

Her people belong to the oldest and best families in the Southern mountains.
. . . She comes of two of the oldest and best families in America, for the sub-
merged millions who live in the Southern Appalachian Mountains are "one-
hundred-percent Americans." Mrs. Stewart's mother was a Halley, and her
father's mother was a Lee, and anybody down there will tell you that the Halleys
and the Lees are of the bluest blood of the mountains. This means that for
generations they have perpetuated certain characteristics that have almost in-
variably marked them as outstanding men and women of their generation.[16]

Cora's mother had Halley blood, but her father was only distantly a Lee,
making her claim to the southern aristocracy somewhat weak. Nevertheless,
Cora was born slightly above the class she sought to uplift, and the distinction possessed some merit, particularly in the South. Southern women, regardless of race, were shaped by a shared regional heritage of both privilege
and oppression, but white middle-class women in particular emerged from
well-educated and influential domestic circles into patriarchal bureaucratic
systems tightly bound in traditional values. They had to find socially acceptable ways of interacting in those realities.[17]

Given her strong personality, love of learning, and experience in nurturing younger siblings, education presented a respectable and attainable career
in a time and place limited in options for women. It is not surprising that she
selected teaching as her life's work, since it was a frequent choice for women of
her generation, many of whom believed teaching was a form of religious, social, or political activism. Moreover, a career in education enabled women of
Stewart's generation to bring about change, whether for themselves as individuals, workers, or citizens or for their community or profession.[18]

Whatever role they chose, family background mattered in the lives of
southern female reformers. And whether they approached public work as a
duty or an opportunity, ancestral prominence and aristocratic connections
counted heavily. The family name of many socially concerned women assured their credibility and trustworthiness and helped deflect criticism. Prominence for women in the late nineteenth century generally depended on the
social standing of the woman's husband or father, but that changed as women
gradually attained prominence through individual distinction in professional
fields or public affairs.[19] Prominent women of Stewart's generation, regardless of what they accomplished in their own right, benefited from the wealth
and social standing of their ancestors. Such "Bluegrass blue bloods" as Laura
Clay and Madeline McDowell Breckinridge used "the trappings of class,
chivalry, and kinship networks" to attain their goals. Southern suffrage leaders came from prominent families, and even those who did not have wealth

claimed ancestral links to such families as the Jeffersons, Marshalls, and Lees.[20] While reform work satisfied Stewart's ambition and provided an outlet for her significant managerial and organizational skills, it also secured her claim to higher class. Like other American women who took up places in the new middle class, she used benevolence work to formalize her station.[21]

The Wilsons, though respected members of the community, were not wealthy. In fact, like most rural practitioners, "Dr. Jerry" was often paid for his services in barter. Patients offered chickens, hog meat, homegrown produce, or perhaps a service such as repairing a wagon wheel instead of cash for medical treatment.[22] The family was at least comfortable enough to afford domestic help for Mrs. Wilson, and Dr. Wilson employed a black hired hand named Cy. This occasioned frequent comment in Morehead, a small town that, like other non-coal-mining rural areas, had only a very small black population. A nephew recalled that Dr. Wilson frequently had to accompany Cy to town to protect him from local ruffians, and on more than one occasion he treated the hired man for injuries received at their hands.[23]

The Wilsons attended the Christian Church (Disciples of Christ), a denomination that encouraged and expected community involvement from its congregation. Through its affiliates, the Kentucky Christian Missionary Society, the Christian Woman's Board of Missions, and its own state board, the Christian Church in Morehead put its members to work in regional, national, and international mission support and outreach. Annie Wilson saw to it that her children served the community through the local church, a commitment that Cora and her siblings observed throughout their lives.[24]

Religion was important to Cora, and in 1924, as she approached the age of fifty, she wrote that even as a child she had sensed a special calling. As she matured, she came to believe that God had a mission for her. She went to pray and meditate in a special place she called a "prayer grove." When Cora was seven, and her seven-week-old brother, Cleveland, fell gravely ill, she called on God to save him, "going often to the grove in childish faith to . . . ask that his life be spared." Cora did not remember the death of her older sister, Viola, but her baby brother Cleveland's death devastated her. She wondered why he had been taken and not her, and later concluded that God had spared her because he had a special purpose for her.[25]

The religious atmosphere of her home and her mother's emphasis on hard work and achievement planted the seeds of an activist social conscience that drove Cora Wilson Stewart throughout her life. Coupled with her own intense desire to lead a spiritual life and to do what she considered God's will, she grew to adulthood with a strong moral imperative that developed into a sense of mission. Like the progressives identified by Robert M. Crunden in *Ministers of Reform,* her faith in God shaped her political and social conscience. Crunden analyzes the "conversion to social reform" experienced by Jane Addams, Ida Tarbell, William Allen White, and William Jennings Bryan, among others, and identifies commonalities in their upbringing, intellectual and psychological makeup, and career choices to inform his conclusions about the nature of progressivism.[26] Whether it was a similarity in backgrounds, interests, or simply a matter of fate, Stewart was drawn to all these individuals and ultimately enlisted the aid of each in her crusade against illiteracy.

Stewart's own "conversion" became a central part of a public image she created, at least in part, to justify her place in the reform movement and profession she had chosen. The idea of calling played heavily in the descriptions of public figures, including Cora's role model, Jane Addams, whose founding of Hull House in 1889 has been described as an "important cultural phenomenon" because of its influence on contemporary women.[27] Cora frequently told the story of her own inspiration to groups of volunteers and retold it in her memoir of the literacy crusade, *Moonlight Schools for the Emancipation of Adult Illiterates,* published in 1922. Biographical sketches, newspaper and magazine articles, and many of her public speeches relate a version of this same story in which she awakened to the need for literacy work because of conditions in her community. The need to act became imperative after three different neighbors came to her for help, each struggling in specific ways to cope with illiteracy.

The first was a mother whose children had all grown up unable to read or write until one enterprising daughter, Jane, went to Chicago, where she educated herself and began to write letters home. Her mother generally took the letters to Cora to read, but during one long spell when the "cricks were too high," she secured a speller and taught herself to read. Stewart quotes the mother, representing her mountain dialect in phonetic spelling (a common practice in the uplift literature of the time): "Hit jist seemed like thar was a wall 'twixt Jane an' me all the time," she said. Unable to bear the wall any longer, the mother taught herself to read and write.

This woman represents one of the most important elements of the illiterate constituency, the isolated rural mother separated from children driven away from home by economic necessity. Stewart wanted to enable them to communicate with their distant loved ones and also prepare them for the progress and change she thought both desirable and inevitable. Cora's second inspiration was a middle-aged man with a great deal of curiosity about the world. When Stewart offered to lend him a book he admired on her shelf, he tearfully refused. "I'd give twenty years of my life if I could read and write," he told her as he left her office, his "head bowed in shame." The man represents the idea that the people of her region were not ignorant by choice or as a result of laziness. Hardworking white Protestants, they were simply unschooled. The third was a young balladeer, known for his sweet voice and lovely renditions of mountain folk songs. Stewart offered him some sheet music and told him he should set his own tunes to paper, only to find that he was in the same "pitiful" condition as the others.[28] These tales, whether symbolic or real, illustrate the centrality of calling on two levels. Not only was it an accepted and even expected aspect of women's career choices in Progressive Era America, but in Stewart's case, it shows the Moonlight campaigns were always about more than simple literacy skills.

The sense of calling that became an important element in her professional identity also reflected her relationship with her father. Biographical material and local accounts of her youth indicate that Cora accompanied "Dr. Jerry" on his rounds in the community, encountering the poverty and illiteracy that characterized much of the region. As she and her father visited in their homes, patients who could not read often asked her to read letters and documents to them. These experiences, she said, illustrated to her the value of education; but just as important, they secured a place for her in the community. Her father was well liked and enjoyed a congenial relationship with most of the county's residents. By association, Cora became someone they knew and could trust as well.[29]

Cora's public image evolved over time, and both her parents and her Lee-Halley ancestry contributed to that evolution. Her mother's reputation in the community gave Cora a claim to piety and goodness that added dimension to her reforming image, while her father's healing power imbued her with public presence, perhaps even the ability to do benevolence work in a community that might otherwise have rejected her. These inheritances assured the young woman a favored position in the community. Stewart's strong sense of calling and her idealistic conceptualization of herself in the role of the southern lady helped create a theoretical and social position from which she could attempt to "heal" the "disease" of illiteracy, a position that was both shaped and embraced by mediated ideals of womanhood.

Cora's heritage and upbringing were important elements of her self-creation and helped define the course her career would take. So, too, did the times. Eastern Kentucky had become famous as the home of "contemporary ancestors," allegedly living in the "land that time forgot."[30] Appalachia's literary image captured the nation's attention as schoolmen and journalists exposed the realities and unrealities of a complex region in the simplest and boldest of terms.[31] Author Durwood Dunn notes in the foreword to the 1998 reprint of Gordon McKinney's classic, *Southern Mountain Republicans, 1865–1900: Politics and the Appalachian Community,* that the older works shaped an enduring image of the region in the American mind. Just as important, he says, they even "helped shape the people of the region's own image of themselves."[32] These literary images permeated Stewart's descriptions of the educational needs of eastern Kentucky and played a critical role in the creation of her public identity. They brought both publicity and financial backing and caused the nation to embrace the cause of Moonlight Schools for rural adults.

Although the isolation, homogeneity, and resistance to change of the region have been overstated, modernization came slowly to this part of the upper South, and bloodshed often accompanied change. Violence in the mountain areas was no more pervasive or destructive than the various riots, strikes, and other civil disturbances that troubled urban areas, but the popular press sensationalized it and characterized it as endemic. The high homicide rate, frequent coverage in the *New York Times* and *Chicago Tribune,* along with a growing body of local color literature, significantly influenced public perception of the region.[33]

Literary depictions of the isolated, backward mountain people created the myth of a peculiarly violent, ignorant, and poverty-stricken area, the darker side of which emphasized lawlessness and mayhem. However, a somewhat more benign but equally inaccurate image proliferated as well. Designed primarily to characterize the mountaineers as sturdy, hardworking, worthy recipients of the dollars being doled out by northern philanthropists in the name of benevolence, denominational missionary literature portrayed them as Anglo-Saxon Protestants who represented all that was good in the nation's past. The antithesis of urban immigrants, working-class poor, and blacks, these Americans were said to be religious, truthful, and hospitable, even if some were much addicted to killing one another.[34] Whether definitions of Appalachian distinctiveness relied on geographic isolation or on the mythology of the region's Elizabethan heritage, mountain folk emerged as elements out of time, dependent on missionaries and philanthropists for their salvation and modernization. And whatever else they might be, the mountain people were white.[35]

These mythical constructions of Appalachia played an important role in Stewart's career. As Karen Tice has shown, education reformers like Stewart faced "pressures to evoke such stereotypes, especially in publicizing their efforts to a wider American public and soliciting financial support."[36] In Stewart's home county, the violent and debilitating Martin-Tolliver feud, also called the "Rowan County War," added to the region's notoriety. The bloodiest feud in the state's history, it surpassed even the Hatfield-McCoy vendetta in numbers of dead. Like Berea College president William Goodell Frost and other purveyors of missionary education in the mountains, Cora used that notoriety to further the campaign against illiteracy. Her depictions of the feuds added romance and excitement to her own past, making her a more dramatic and colorful speaker. More important, she took advantage of these tales as publicity devices and used them to illustrate how desperately the mountaineers needed the reforms she advocated.

The characterization of Appalachian illiterates as victims served another purpose. In addition to striking a resonant chord with prospective patrons and philanthropists, it allowed Stewart to fulfill the benevolent role of her class and gender by rescuing those who, through no fault of their own, suffered from the affliction of illiteracy. Moonlight Schools enabled them to move out of their "darkness and isolation" and equipped them for participation in modern society, in effect transporting them from the dark days of the feudist and moonshiner into middle-class American life through the vehicle of the Moonlight Schools.[37]

The Rowan feud, which began when Cora was nine years old, left a profound mark on her imagination. It colored her perceptions of her region and shaped her opinion of its residents and their needs. She told her audiences she grew up in a "feud county" and often emphasized the difference the literacy crusade made in her "feud damaged" community. She often quoted the old "Moonlighter," who said: "Things certainly have changed in this district. It used to be that you couldn't hold meeting or Sunday school in this house without the boys shooting through the windows. It used to be moonshine and bullets, but now it's lemonade and Bibles."[38]

Her own childhood experience in the Rowan County War and the rhetoric of benevolence work and education shaped her understanding of the mountain people's circumstances and environment and led her to invoke their colorful past as she promoted the literacy campaigns, claiming that Moonlight Schools had taken them from lawlessness to order and from sin to salvation. That these descriptions of the rural night schools contributed to strengthening the stereotypes Stewart abhorred is one of the ironies of the literacy crusade.

Rhetorical representation of the mountain region and its people had consequences. "Writing and description are political acts," argues Karen Tice, and mountain settlement workers addressed a public familiar with the literary stereotypes who expected them as a frame of reference. At the same time, reformers addressed the community they sought to uplift and could ill afford to alienate by condescension or ridicule. Many in rural uplift work shared this classic quandary: "Perhaps in real life Lizzie Ann is no longer barefooted, but if we show a picture of Lizzie Ann wearing shoes and stockings, it is doubtful whether she will appeal so greatly to the hearts of those on whose gifts the work depends."[39] Stewart believed education had already changed the region and that Moonlight Schools could improve people's lives, especially if they embraced the idea that community betterment could be accomplished by social intervention.

Stewart also capitalized on the feud experience in another way, using it as a theme in the fiction writing she did to earn extra money. Her short story "The Rowan County War" appeared in a 1902 edition of *World Wide Magazine* under the pen name Edward T. Moran. The pen name protected her identity in a county that has always preferred not to discuss the feud either publicly or privately. Two later stories, "The Feud of Fire" and "How the Feudist Was Captured," both written under her own name, romanticized and sanitized the conflict but did not depict the mountaineers as ignorant, violent, gun-toting moonshiners. Instead, both reflected her understanding of the feud as a political conflict, exacerbated by familial ties, nineteenth-century concepts of honor, and government interference, all more palatable themes for middle-class eastern Kentuckians offended by the ignorant hillbilly stereotype and the constant negative attention of the popular press.[40]

A blood feud no doubt represented high adventure to an imaginative child like Cora, especially because she knew most of the participants. She recalled that Boone Logan, who lost two brothers in the feud and finally marshaled the forces that ended the "war," was her first teacher, and that Craig Tolliver, the leader of the opposite faction, held her on his knee when she was a girl and sang mountain ballads to her. Despite their acquaintance with many of the participants, her family did not take sides, although her father was frequently called to treat the wounded.[41]

Hostilities had erupted into open warfare on an August election day in 1884 when old political rivalries ignited in a shooting incident that left one man dead and another severely wounded. Authorities never positively determined who did the shooting, but relatives and supporters of two families, the Martins and the Tollivers, lined up on either side of the issue until virtually the entire county, including reinforcements from some adjoining counties, were involved. Outbreaks of violence over the next three years wounded sixteen people and killed more than twenty, but law enforcement officials failed to secure a single conviction for murder, manslaughter, or assault. Children feared the walk to school, local churches locked their doors, and rural people remained indoors, particularly at night. Finally the Kentucky General Assembly revoked Morehead's city charter because local law enforcement officials had failed to bring peace to the region and the perpetrators to justice.[42] The feud finally ended in June 1887 in a two-hour gun battle that killed Craig Tolliver and several of his family members and supporters. In the once-booming town of Morehead many businesses failed, and the population declined from 700 in 1885 to 296 in 1887.[43]

They had not taken sides, but like many families in the county, the Wilsons longed for the feuding to end and volunteered to do their part when the Kentucky Christian Missionary Society, an affiliate of the Christian Church, decided to send a missionary to Morehead. Conditions were so bad that the group debated whether to send the gospel or the militia, but it concluded that a mission school was the best way to fight the "feuding sin." Prominent churchman and former Confederate general William T. Withers contributed $500 toward establishing a school at Morehead, hoping that education would end the political and economic causes of the violence. The Christian Woman's Board of Missions (CWBM), on which Cora's mother served, provided moral support and additional funds. The board called for someone to lead a mission school in Morehead, someone who could teach as well as spread the gospel to the "uncivilized mountaineers." Phoebe Button and her son Frank answered the call.[44]

Three months after the shootout, the first students entered Morehead Normal, which required daily church attendance in addition to the academic curriculum.[45] Local residents generally credited the school that later became Morehead State University with ending the feuding.[46] Whether or not it actually did, this belief mythologized the feud experience and promoted the idea that education fostered radical change, a lesson that was not lost on young Cora Wilson, who was twelve years old the year the institution was founded and the Rowan County War ended.

The Rowan conflict was only one of many feuds that rocked the mountains in the 1880s and 1890s, and their bloody legacy, combined with political assassination, vigilantism, and racial violence after the turn of the century, convinced residents of the state and much of the rest of the nation that Kentucky was a dangerous place. The state's homicide rate was among the highest in the nation, and what some have called a "subculture of violence" permeated the state, producing aggressive behavior that met only limited resistance from law enforcement agencies and legal authorities. Sensationalized in the *New York Times* and other newspapers and popular magazines, the state's image as a "dark and bloody ground" hindered economic growth and development.[47]

Feuding was only one of the problems eastern Kentucky faced in the opening decade of the twentieth century. Poor roads, the exploitation of land and labor by timber and mining companies, political corruption, and substandard education loomed as the region faced an uncertain future. But the winds of change were blowing, and across America feminine reformers entered public life in unprecedented numbers as more and more educated women found ways to put their knowledge and expertise to work for the public good. The emerging progressive belief that local, state, and national governments were bound to serve and take care of their citizens enabled them to step out of the domestic circle into the wider world of politics and reform.[48]

Cora Wilson, like most women of her time and place, held many of the traditional values and principles of her region and sex. Born into a world in which women nurtured and men protected, she heard men preach and watched women fill the church pews. In religious benevolent associations, men often held the paid jobs and positions of official leadership while women taught the Sunday school classes and formed auxiliary associations. As women gained experience, they sought independence and additional responsibilities within the church structure. The CWBM, which claimed the service of all the Wilson women, ran Morehead Normal for more than twenty years. Cora served as district director for many years and through her contacts with the group secured both moral and financial support for public school improvement and in the crusade against illiteracy.[49]

The CWBM and organizations like it reinvigorated missions in Appalachia. By 1907 more than five hundred students attended the school at Morehead, and more than three hundred boarded at Hazel Green, a nearby mission school. Mission school advocates believed boarding schools rather than public day schools provided the best means of educating rural children because unfordable creeks, a lack of bridges, poor or nonexistent roads, and constant flooding created an environment in which day schools could not flourish.[50] In some of the more isolated areas, mission schools provided the only instruction available to school-age children. Women, with financial assistance from northern philanthropists, provided critical leadership in these institutions.[51]

Cora learned from the mission school phenomenon. Her memories of the Rowan County feud and her perception of the mission school's influence on the region shaped her professional identity, colored her understanding of eastern Kentucky's problems, and offered an important context for understanding her world. Thus Cora's upbringing, Christian faith, and belief in the power of education to change lives translated into a sense of calling, and her environment provided a ready-made mission field.

Cora Wilson stepped into that field in 1890 at age fifteen as a teacher in a one-room school. Only one year older than the school's oldest pupil, she had no formal training other than her own public school education. Despite its reliance on young classroom teachers with only common school diplomas, Kentucky surprisingly occupied a respectable position compared with other southern states. In 1900 it ranked fourth in per-pupil expenditure and third in average length of school term with more than 115 days, and it was the only southern state with a compulsory education law. In 1904 the state lengthened the school term from five to six months, but education gradually lost ground in succeeding years in the face of public opposition to the mandatory reduction of the child workforce. Although the commonwealth fared reasonably well in comparison to other southern states, support for public schools in the South lagged far behind the national norm, and, per pupil, Kentucky spent only about half the national average.[52]

In a part of the country where "antiquated social institutions protruded like primeval rock from smooth pavement to obstruct the traffic of progress," 50 percent of all blacks and 20 percent of all whites could neither read nor write. Segregation meant the additional expense of two separate school systems for the two races, with two corps of teachers and two sets of physical equipment. Not all communities enjoyed access to schools, and children often walked several miles in a region that was 80 percent rural. School met only three or four months of the year in many parts of the South and served little more than half the eligible school population. In addition, only a small portion of the tax dollar in that region supported public education, ensuring a pitifully low per-pupil expenditure. Rural areas simply lacked the tax base required to sustain the growing needs of the public education system.[53] In Kentucky, fifteen cities raised $600,000 per year for a school population of 150,000, while the rest of the state, with four times the number of pupils, raised less than half that amount. Funding in the state's poorest counties remained low.[54] In addition, localism drove school administration in Kentucky as it did in most of the nation.[55] Because policy mandated a district wherever up to one hundred school-age children lived, the state had eighty-five hundred districts. Three elected trustees, at least a fifth of whom could neither read nor write, administered these districts. Corruption, job selling, nepotism, and incompetence assured that many school districts in the state operated as little more than minor political fiefdoms. Rural school districts, in particular, suffered from poor funding. Their one- and two-room buildings were often drafty, poorly constructed, inadequately equipped, and uncomfortable.[56]

Poor funding kept teacher salaries low; consequently, when Cora Wilson entered the classroom in 1890, women dominated the profession, especially at the elementary level. By 1900, two out of three professional women were teachers, and three out of four teachers were women.[57] Elected school board officials rarely paid teachers more than minimal wages and generally refused to grant professional status to the men and women who taught their children. Women typically earned only half as much as male teachers.[58] Both were in short supply in rural and mountain areas such as Morehead, and even when they could find qualified teachers, local trustees often caved in to political pressure and chose poorly trained or even untrained local candidates over more qualified applicants from outside the district.[59] A contemporary observer noted that rural mountain schools were often "cousined to death."[60]

But Cora Wilson wanted to be a teacher, and she began as many young teachers in the one-room schools of the South did—"apprenticed" to an experienced teacher, the Reverend J. R. Powers in the Morehead Public School. She also enrolled at Morehead Normal, where she secured a teaching certificate in two years. Between public school sessions, she attended the National Normal University in Lebanon, Ohio. At age eighteen, Cora accepted a teaching position at Morehead Normal, but she left it two years later to return to public school work, where she remained for almost five years. She found the work stimulating and interesting and earned rapid promotions, going from primary to intermediate grades and then becoming principal of the school at Morehead. "That was all one could achieve in the school where one started," she noted.[61]

Women of Cora's generation entered the profession at a time of increased opportunity for female educators. Women not only dominated teaching in the early decades of the twentieth century but also attained school leadership positions in unprecedented numbers. Since Ella Flagg Young's election as superintendent of the Chicago city schools made her the first woman in the country to hold such a powerful executive position, thousands of women took on leadership roles in school systems, large and small.[62] In the South, educational leadership often required improvisational or intuitional action, since support networks were eclectic and diffuse and institutional support virtually nonexistent. Some scholars have argued that differences between male and female administrative styles better equipped women to cope in these kinds of environments, and they maintain that female pedagogy and leadership were less authoritarian and more democratic, less focused on abstract goals and more concerned with the humane elements of relationships and growth. According to this interpretation, these qualities placed them at odds with the male-defined model of school administration that emerged in the early decades of the twentieth century.[63] While there is some truth to this argument, it is equally likely that ideas of fairness combined with strong personalities to cause resentment against male-dominated leadership, and that female classroom teachers learned practical and pragmatic problem-solving and networking skills at the point of contact, making administrative plans and oversight if not irrelevant, at least moot.

Cora Wilson was ambitious, energetic, and determined. Teaching and school leadership empowered her, as they did many women of her generation. Despite low salaries and lack of professional prestige, the women and men with whom she interacted valued their work and encouraged one another. One of the most influential and powerful educators in the region, Frank C. Button, mentored Cora, and for some years she and two close friends boarded in his home. The first principal of the Morehead Normal School and minister at the First Christian Church, he had recruited her to teach at Morehead Normal.[64] Cora was a friendly and outgoing young woman whose warm personality and interest in people endeared her to local school trustees and family acquaintances. Through these associations she began to understand the problems and needs of her rural neighbors but also to respect their independence, resourcefulness, and pride.[65]

In 1895, at age twenty, Cora married Ulysses Grant Carey, but unlike most young women of her time, she continued to teach. Little is known about this marriage, but when it ended in divorce in June 1898, Cora reclaimed her maiden name.[66] She also enrolled at the Commercial College of Kentucky University in Lexington. At that time many single women were taking jobs as typists and stenographers. Jobs requiring this new skill often paid more than public school teaching, so it is likely that Cora made the move for that reason. Within a year, she accepted a faculty position there and became the school's first female instructor.[67]

In August 1900 Cora was called home to care for her seriously ill mother, who died shortly after Cora's return to Morehead. A long illness, probably tuberculosis, claimed Annie, and her death left Cora and her family devastated.[68] As the eldest daughter, Cora felt responsible for helping her younger brothers and sisters finish their schooling. Using the skills she had learned at the Commercial College to secure secretarial employment with a lumber company in Huntington, West Virginia, and with help from brothers Clefford and Bunyan, she undertook the financial responsibility and care of the three younger siblings. Although her father was still living, he "courted" several women during this time, and Cora took considerable exception to his remarriage in 1902, perhaps because her new stepmother, at nineteen, was eight years her junior.[69]

Her mother's death and Cora's sense of obligation to her family may have caused her to reconsider what she wanted in life. In 1901, twenty-six-year-old Cora left the job in Huntington to return to Morehead, where she became a candidate for county school superintendent. This was a unique opportunity, one her county had never extended to a woman. Her brother Bunyan Spratt Wilson, after graduating first in his class at the University of Louisville College of Law, had assumed an active role in local and state Democratic politics. He was Morehead's first mayor, and although it would be erroneous to assume that Cora rode to office on his political coattails, his contacts were no doubt important in both her nomination and her election.[70]

Political power was still hotly contested in Rowan County, and although disputes were no longer settled with bullets, Cora's election was hardly a foregone conclusion. Claiming to have the best interests of Rowan's school-children at heart, she waged an energetic campaign against a Republican opponent. She won the backing of several local newspapers as the "Children's Friend." Cora's connections with the public schools and Morehead Normal served her well, and she won her first election by a comfortable margin.[71]

Although it was a definite step up for a teacher, at the time of Cora's election as county superintendent, holding that office required only a state diploma, a state certificate, or a special certificate. A state diploma covered some high school subjects and was considered superior to the state certificate, but the special certificate signified little more than the completion of common-school subjects.[72] County superintendents often were not educators but ministers or businessmen devoting most of their time to other interests. Unlike such part-time administrators, Cora literally worked day and night, and her activism stood in stark contrast to those superintendents with no real interest in education. Often such men were chosen less for their ability than because they were "the only men to be had at the price fixed by law." The price fixed by law in Rowan County was $500 per year, to which was added $104.40, Cora's salary for teaching.[73] As superintendent, she supervised four educational divisions with fifty-two subdistricts (fifty-one white, one black) and fifty-eight teachers (thirty-three male, twenty-five female). Cora's report for 1910 showed that the average per capita expenditure per child was $4.36, one-fifth the national average.[74]

While Cora was the first female elected Rowan County superintendent, the position afforded women in Kentucky who met specific literacy requirements rare access to elected office at a time when they could not vote. Some twenty women filled county slots statewide. By 1914, a total of 495 females held elected county superintendencies in the United States, nearly double the number at the turn of the century. In the commonwealth, women did not gain the vote until the ratification of the Nineteenth Amendment in 1920, but if they met educational requirements, single women and widows with school-age children had been able to cast ballots in school board elections since Kentucky voted limited school suffrage for women in 1912.[75]

Upon election to the presidency of the National Education Association in 1911, Ella Flagg Young, the superintendent of Chicago's city schools, claimed that women would become key leaders in public education. Although Young's prophecy was not fulfilled, women teachers in several major cities had begun to protest the domination of top administrative positions and professional associations by men and the higher salaries male teachers received.[76] The number of women holding these offices increased, but only temporarily, since male professionals soon began to lobby for the replacement of elected positions with appointed "professionals" trained in men's postsecondary institutions.[77]

As superintendent, Stewart forged strong friendships and established valuable professional connections with many of the state's school superintendents. Her circle of friends also included Mattie Dalton, a staff writer and editor who worked for Rice Eubanks editing the *Southern School Journal,* the official organ of the Kentucky Education Association. Dalton often criticized the male professional hierarchy in long, advice-filled letters that strongly influenced Cora in her career choices and political decisions. Dalton introduced her friend to Nannie Faulconer, the superintendent of schools in Lexington, and to other female educators throughout the state. She also prodded Cora into a friendship with a young man named Nat Sewell, who later became a state examiner and important political ally. Dalton's insistence that Cora write a regular column for the journal provided statewide visibility for her protégé.[78] These friendships connected Cora to some of the state's most influential people, brought her into the politics of education, created a constituency that supported and assisted her work, and formed a base for her political connections and influence. Over time, it became obvious to local and state politicians that she represented two developing constituencies, teachers and women, and support from both groups was important to both political parties.

Within two years of her election, colleagues urged her to run for state superintendent of public instruction. Superintendent D. F. Gray, of Elliott County schools, wrote to her in August 1910, saying, "It would be real nice to have one of our home county girls at the head of the educational affairs of our state and I hope you will not hesitate to take advantage of any opportunity that may come your way."[79] Women were ineligible, however, and in a letter to Button, Cora requested that he get her brother Bunyan "to have someone introduce a resolution to the constitution permitting a woman to hold the office of State Superintendent." "Now Brother Button, please have him attend to this at once," she wrote, "and if he forgets it, jog him up again. Also, I want some information on the good roads measures before the General Assembly."[80] Avidly interested in local and state political issues, Stewart cultivated many political friendships, including with James B. McCreary, U.S. senator and twice governor of Kentucky.[81]

An activist superintendent, Cora broke precedent to open the office every day and to regularly visit each of the county's fifty-two schools. She aroused public interest in the physical condition of the schools, persuading school trustees and parents to spruce them up, repair windows and doors, and beautify the exteriors. She even renovated the superintendent's office, although this was done at her own expense.[82]

A frequent speaker at civic, church, and professional meetings, she touted the benefits of "modern" civilization, trying always to convince her audiences of the importance of formal education and to urge them toward her vision of progress for the county. Her lectures and speeches offer hints of the reform agenda that was soon to emerge, and her views, which found expression in speeches to local gatherings, are an important part of her developing professional identity. She rejected media depictions of mountain people as lazy and lawless hillbillies, seeing them instead as victims of their environment. In her talks, she praised their moral character, pride, and devotion to hard work, even as she lamented their endemic isolation and ignorance, twin problems exacerbated by the feud experience and the advent of industrialization.

The "Mountain Jewels" speech, first delivered at Soldier, Kentucky, in 1902, became one of her most popular orations. In it she condemned the poverty and lack of educational opportunity in the region. Mountain children were, in reality, "rough gems, needing only the polish of education." Her words echoed the uplift rhetoric of the time and cast eastern Kentuckians as a "people of arrested civilization . . . a noble people" who possessed great intelligence and an insatiable desire for knowledge. They constituted "a buried treasure of citizenship richer far than [Kentucky's] vast fields of coal, its oil, its timber or mineral wealth."[83] Mountain children were pure of heart, their minds "fresh and vigorous," she said. But opportunity eluded them. Short school terms, the frequent change of teachers, and the "poverty of parents in some cases and criminal negligence in others have combined to rob our precious jewels of the continuous advancement enjoyed by others."[84]

In this address, "Miss Cora," the respectable schoolmarm, with just a hint of "the General" that her father had identified, encouraged fathers to eschew alcohol and mothers to improve their minds. "How important it is that the mother be cultured," she intoned, as she recommended that instead of gossiping or discussing trivial affairs, women at home devote their spare moments to reading the *Ladies' Home Journal* or *Twentieth Century Home*. They could take up "nature study or ornithology" or some other interest, and no doubt be surprised at "how much culture they could take on in a year."[85]

Perhaps from her somewhat contrived position as a southern lady, she had not realized that reading *Ladies' Home Journal* was simply not an option for illiterate women living in the mountains of eastern Kentucky. Even if they had been able to read, such magazines probably had little applicability to their lives. However, just as women reformers in the cities tried to remake working-class mothers in their own middle-class image, urging them to accept ties to home and children that reformers themselves often rejected, Cora sought to impose common middle-class ideals of Victorian family life on her rural neighbors. Like her counterparts in the city, Cora's conceptualization of the home and family was traditional, middle-class, and often far removed from the lives of those she sought to uplift, but as she matured and gained experience, she lost much of the condescension and insensitivity that marked this and a few other early speeches. Nevertheless, as her crusade against illiteracy developed, the image of the genteel schoolmarm dispensing knowledge, culture, and middle-class values endured.

The "Mountain Jewels" speech is important for its rhetorical value but also because it indicates her priorities and sets the course for her work. It also reflects Cora's traditional understanding of the role of the school and the teacher in society, a role that profoundly shaped her reform vision and self-creation, for since the days of Catherine Beecher, the ideal schoolteacher had instilled the values of neatness, order, and thrift; introduced her pupils to the broader culture of learning; inspired the principles of morality; and modeled Christian virtue.[86] In typical Progressive Era fashion, Cora extended that role into the home by informing parents that they, in partnership with the schools, were responsible for what their children became. Given her emphasis on the importance of the parental role, it is easy to see how the "children's friend" focused her attention on educating illiterate adults. If they were to value education in the lives of their children, parents first had to see its importance in their own.

Because of her intense devotion to her work, Cora's professional life took precedence over her private life, but she still found time for family and friends. Her modest salary provided for her own needs and enabled her to assist younger siblings toward self-sufficiency or marriage. Always well groomed and as well dressed as her pocketbook would allow, she walked with her shoulders back and her head held high. A handsome, "classy" woman, she met the camera's eye with a steady and composed demeanor. Still single at age twenty-nine, Cora was strongly independent, but she was also witty and likable.[87] In her day, unmarried women in their twenties became "old maids" who were expected to devote their lives to caring for other people's children. In fact, women in education remained unmarried to a larger extent than women in other fields. Only 40 percent of female educators of that time married at all, and of them, only 25 percent had children. Moreover, nearly 18 percent of the marriages of career women ended in divorce, a rate two and a half times the national average.[88]

Cora was not a spinster, however. After a brief courtship, she married Alexander T. Stewart, a schoolteacher several years her junior. The couple married on 24 September 1902, but divorced on 7 March 1904. They remarried in June of that same year, but the second attempt was no more successful than the first. Alexander, known as A.T., was moody and often drank heavily, a situation Cora simply "would not tolerate." The situation worsened over time, and he began to abuse his wife both verbally and physically.[89]

The abuse worsened, finally reaching the point where Cora feared for her life. Following an incident in which she alleged that her intoxicated husband broke into her house, "burst open the door" of the room where she and her sister were sleeping, and threatened to shoot her with a pistol, she petitioned the court for protection. She was convinced that her husband intended to make good on his threats to kill her, and perhaps himself. Although much of the abuse took place when he was intoxicated, Cora charged that "his cruelty is not confined to his drunken hours [and his] vengeful nature is manifested without regard to his condition as to liquor." Depositions of her sister and a neighbor support Cora's claims of brutality and drunkenness.[90]

In her petition against A.T., Cora alleged that the abuse had gone on for nearly five years. If that is so, it had begun before the birth of the couple's only child, William Halley Stewart, who was born in August 1907 and died ten months later. Cora also charged that her husband had failed to "seek or carry on any employment" and had for the last four years refused to "furnish her with any of the . . . necessities, or to aid her in making a living." She had even purchased their home with her own money, she said, "in her own separate right with legal title in herself." The wording of the divorce petition and the various affidavits associated with it indicate that the couple's marital problems, although perhaps exacerbated by the death of their child, may have resulted from Cora's status as a working wife. A.T. may have resented her work because it kept her from her household duties, and he may have believed her job infringed on his role as sole breadwinner. He may also have resented her prominence in the community and felt inadequate by comparison, hence his failure to hold a job or contribute to her support.[91]

Although many respected and admired her work, after her marriage and particularly after the birth of her child, some in the small town of Morehead criticized Cora for being a "working woman."[92] Possibly as a result of this criticism and her husband's wishes that she devote more time to domestic pursuits, she did not stand for reelection as county superintendent in 1905. She did not give up her work, however. Instead she accepted frequent speaking engagements and organized teacher training institutes throughout the state. She also served as principal of the Morehead Public School (1906–7) and the model school at Morehead Normal (1908).[93] When she gained reelection as county school superintendent in November 1909, the marriage had probably deteriorated beyond repair, but her choice to resume such a demanding job may have hastened the end. The divorce decree, granted in June 1910, faulted A. T. Stewart for his "habit of drunkenness" and the "wasting of his estate" in his failure to provide for his wife.[94] Following the divorce, an important element of her self-creation emerged. Despite the unhappiness of her marriage, Cora chose to retain her former husband's name and was known for the rest of her life as Cora Wilson Stewart. Perhaps she wanted the world to recognize that she was not an "old maid."[95]

For her, as for many others, the tension between family and career caused intense personal conflict. After the death of her son, private criticism escalated to public gossip, with many people in the county chastising her for not devoting her full time and attention to her home and child. The visibility of her job and the size of the community no doubt intensified the scrutiny. Devastated by the loss of her young son, bitter about the criticism but determined to ignore it, she plunged herself even more deeply into her work.[96]

It is significant that no diary entries or correspondence records the death of her child; only the obituary clipped from a newspaper notes the cause of death as "three fatal diseases."[97] Given the fairly frequent references to the deaths of siblings, her mother, and later her father, the omission probably indicates the episode was simply too painful to recall. In the wake of her loss, Cora embarked upon a grueling schedule of professional, church, and civic activities that occupied every waking hour. It was work she loved, and perhaps the frenetic pace dulled the ache of private pain.

Cora's rhetorical skills had made her one of the most sought-after institute speakers in Kentucky, and since teacher training institutes were held annually in most districts, she kept busy. Superintendents and school administrators who heard her heartily recommended her to their colleagues, and soon she had more requests than she could handle. Although she may not have been fully aware of it at the time, these connections, particularly with women teachers and school administrators, formed the basis of a critical mass of volunteers who later assisted her in teaching illiterates in her home state and elsewhere. In addition, this constituency helped make her a powerful woman in political circles, particularly once woman suffrage passed. Conducting institutes also had the practical benefit of supplementing her salary. She received between thirty and fifty dollars per session, plus reimbursement for travel and lodging.[98]

The institutes also enabled her to expand her acquaintances with prominent educators in the state. She formed a lasting friendship with Dr. John Grant Crabbe, Kentucky's progressive superintendent of public instruction, to whom she often turned for advice and encouragement.[99] Like Button and Stewart, Crabbe focused on rural school improvement, and like her he spoke out energetically on the subject. He noted that Kentucky's citizens were "clamoring" for better schools, and that "men who heretofore have failed to connect material progress with educational progress" now understood that the two go hand in hand.[100]

A Republican, Crabbe had drawn education to center stage in the commonwealth, where it remained throughout 1908 and 1909. His "Whirlwind Campaign" aroused interest in education and rallied women's clubs, businessmen, civic leaders, and newspapers to the cause. Kentucky's "Educational Legislature of 1908" responded to increased public interest by passing a county school district law and a compulsory attendance law.[101] Crabbe charged that their home state stood near the head of the list in per capita expenditure for education (nearly $3 million), but in actual returns stood near the bottom. Of the fifty-two states and territories, Kentucky ranked forty-ninth in the number of illiterate white voters, leaving only those of North Carolina, Louisiana, and New Mexico with higher numbers.[102]

The excitement of Crabbe's campaign, the encouragement of friends, and perhaps the realization that her marriage had deteriorated beyond repair compelled Cora Wilson Stewart to seek another term as county superintendent. In November 1909 Stewart challenged female incumbent Lyda Messer in a vigorous campaign in which her opponent sought the "sympathy" vote, maintaining that she "needed" the job to survive. Stewart relied on her professional reputation, carefully avoiding any reference to personal matters. She feared that her marital problems would influence public opinion against her, although friends assured her that she was well thought of despite her domestic difficulties. Cora won the election by a comfortable margin and, with characteristic vitality, immediately embarked upon a number of important local and state projects, including financial aid, vocational education, and agricultural training.[103]

Her activism made her the logical choice to head the Kentucky Education Association (KEA), but when colleagues urged her to run for president of that organization, she again worried that exposure of her private life would tarnish her professional image, undermine her position in the state, and ruin her work. She nearly declined the nomination because she feared her status as a divorced woman would become a point of public discussion and turn people against her. Fellow superintendent Jessie O. Yancey wrote that she had not heard Stewart's "domestic troubles" mentioned, except "in a fearful way by one who loves you most dearly and that was Mrs. Faulconer."[104] Stewart kept her life private, but those who knew of the divorce offered moral support and tried to convince her it would not interfere with her professional ambitions. Some supporters even believed she had derived strength from her ordeal. One wrote: "I have often felt while in your presence that you had cares that were burdening you down, and longed for a word that would lift a burden. . . . We know that the 'crushed flower yields the sweetest fragrance.' You have many admiring friends that have been won by reason of your troubles and your fortitude."[105]

Her friend Mattie Dalton took the argument a step further and urged Cora to consider her divorce as necessary for her own fulfillment: "Time was when the idea of divorce horrified me. . . . I think that seven out of ten marriages, looked at from my point of view, are little more than legalized prostitution; and the realization that such is the case is the cause of the numerous divorces of today. Women are thinking a little more and in consequence they value themselves more highly than they used to do, when they placidly accepted the valuation of their men-folk as being correct."[106] She also urged her to take strength from her ordeal: "It is barely possible that you have improved because of the hard blows you have had to withstand. . . .

Perhaps you are stronger or sweeter because of your troubles." Dalton urged Cora to ignore past criticism and forge ahead:

> But for God's sake, Cora, for the work that you ought to do and can do in this world, stop crucifying your soul because of those besotted fools. . . . Say what you please, but I can never believe God is either a fool or cruel. That you or any blameless woman should suffer unnecessarily because of the mistakes of a blind age, is not God-like in my mind. . . . The Bible is the greatest book in the world, but it does not fit every condition of the present day. Don't abuse God by making him so narrow, cruel, or short-sighted.[107]

Regardless of her marital status, Stewart's friends and colleagues believed she was a capable woman and wholeheartedly supported her candidacy. Dalton and Rice Eubank, editor of the *Southern School Journal,* KEA's official journal and the official publication of the Kentucky State Board of Education, used their influence to assist in her election to the KEA presidency. Dalton reminded a group of women educators that their colleague could "handle public conventions, speaks well, has some back-bone, and will make the best officer of all the women in the state." "If you elect her," she said, "the men who are aspirants will not be able to wrangle much, for they will hesitate to 'oppose a woman,' and she will be the most active in promoting the welfare of the organization of all the county superintendents in the state."[108]

Buoyed by the election of Ella Flagg Young to the presidency of the National Education Association the previous year, Stewart and her female colleagues hoped to follow the national precedent. Young said education administration was "woman's natural field and she is no longer satisfied to do the larger part of the work and yet be denied the leadership." "This is woman's year in school affairs," predicted Dalton.[109] She was right, and Stewart became the first woman president of the KEA.

A number of male colleagues also supported her election and promised their support, including J. H. Boothe of Eastern Kentucky State Normal School and D. M. Holbrook of Richmond. Even T. J. Coates, the former president of KEA, whose arrogance had sometimes provoked blistering comment from Stewart and her female colleagues, managed a backhanded compliment: "The educational forces of Kentucky looked all over the state and not finding a man big enough to fill my place had to elect a woman." Stewart received a cordial letter from her friend Dr. Crabbe, a Republican, then president of the Kentucky State Normal School at Richmond, who wrote a congratulatory note: "I rejoice with you at the signal honor which has come to you and I am sure that the association will prosper under your leadership."

Below his signature, he penned, "Count on me!"[110] Her hometown also took pride in her achievement, and past criticism seemed forgotten. A local headline read: "Rowan in the Lead in Education: Our Brilliant and Able Superintendent of Schools Chosen to Head the Educational Forces of Kentucky."[111]

As KEA president Stewart championed vocational education and modernized consolidated schools, especially in rural communities. Rural life had become a hot topic across the nation, and a report issued by President Theodore Roosevelt's Country Life Commission reflected the concerns of the Country Life movement, a disparate and diffuse effort that focused on inadequate farm profits as the reason for widespread poverty in the South and attempted to teach farmers more efficient agricultural practices. Some Country Lifers thought rural education had failed and should be changed to inculcate both a love of country living and an appreciation for scientific farming methods. One result of the growing concern over rural life and farm income was the beginning of agricultural extension work, a classic example of the use of education to secure social progress. The General Education Board, the arm of the Rockefeller Foundation in the South, decided to educate farmers about new forms of scientific agriculture that would ultimately increase both production and agricultural earnings. Toward that end, philanthropists formed an alliance with Department of Agriculture officials to support extension work that enabled experts to bring experiment stations and other research directly to farmers.[112] Convinced that such programs could enhance economic development and therefore progress in the region, Stewart took an active role in facilitating extension and demonstration work in her home county and throughout the state. Since educating adult farmers was not within the purview of the state's public schools, she said educators should focus their attention primarily on young people whose agricultural knowledge and practical skill could be shaped by extension programs for students. Stewart's work at the state and local level earned her a place on the program when Kentucky's commissioner of agriculture called for hearings in Frankfort on the subject.[113]

Stewart believed that the state's young people, especially those in rural areas, needed training to prepare them not just for farming, but for industrial jobs, so she pushed for public school programs in vocational education. She resisted the idea of preparing rural Kentucky youth for industrial work, primarily because it meant they would leave the region, but she remained committed to the idea that certain types of vocational programs could benefit and prepare young people for work in the changing rural economy. Although she supported it, she feared that vocational education had come nearly too late in her own region. In her KEA presidential address, she argued that had vocational education been provided "forty years ago, seventy-five percent of the natural resources of the State would not be in the hands of foreign capitalists, and the youths whom Kentucky has given to other states for governors would, doubtless, have remained at home to help solve her problems and enrich her history."[114]

Unlike some educators who embraced vocational education as a means of ensuring class stratification, Stewart believed it was dangerous. She reminded the KEA membership that there were two groups of educators, each trying to "bend the trend of public school progress in its direction." One group, she said, had lost sight of the fact that "men are beings of flesh and blood, to be housed, clothed, and fed." The other group "sees little in life beyond earning a living and making money, and would cast overboard the languages and every other subject that does not contribute clearly and directly to strictly utilitarian ends." Adopting a "golden mean" would enable Kentucky's young people "to be great scholars, but no less good breadwinners and good homemakers."[115] These ideas formed an important part of her philosophy of education and influenced her thinking when she switched her focus from children to adults.

Stewart wanted to broaden school programs and functions to include a direct concern for health and the quality of family and community life. Progressive education called for the application of innovative pedagogical principles derived from new scientific research in psychology and the social sciences, and advocated tailoring instruction to meet the needs of "real life" children.[116] One of the needs of "real life" children (and adults) in her region was health education, which became an important goal in every school in Kentucky in 1911 when state officials mandated its inclusion in teacher-training institutes.[117]

Stewart took on a formidable workload in order to implement these programs. Her activism at the local level and her presidency of the KEA brought her into the mainstream of education reform, widened her network of contacts, and enabled her to broaden her efforts on behalf of her local constituency. It also enabled her to see local needs in a broader perspective and to provide remedies from both inside and outside.

Like many reformers of her generation, Stewart also tapped the valuable resource of organized women. Her own experience with the CWBM led her in that direction, as did her understanding that most women involved in public work, whether professionals or reformers, got their start in a voluntary association, were supported by one, or belonged to one. Clubwomen had been involved in education reform since before the turn of the century and seemed to Stewart a natural ally. Lexington clubwoman and suffragist Madeline McDowell Breckinridge traced GFWC educational activity in Kentucky to the traveling library movement, which by 1908 saw more than fifty-four hundred volumes circulating in twenty-five mountain counties. Federated clubs were common in the Bluegrass region and more heavily populated cities, but Stewart's hometown had none. Never one to wait for progress, Stewart founded and became the first president of the Morehead chapter of the Kentucky Federation of Women's Clubs (KFWC).[118] Local clubs took on both moral and financial support for educational outreach in their communities, and the Morehead Women's Club connected Stewart and the literacy movement directly to the broad network of state clubs and the General Federation of Women's Clubs.[119]

The Morehead chapter took on a variety of causes but retained its particular involvement in education affairs. Kentucky clubwomen campaigned for school suffrage in the winter of 1910, and Stewart honored the state federation's request to devote one full meeting to the subject.[120] Madeline McDowell Breckinridge asked her to distribute school suffrage leaflets to teachers to better inform them of the issues. Breckinridge, legislative chairman for the KFWC, successfully lobbied the legislature for the bill granting women the right to vote in school elections that passed in 1912.[121]

It is easy to overlook the accomplishments of rural clubwomen because they were fewer in number and lacked the financial resources of their urban counterparts, but Paula Baker has shown that women in small towns, villages, and rural hamlets actively participated in social reform, "child-saving," and moral order campaigns. They commonly looked beyond their immediate communities, where resources were scarce and traditions entrenched, to urban, state, and national women's groups, developing a strong habit of side-stepping local authority in favor of state and federal action. The absence of a large community convinced them that the state could accomplish tasks that localities dodged.[122] A country woman herself, Stewart saw public activism as a natural extension of woman's domestic role and believed women in rural areas and small towns could band together just as effectively as women in urban areas.

Stewart believed women needed education just as much as men, and in an oratorical offering called "Mountain Girl," a sentimental paean to the service ideal, she expounded on that need. Like many of her prepared talks, the speech reflects the tensions between reality and the ongoing rhetoric conceptualizing mountain people not as archetypal feudists and lazy moonshiners but as pure Anglo-Saxons whose honesty and integrity made them worthy of uplift. This speech illustrates her skillful manipulation of class values and attitudes, and points up her ability to match her rhetoric to her audience. In it, she encouraged rural folk to pay closer attention to the education of their daughters, noting that there was "a Cinderella" in the commonwealth household, but when educated, "She may lead the blind, teach the illiterate, cheer the faint, uplift the fallen, and do God's service to all mankind. . . . Every dollar that is spent in equipping her for service, the mountain girl will send back into the treasury of the state, into the collection boxes of the church and Sunday schools, yes, even into the mission fields of India and of Africa—and so money spent in these splendid institutions for her advancement is but being put in interest for Kentucky and for Christ."[123]

Stewart lived the service ideal. Between 1910 and 1912 she served as district director of the CWBM and as secretary to both the Rowan County Sunday School Association and the Rowan County Ministerial Association. Frank C. Button, president of Morehead Normal, appointed Stewart to the all-male advisory board for the school. She also served as a paid correspondent for the *Ashland Daily Independent,* wrote occasional articles for the *Lexington Herald,* prepared a monthly column for the *Southern School Journal,* and earned a commission on subscriptions for all three.[124] Although the money supplemented her income, equally beneficial were the public exposure and the opportunity to report on various educational initiatives across the state. In her *Southern School Journal* column, she related the activities of superintendents across the state and commented on the efficacy of their work. This statewide contact with superintendents through the KEA journal further extended and strengthened her developing network of professional colleagues and like-minded associates. Her *Journal* columns modestly glossed over her own accomplishments, causing her friend Mattie Dalton to chastise her for not reporting her own efforts fully enough. But even if she did not "beat her own drum loudly" as Mattie suggested, her early journalistic efforts and the response from education professionals and the general public served her well and made clear to her the role the press and a support network could play in any campaign.[125] These were important years for Stewart, for they were a time of self-creation and professional identity development. But they were also critical because they connected Stewart to individuals and groups that formed the infrastructure of her reform network.

One of her tasks as KEA president was planning the program and presiding over the annual meeting. For this important event, Stewart brought Philander P. Claxton, U.S. commissioner of education, and David Starr Jordan, president of Leland Stanford University, to address the gathering, and she invited Ella Flagg Young as the keynote speaker.[126] All three became members of her growing network of professional acquaintances and associates. Later in her career Stewart received the prestigious Ella Flagg Young award for achievement in the profession and served with Claxton on several national boards and committees. Jordan spearheaded the illiteracy campaign in his home state of California.

As KEA president Stewart also represented the commonwealth's teachers and acted as their spokesperson, particularly on legislative matters.[127] She used her office to advocate increased salaries for teachers, but she also believed teachers needed better training: "An elevation of both their salaries and qualifications should receive the careful consideration of those who are interested in the educational welfare of Kentucky," she maintained. But "fairness and justice . . . demand that salary and standard rise together."[128]

Stewart had of course known for a long time that many Kentuckians could neither read nor write, but as she visited schools in the district, talked with parents of schoolchildren, or transacted business at her office, she was forced to confront the appalling lack of literacy and its effects. Many rural Kentuckians took no part in local politics, Sunday schools, or school-related affairs because they could not read or write, and their ability to transact the business of everyday life suffered as well. Overseeing the affairs of the public schools heightened her awareness of illiteracy, and she became convinced that in order for educational progress to take place, schools had to reach parents as well as children.

Throughout her life Stewart had served as a literate interpreter for local residents, reading letters from distant relatives and penning their own letters in reply, but she came to believe reading and writing for them did illiterates a grave disservice. She needed to address the problem at its source. Adult illiteracy, she decided, demanded attention. But what to do? Her answer was a new crusade, a classic Progressive Era campaign to eradicate a social evil. She announced her intentions in her presidential address to the KEA and asked her colleagues in the organization to help:

> We have solved, in a measure, the compulsory attendance law and other problems—but Kentucky has yet other vital education problems to solve. . . . The greatest stigma which rests upon Kentucky today and the greatest problem which confronts Kentucky educators, is her appallingly high percentage of adult illiteracy. The days of the night rider, the feudist and the moonshiner—those dark pages of Kentucky's history have passed. . . . the only cause . . . for shame or humiliation is the persistent report . . . that Kentucky has stood for more

than a decade fourth from the bottom on the scale of literacy. . . . 132,000 [Kentuckians] are handicapped by a lack of learning. . . . Surely this association, which is supposed to inaugurate and to foster all education reforms in the State, has no more imperative duty than to foster the movement to abolish illiteracy from the borders of the commonwealth.[129]

Cora Wilson Stewart had found the mission that would occupy the rest of her life. Her calling had become clear, and she expressed it in the uplift rhetoric of her time: "If they were blind and I could open their eyes by an operation, my duty would be plain. Are they not mentally blind? Can I not open their minds? Have I not the instruments right at hand?"[130]

TWO

The Moonlight Campaign

W hen Cora Wilson Stewart celebrated her thirty-sixth birthday in January 1911, her only child was dead and her marriage was over, but she believed she had found the work God intended her to do, and with characteristic determination, she began. Having given the issue of illiteracy a lot of thought, like many of her contemporaries in mountain mission work, she agreed with Berea College president William Goodell Frost and others in their interpretation of the mountaineers as "a people of arrested civilization," living much as their ancestors had generations earlier. In her speeches and in her book *Moonlight Schools for the Emancipation of Adult Illiterates* (1922), she used the rhetoric of Appalachian worthiness to justify the time, money, and energy necessary to bring this group into the twentieth century. A "noble people," the mountaineers stood eager and hopeful, "anxious to enter in and take their part in the work of the world," she wrote, citing Theodore Roosevelt's description of the hardy Scotch-Irish Presbyterian backwoodsman in "Winning of the West."[1]

At first glance the missionary uplift rhetoric appears to present a faith in education that rivals novelist Horatio Alger's belief in the transformative power of the almighty American dollar. Just as the heroes of the dime novels needed only one lucky break and their own determination, hard work, and native intelligence to turn their rags to riches, these mythical Anglo-Saxon Appalachian mountain folk appeared to need only the benefit of education to revolutionize their lives and landscape. Just as the dime novels sold the working poor a capitalistic bill of goods, holding out the promise of wealth and power to the poor and powerless, on the surface it appears that schoolmen and schoolwomen held out the promise of equally unlikely transformations among the mountain folk. In this rhetoric, however, exists a fine and elusive line between myth and reality. Although Cora Wilson Stewart understood and employed this rhetoric, it is also likely that she, Frost, and others actually believed much of what they said, even though their intentions were partially subsumed in the language of benevolence work, fine-tuned to the ears of wealthy philanthropists.

Although the rhetoric of benevolence work overstated both the negatives and the positives, upward mobility in Progressive Era America was a distinct possibility. And just as city dwellers and some immigrant groups could move, if not from rags to riches, at least from rags to respectability, so could rural folk move from poverty to reasonable comfort. While it is easy to criticize uplift as little more than social control—a misguided attempt to fit the poor to their circumstances—and its rhetoric as opportunistic and denigrating, Stewart believed that education enabled the rural poor to acquire some of the benefits of modern life. She saw that as a good thing.

Moreover, acknowledging that schooling is deeply connected to the mutually reinforcing class and economic structure of capitalism and that women chose careers in teaching because it was socially acceptable does not preclude analysis of Stewart's life and work from the perspective of individual and gender agency. In fact, Stewart, whether or not she considered herself a feminist, was an educational activist who chose her profession for a variety of reasons—not the least of which was a desire to improve rural society.

Historians generally call women of Stewart's generation social feminists and tend to overlook or minimize the degree to which they pursued political goals and political activity, and Stewart has been placed in this category.[2] Historian Nancy F. Cott has assessed some of the limitations and problems of casting Progressive Era women solely in the role of social feminism and has urged historians to expand the vocabulary of women's history. She also points out that "the use of social feminism as an umbrella term neither deals with the broad political spectrum from left to right that women's politics occupied (as men's did) nor recognizes that women's loyalties and alliances outside of feminism shaped their woman-oriented activities."[3] Cora Wilson Stewart's life history illustrates some of the shortcomings of wholesale application of the social feminist paradigm to women based on their location in time and circumstance. Of broader applicability is the category of "maternalism," which initially defined a type of activism that used the language of motherhood to justify women's political activism. This analytical framework has broadened to include a variety of reform initiatives begun and supported by individuals and organized women, and thus it is a somewhat more useful term for Stewart when definitions are necessary.[4]

Despite the contradictions inherent in the literacy movement and the problems its leader presents to analysts seeking to attach a label, the Moonlight School movement adds dimension to historical understanding of efforts to combat illiteracy over both time and location, but only Katherine C. Reynolds and Susan L. Schramm have examined the important policy dimensions of the literacy crusade. Calling Stewart a "systems thinker," this brief analysis by education historians locates her in the "Separate Sisterhood" of women who shaped southern education from the 1890s through the early 1920s and draws parallels between her work and that of South Carolina's Wil Lou Gray, whose own work grew out of Stewart's literacy efforts there.[5] They correctly attribute Stewart's limited mention in educational history books to the fact that she served a predominantly rural population that was both undervalued and marginalized by the larger society. Like Willie Nelms in his biography of Stewart, they note that she was a woman operating in the public sphere of men and point out that she lacked the graduate degree credentials of some of her professional counterparts. These assessments are accurate, but a closer look at Stewart's strategies, tactics, and ultimate goals does not fully support their contention that she was a "safe" woman or Nelms's conclusion that she was a "moderate" feminist whose demands did not threaten the status quo or male power structures. Moreover, Reynolds and Schramm fail to acknowledge that the Moonlight School movement included African Americans, albeit separately, a point that Nelms documents.

Recent research in the history of education in the United States reveals a "broad network of like minded women across the country" who, with only tangential connections to each other, used political and professional activism to promote an inclusive and expansive understanding of democratic civic ideals with the understanding that it would enable people to improve their lives. Because of the narration of the history of education in terms of progress toward greater sophistication of organization and emphasis on higher levels of licensing to define professional accomplishment and competence, these same women have been labeled as obstructionist or retrograde. Their support for the normal school as adequate preparation for teaching, their demands for a greater role for the teacher in decision making, and their criticism of centralization and bureaucratization as stumbling blocks to meaningful school reform and progress—in fact, their overall refusal to embrace the revision of education according to the values of corporate culture—

marginalized them and assured their exclusion from histories of the progressive education movement.[6] Examining Stewart's work and particularly her interaction with adult education professionals in the context of this identified trend sheds new light on her motivations and goals, allowing a fuller understanding of her contribution by demonstrating that her reactions and decisions did not emerge solely from a desire to exercise total control over the literacy crusade or to promote her own accomplishments.

Stewart actually wanted more than literacy for Moonlight pupils. In addition to basic skills, she wanted them to absorb what she called the "classical benefits" of literacy, an appreciation and love of learning for its own sake. If Stewart oversold the benefits of a practical education, she was not alone. Equating literacy with progress was a hallmark of progressive thought, and at the time, confidence in progress ran high. She shared with other progressives great confidence in the power of education not only to equip individuals for productive work but to facilitate the acquisition of traditional values, a love of learning, and an appreciation for higher-order thinking and reasoning skills. Sometimes called the "mystique of literacy," this ideal developed in late nineteenth-century and early twentieth-century America, reflecting both literacy's utilitarian, functional uses as a vehicle of progress and its aesthetic and spiritual value.[7] Some critics say this ideal creates false hope and call the idea that education automatically improves earning power a "myth" perpetrated by the educational establishment on a trusting public.[8] Other analysts validate the progressives' faith and argue that literacy actually promotes more literacy because as more people become literate, the amount of printed material in circulation increases, providing more motivation for people to learn to read. As schools produce more literate people, the job structure improves and in turn affects future demands placed on the schools.[9]

Stewart envisioned instruction that would enable adults to function in a modernizing society and economy, provide the ability to read and write basic sentences, conduct simple business transactions, and read a few verses of the Bible. In effect, students who completed the Moonlight curriculum acquired functional literacy, although that term was not introduced until World War I and did not come into widespread use until World War II. Functional literacy came to mean "the capability to understand written instructions necessary for conducting basic military functions and tasks" at a fifth-grade reading level.[10] In two six-week sessions, Moonlight pupils generally gained the ability to sign a document, make basic mathematical calculations, write simple letters, and read a few verses of the Bible.[11] Stewart did not set grade-level equivalencies, perhaps thinking that to do so might insult or demoralize adult pupils; instead, completion of the second six-week session marked the point at which they moved from illiteracy to literacy.[12]

With no set standards defining literacy, no experts to consult, no professional standards to guide the work, and no means of paying teachers for their services, Stewart simply planned as she went along, learning from experience and making changes as necessary. Flexibility was essential, since those who had not gone to school had missed more than just the basics of reading, writing, and arithmetic; lack of formal schooling had left many adult Kentuckians with an intensely narrow and parochial social vision. Progressive educators like Stewart generally saw the public schools as socializing agents, teaching the norms necessary to adjust the young to society's more modern values and to its changing economic systems.[13] Moonlight Schools could serve this same function for adults.

Stewart wanted the schools to pass on some of the values of middle-class American culture, including respect for hard work, cleanliness, order, and a desire for upward mobility, if not for the adult students, at least for their children. Although she realized the limitations of that mobility in rural eastern Kentucky, she nevertheless hoped that education would raise individual quality of life and earning power and improve both the region's economy and its public image. Stewart thought she fully understood the needs of rural illiterates, respecting them for the hardworking simplicity of their way of life, but she had committed herself to an ideal of progress that required fundamental change if they were to realize its potential. Stewart criticized the coal and timber industries for damaging the rural landscape and taking advantage of the mountaineers, but like many progressives, she seems to have accepted industrialization as a necessary evil that required accommodation because it provided the essential means of economic development.[14]

Stewart also knew that change could not take place overnight, since even the most industrious adult students could not make up for years of missed schooling in the short time available to them. Once introduced to the world of letters, however, they could progress rapidly on their own, continuing their quest for knowledge once they had basic instruction in English, mathematics, science, history, and literature, and as much practical information as the teachers could supply. *"Just to have a chance with the other folk— to be something and to do something in the world!"* was the hope of mountain people young and old, wrote Stewart.[15]

When, as county superintendent, Cora Wilson Stewart asked the teachers of Rowan County to help "those whom the schools of the past had left behind," they probably had no choice but to rally to the call, but all of them signed on. In their first meeting, Cora imbued the volunteers with her own sense of mission and calling to the literacy work as she explained the positive effects of adult literacy on the day schools and on the community as a whole.[16] Although she originally considered incorporating adult learning into the public day schools, Stewart soon realized that was impossible, since people had to work during daylight hours and the schools were already overcrowded. As an alternative, she settled on evening instruction. The county's violent past and the conditions of rural roads meant she had to choose dates carefully to ensure good attendance, and since the almanac promised a full moon on 5 September 1911, she selected that evening for opening night.[17]

Volunteers promised to visit each home in the district and issue a personal invitation to every adult in Rowan County. Teachers told day school pupils to encourage their parents to attend. They enjoined ministers to spread the word from their pulpits and storekeepers to notify and urge their customers to participate. Based on available information on families in their districts, the group expected and prepared for 3 or 4 pupils per school, or about 150 for the county. This, they thought, was a manageable number given the size of the one-room schoolhouses, the availability of materials, and the capabilities of the instructors. Almost one-third of the county, nearly 1,200 people, turned up on opening night.[18] Ranging in age from eighteen to eighty-five, they sat on small benches in the little schoolhouses, confronted marks on the tablets in front of them, and examined chalked images on the blackboards. They sang songs and visited with neighbors, and took home that first night a vision of what it would mean to be able to read and write.

For the teachers, the huge turnout presented immediate problems, the most pressing of which was a scarcity of materials and personnel. Education funding was a relatively low priority throughout Kentucky, which ranked forty-first in the nation in terms of overall education provision.[19] Rowan County had no funds for night schools, so Stewart asked women's organizations to donate money, writing tablets, and other supplies. The Morehead Women's Club, which she had helped found, and the Christian Woman's Board of Missions responded. To secure more teachers Stewart appealed to all church- and clubwomen within traveling distance. Volunteers, some of whom boarded with local residents in order to teach in the schools, came from as far away as Louisville, where clubwomen had an active tradition of educational work. Thirty-four teachers taught in the schools over the next three years. One even wrote a "fight song" for the movement, entitled "Onward Rowan

County," to be sung to the tune of "Onward Christian Soldiers." Many retired teachers also offered their services.[20]

Designing a curriculum for adult learners was the next step. Although they were readily available, Stewart opposed using children's primers because she feared their child-directed language and topics would insult people already embarrassed by their illiteracy. She wanted books created specifically for adult learners, but since none were available, Stewart published a little newspaper, initially called the *Rowan County Messenger*, as a text.[21] The newspaper not only provided basic reading skills but also connected readers to their community by stimulating interest in local activities and events. It continued to serve that purpose even after adult readers appeared, but its circulation area doubled, and it was renamed the *Mountaineer*.[22]

Moonlight teachers lacked not only materials but also experience dealing with adult learners, but Stewart told them simply to be practical and resourceful. She encouraged them to teach history in "homeopathic doses" instead of presenting hundreds of "cluttering up facts," instructed volunteers to pay particular attention to regional speech patterns, and stressed the importance of teaching language skills. They needed to reinstate "-ing" to its proper dignity, she said, and eliminate the use of such words as "seed" for seen, "crick" for creek, "git" for get, "hit" for it, and "haint" for has not. By emphasizing correct grammar and pronunciation, volunteers attempted to create a "language conscience," what Stewart called "a pathway" that would lead to "the broad highway of better, if not perfect, speech."[23]

The issue of changing mountain speech drew a variety of opinions from analysts and those involved in education in the mountains. James Watt Raine, head of the Department of English at Berea College, claimed that the "language of the Mountain People has been much maligned." He said it was neither "careless nor degraded" and charged that "our magazine writers usually overdo the dialect in stories of Mountain life." He claimed there were pure links to Elizabethan English and that mountain dialect was creative, spontaneous, and utilitarian, explaining that "here language is still spoken thought, not something written down and analyzed."[24] Although she valued mountain people's heritage and many of their colorful expressions, Stewart did not share this popular contemporary analysis. To her, some speech patterns were simply bad grammar.

The task ahead was a daunting one, and to maintain momentum Stewart and her volunteer teachers sponsored competitions among students and districts, awarding incentives and prizes such as Bibles, pencils, paper, and books to students for individual accomplishment. Cash awards from donated funds went toward general day school improvement. Announcements appeared in the *Messenger* in simple, readable text:

> Can we win?
> Can we win what?
> Can we win the prize?
> Yes, we can win.
> See us try.
> And see us win![25]

Moonlight schools met Monday through Thursday evenings from seven to nine o'clock for six weeks. Sessions began promptly at seven, with a fifteen-minute devotional that generally included singing. Reading lessons took twenty-five minutes, writing exercises another twenty-five, followed by twenty-five minutes of arithmetic. Teachers then led two fifteen-minute drills in basic history, civics, health and sanitation, geography, home economics, agriculture, and horticulture. Students left promptly at nine.[26]

Stewart visited as many of the Moonlight Schools as possible, riding horseback or traveling in a small buggy throughout the county, generally alone, to check on their progress and offer encouragement to pupils and teachers. A "graduation" ceremony ended the second session, in which students learned to read from the Bible and the newspaper "with reasonable facility" and to write a legible letter. Some students graduated after one six-week session, particularly those with some previous schooling, while others attended several sessions before mastering the basics.[27] The ceremonies took on the ambience of a social event, complete with cookies and lemonade. Stewart generally gave an inspirational address, and graduates received diplomas and Bibles. In her memoir and history of the Moonlight movement, Stewart described the first graduation: "The newly learned gave an exhibition of their recently acquired knowledge. . . . They were next presented with Bibles, and as they came up one by one, some young and stalwart, some bent and gray, to receive their Bibles with gracious words of thanks, it was an impressive scene—and when the Jezebel of the community came forward and accepted her Bible and pledged herself to lead a new life forevermore, there was hardly a dry eye in the house."[28]

Literacy sparked less dramatic changes in the lives of most Moonlight students, but their participation in graduation ceremonies validated Stewart's faith in education's ability to renew its beneficiaries and provided a theme as she extended the campaign beyond Rowan County. With intense pride in the accomplishments of Rowan's first night school population, she frequently spoke of changes the schools had wrought there. Saving letters from the students as evidence of what they had accomplished, she used them to convince teachers, patrons, and eventually legislators that contrary to popular opinion, adults could learn to read and write at any age.[29] Some educators still believed knowledge had to be acquired during the impressionable years of youth and that it was wasted on those who missed that chance. Her students had not rejected education, she believed. Instead, the vicissitudes of rural life and poverty had deprived them of it, a situation she intended to rectify.

The first session of Moonlight Schools convinced Stewart that hers was an idea whose time had come, and although it presented problems of logistics and supply, the huge enrollment indicated that illiteracy was even more widespread than she had believed. She knew it was a complex problem that seemed to perpetuate itself, and without the active intervention of educators, the cycle would continue. Once the first session of Moonlight Schools in Rowan County was under way, Stewart visited nearby school districts to tell of their success and to urge the creation of night schools in every rural community. Showing photographs, she told of "stalwart men" standing at the blackboards after a few evenings' training and "writing their names with greater pride than ever filled the heart of a graduate from Harvard upon receiving his degree."[30] One young man's joy upon learning to write his name was so complete, said Stewart, he etched it in several trees on his way home from school, then carved it on numerous fence posts the following day, and continued to place his name on public property throughout the county until requested by the sheriff to desist.[31] These tales, although somewhat lighthearted, related the story of the Moonlight Schools in the romantic, expressive prose of the day. Modern readers may see them as overstated and sentimental, but they reveal a great deal about the literacy crusade and the value both teachers and students placed on the simple ability to read and write. Stewart asked each student to write her a letter that she could keep, and she used these samples to demonstrate the efficacy of the schools.[32]

Her work caught the attention of progressive educators, and Lexington's M. A. Cassidy, president of the Southern Education Association (SEA), the largest professional education organization in the South, asked her to address the annual meeting in Houston, Texas, in December 1911. Cassidy asked her to "show what you can do. Not only can you estimate the worth of the mountain child, his value to society if properly educated, but, in graphically outlining his lack of educational facilities, [generate] much good will."[33] In a speech titled "The Education of the Mountain Child," she told the SEA that the only hope for economic development in the mountains was better education, and that had to begin with parents. Following Stewart's explanation of the inherent worthiness of mountain children and her description of the recent success of the Moonlight Schools in her county, the SEA voted an endorsement to the work, calling it the "most practical plan" for eliminating illiteracy in the South.[34] Educators from all over the South heard her address at the SEA, and in the next year she accepted speaking invitations from many of them.

In the fall of 1912, Stewart organized a Moonlight teachers' institute in Morehead in which she and the teachers who had taught the first evening sessions instructed others who wanted to conduct schools of their own. Attendance was completely voluntary, and teachers paid their own expenses and were able to compare experiences, learn from one another, further develop the curriculum for Moonlight Schools, and address their primary concern, the lack of materials for adult learners. Veteran teachers also began to conduct workshops for educators who wished to open schools in the surrounding counties.[35] The institutes were very popular and quickly became Stewart's primary source of income, enabling her to travel extensively on behalf of the literacy cause.

Fortified by their institute training, volunteers in Rowan County taught more than sixteen hundred adults in 1912. Students who could not attend because of illness or infirmity received instruction in their homes. Not all these students were illiterate; many had some reading and writing skills. In fact, in the 1912 session, only three hundred were unable to read and write at all. Another three hundred had acquired basic skills in the first Moonlight session, and the remaining one thousand "were men and women of meager education." In one school of sixty-five pupils, only twenty-three were classified as illiterate. In another, three of the eight students could neither read nor write. One school included a carpenter, a preacher, a postmaster, a school trustee, five former teachers, "many educated persons, and eight illiterates."[36] At the close of the next year's campaign in Rowan, Stewart calculated that only twenty-three illiterates remained in the county. Six of these were blind or had defective sight, five were "imbeciles or epileptics," two had moved into the county as the session closed, and four "could not be induced to learn."[37]

Stewart's statistics may have been inflated and the standard of literacy low, but the first Moonlight session was a phenomenal event. The *Lexington Herald,* the newspaper that most consistently supported Stewart's efforts, ran a full-page article complete with photographs.[38] Under the headline "The

Moonlight Schools of Rowan County" was a glowing account of the program's results: "The effect on the county . . . has been wholesome. Some of the night schools have resolved themselves into Sunday School classes; . . . education is more popular; there is an increased respect for law and order; an intensified love for the Bible, the Sabbath school and all religious institutions are manifested; all hearts are happier and the people are firm believers and advocates of 'Moonlight Schools' as one of the greatest blessings which has come to uplift them."[39] This type of publicity drew attention to the Moonlight Schools and moved them quickly beyond the boundaries of Rowan County.

Across the country, individuals like Cora Wilson Stewart, in concert with reform groups and civic and church organizations, had begun to examine the social implications of their Christianity and to act on their missionary impulses in their own communities. Taking full advantage of a pervasive religiosity, southern Christian progressives saw their involvement in the betterment of society as a moral imperative.[40] Despite the South's reputation as "a land of piety and tradition," historian Dewey W. Grantham shows that there was an active, if disparate, Social Gospel movement there, although much of the humanitarian work was done by religious groups outside the denominational churches. Groups like the Men and Religion Forward Movement, the Young Men's Christian Association (YMCA), the Women's Christian Temperance Union (WCTU), and the Young Women's Christian Association (YWCA) supported a variety of causes, including education reform, child labor legislation, prohibition, and prison reform.[41] Public education was a crying need, and reformers had come to understand that community neglect and indifference guaranteed weakness in the schools. "The deficiencies of rural schools reflected not only rural poverty but rural apathy," concluded William A. Link in his study of southern progressivism.[42] In Kentucky, as in other states, shifting coalitions and disparate reform efforts waxed and waned, but individuals and groups in urban and rural areas focused a great deal of attention and effort on the issue of public education. Public information and inspiration were important elements of every campaign.

Cora Wilson Stewart was very good at this; thus, the illiteracy campaign grew exponentially. Churchmen and churchwomen, the YWCA, mission boards and societies, and local Sunday school circles all rallied to the cause, donating money, supplies, time, and expertise. Stewart's success in bringing these organizations into the fold is significant given the fact that southern Protestantism "did more to conserve than to undermine" the region's dominant cultural values.[43] But the literacy campaign was not designed to realign the economic structure or subvert cultural values; it was simply intended to raise the standard of living by enabling people, through education, to better themselves. Although Stewart frequently criticized the powerful timber and coal industries for what she saw as the pauperization of the mountain people, the literacy campaign created opportunity through self-help without engaging in economic redistribution, hence its appeal, in part, to conservative southern progressives. Professional educators, businessmen, clubwomen, and the press got on the rural night-school bandwagon to help Stewart promote her "cure" for the "disease" of illiteracy. They shared her optimistic hope that education would bring progress in the form of economic development. Their faith found expression in what some have called a "new interventionism," a reconceptualization of the government's role in a free society.[44]

There was real hope, since students in the first sessions had already disproved the prevailing belief that age was a barrier to learning. The Rowan County Moonlight Schools served all ages, including eighty-seven-year-old "Uncle" Martin Sloan; the youngest was a sixteen-year-old. Photographs of the early sessions show elderly, bearded men sitting at small desks alongside men half their age, poring over writing tablets with the intense concentration of schoolboys. Dressed in their "Sunday clothes" and appearing vaguely uncomfortable at the prospect of a spelling bee or a drill at the blackboard, Cora Wilson Stewart's neighbors to some degree represent the romantic image of a bygone time. Photographs show that many are neatly and carefully dressed and appear well groomed and healthy, despite their lack of opportunity. Stewart described them as follows:

> There were overgrown boys who had dropped out of school and been ashamed to re-enter. There were girls who had been deprived of education through isolation. There were women who had married in childhood—as so many mountain girls do—and with them came their husbands, men who had been humiliated by having to make their mark or to ask election officers to cast their vote for them. There were middle-aged men who had seen golden opportunities pass them by because of the handicap of illiteracy—men whose mineral, timber, and other material resources were in control of educated men who had made beggars of them.[45]

The romanticization and overstatement of their condition was part of the rhetoric of the crusade, meant to entice financial and moral support from the educated community and to play on public sympathy for the benighted mountaineers, worthy whites more deserving of uplift than blacks and immigrants.[46] In all mountain uplift work, race and class were the determinants of worthiness, and on both issues Stewart played the public relations game.

Nevertheless, she saw to it that Moonlight Schools were established for black rural and small-town illiterates as well. In fact, by 1915, at least fifteen Kentucky counties conducted schools for black students. Stewart reported that the "best" schools were in Maysville, Winchester, Mount Sterling, and Paris, with Clark County (Winchester) reporting an enrollment of 203. Mercer County held sessions in "each and every colored district."[47]

Buoyed by favorable publicity, armed with progress reports, and convinced that what had worked for Rowan County would work for the entire state, Cora Wilson Stewart embarked on a statewide promotional campaign in late 1912. Ten Kentucky counties immediately implemented Moonlight programs, and dozens more began to examine the problem of illiteracy. When several surrounding states expressed an interest, Stewart began to travel more widely to spread the message. Although many believed that illiteracy afflicted only mountain people and those who lived in isolated rural areas, it quickly became obvious that cities and towns had their share as well. In less skillful hands, this revelation might have provoked a hostile or defensive reaction from teachers and public school administrators, but Stewart had already established herself as a woman who could be trusted with the educational interests of the people of her state. Her reputation, her presidency of the KEA, and her ability to link adult literacy with progress and moral good ensured an enthusiastic response and made opposition nearly impossible. Who could, in good conscience, oppose a program whose goals were so basic to a democracy—the ideal of self-improvement and the tradition of a literate citizenry upon which the nation was founded? Who could criticize schools that taught people to read the Bible and increased both church attendance and respect for the law? School authorities could only rejoice when she promised increased attendance at the day schools and enhanced respect for the educational process. And politicians could offer no objection, since the schools did not place any demands on the public purse.

Moonlight Schools caught on quickly, and soon most counties in Kentucky and several other states had adopted them. They were inexpensive and promised immediate results. In fact, Stewart's rhetoric had imparted to them an almost magical quality. As she traveled throughout Kentucky and neighboring states, Stewart touted grassroots organization and public enthusiasm as the keys to success. She also recommended enlisting the "half-educated" along with the most influential and intelligent individuals in the community, and told volunteers to carry enrollment books for recording the names of all who were willing to come. Their enthusiasm would be contagious, she promised. She further instructed organizers to choose dates for their sessions carefully, using almanacs to pick "the finest moonlit night in the month." They were to avoid rainy, dark nights and limit classes to two hours. If volunteers cleaned up the schoolhouses, trimmed the wicks on the lanterns, and provided plenty of "bright lights," she said, their efforts were sure to succeed.[48]

It would be easy to dismiss Stewart's optimism as vainglory and her rhetoric as hollow, but it must be remembered that many of the mountaineers she wanted to educate were friends, neighbors, or parents of children whom she had taught in the public schools. Some were lifetime acquaintances. Their families had shared the same ground for generations. These people were certainly worthy, in her eyes, of any and all efforts to educate them, and their eager enrollment in the Moonlight Schools indicated their strong interest and desire to learn.

Stewart wanted to reach all the illiterates in the state; therefore, she needed to develop a clearer understanding of where and who they were. As an experiment that she later recommended statewide, Stewart enlisted volunteers in Morehead to take a census of the illiterates in the county. She asked school trustees to create a census report on every illiterate in every district.[49] Many of the surviving census entries are in Stewart's handwriting and generally include the individual's name and age; most include some type of personal information along with such statements as "can read a little," "can read some but cannot write," and "cannot read or write."

Typical of the entries is one for Mr. Chas Thompson, aged fifty years: "Hearing not good. Has a little girl, Marie Thompson, age 11. A bright little girl, and takes interest in school work. Is devoted to this child. Have her teach him." Another described a twenty-five-year-old man named John in District 1 as "rather half-witted. Has small daughter. Can be persuaded by Co. Supt. and taught by Supt. & daughter." This entry reflects Stewart's strong confidence in her ability to teach anyone, but another record shows there were other means of dealing with the same problem. One canvasser reported that "he was going to abolish illiteracy in his district by moving Tom Morrison out."[50]

The census proved a valuable tool, for it helped volunteers identify and reach those in need and convinced Stewart to recommend it as standard procedure for all school districts engaged in the Moonlight work. Each teacher received the record of illiterates in his or her district, along with instructions to call upon them all before the term began. Volunteers also established a home department to deal with "the obstinate, the decrepit and the disinclined," who would be instructed in their homes by a teacher or someone under the teacher's direction. Because identifying and reaching all illiterates in a given area required the involvement of the entire community, Stewart developed ways of mustering volunteers and directing their various talents toward the task at hand: "We enlisted every educated person possible to campaign, to speak or to teach. Ministers, doctors, lawyers, stenographers, merchants, school children and even many of the illiterates themselves as soon as they passed out of the illiterate class, began to teach members of their families and their friends."[51]

The illiteracy work gained national attention when, in 1913, the U.S. Bureau of Education issued a special bulletin, "Illiteracy in the United States and an Experiment for Its Elimination." Using Stewart's efforts as a case study, commissioner of education Philander P. Claxton's introduction noted that the Moonlight School experiment provided strong hope that illiteracy in America could be eliminated.[52]

Using census data, the booklet made it clear that illiteracy was not solely a southern problem. Statistics from the 1910 census indicated that 5,516,163 Americans, or 7.7 percent of the population ten years of age and older, could neither read nor write. Fifteen pages of tables and charts showed higher rates of illiteracy among individuals over twenty years of age, among foreign-born whites in urban areas, and among blacks in general. In the New England, Middle Atlantic, and East North Central states, the percentage of urban illiteracy exceeded that of rural areas, but for the rest of the country, the percentages at least doubled in rural environs.

Couched in the dramatic rhetoric of uplift, the booklet introducing the illiteracy crusade to the nation also reflected the prevailing Progressive Era fear of revolution and the desire for an Americanized community, two impulses Cora Wilson Stewart refused to embrace. The characterization of the nation's illiterates as a "mighty army" whose "banners of blackness and darkness inscribed with the legends of illiteracy, ignorance, weakness, helplessness, and hopelessness" were too large "for the safety of our democratic institutions, for the highest good of society, and for the greatest degree of material prosperity," however, was pure Stewart, reflecting her penchant for martial language urging quick action.[53]

At this stage, the literacy effort still operated as a grassroots movement whose success depended on community action. Volunteer teachers used the public schools for classes, but Stewart also encouraged every literate person to participate. Using the motto "Each one teach one," she urged everyone who could read to teach one person who could not. Those who could not teach could call on their neighbors. Local ministers could preach the message of literacy from their pulpits, newspapermen could write about it, schoolchildren could sing about it, and virtually everyone could contribute at least a few cents to the cause.

As the movement grew, the limitations of community action became apparent, even to the optimistic Stewart. Illiteracy was far too widespread and dispersed to be eliminated solely through voluntary efforts. Realizing that state action was necessary if illiteracy were to be eliminated, Stewart undertook a campaign to win government backing of the work.

Activists in suffrage, temperance, and child saving all looked toward expansion of state services to further their causes. Rural women turned more quickly to the state because they lacked the sheer numbers and volunteer infrastructure that served urban women so well. But there was also an active movement to locate public authority and responsibility with state governments, and nowhere was this development more apparent than in education. Many states, under pressure to increase appropriations for public schools, had begun to provide training institutes, create normal schools, set more rigorous standards for teacher certification, mandate school consolidation, and pass compulsory attendance laws.[54] Education clearly came under state purview, and it seemed obvious to Stewart that state government should help support the education of rural adults as well.

In Kentucky, education was a political issue, and candidates from both parties used local influence as an electioneering tool. A party insider serving in an elected office, Stewart as county superintendent possessed considerable political influence and did not have to fight the local male political establishment, since it was dominated by her brother and several close friends.[55] But power at the local level was not enough. Only legislative support could supply the resources needed to eliminate illiteracy in Kentucky.

Many of the state's politicians, including Senator Ollie M. James, Congressmen William J. Fields, J. Campbell Cantrill, and Jonathan W. Langley, endorsed the work early on, as did Kentucky-born Missouri congressman and Speaker of the House, Champ Clark.[56] Their support was essential because Stewart wanted Kentucky legislators to establish the nation's first state illiteracy commission. In 1914, her initial inquiries met staunch resistance from several representatives who maintained they had no illiterates in their districts. A few county superintendents, perhaps jealous of their own power and resistant to change, opposed the creation of the commission, charging that illiteracy in their counties and in the state as a whole had been overstated. While visiting the nation's capital, Stewart enlisted the aid of her friend Congressman William J. Fields and Kentucky senator Ollie James, who together prevailed on the chief of the U.S. Census Bureau to give her the names of Kentucky illiterates, listed by county of residence, a practice that continued for the next fifteen years at no cost to the state.[57] Stewart presented one doubter with the list of illiterates in his county. Newspaper coverage of the confrontation helped solidify her reform identity throughout the state and demonstrated to Kentucky politicians that she understood the importance of rhetoric and public gestures as well as they did.[58] It also made a few enemies.

Securing the creation of a state illiteracy commission required organization, timing, and skill. With an already impressive list of backers, Stewart had enlisted her friend Governor James B. McCreary, who, once convinced that the people were against illiteracy, became an ardent backer of the cause. He coached her on the February 1914 speech she delivered to a joint session of the legislature requesting formation of a state illiteracy commission. In an address that made the front page of the *Lexington Herald,* she called upon legislators "to blot illiteracy out of Kentucky." Press reports of the session tell a dramatic story of Mrs. Stewart "sweeping" the legislature "off its feet by her eloquence. Not only did her eloquence appeal to the members but the indisputable facts she adduced were equally impressive." One report indicates that after hearing her speech, legislators

> crowded around Mrs. Stewart seeking an opportunity to congratulate her and encourage her. A vote of thanks was expressed by the House and Senate on the motion of Representative Coke, of Logan County for her splendid address. Representative Saufley moved that the regular order of business be suspended and that the bill providing for the Illiteracy Commission be put on its passage. This was done without objection so that Mrs. Stewart had the pleasure of witnessing the effect of her thrilling address. It also gave her the opportunity to realize that by eloquence and facts she had accomplished something in legislative history that had never been done before, as the honor of such a proceeding was given to her.[59]

The ease with which Stewart secured passage of a bill creating the Kentucky Illiteracy Commission (KIC) can be attributed to the fact that she asked for no money, but there were other reasons for the legislature's willingness to grant her appeal. More than a hundred clubwomen and teachers accompanied her to the capital, and they represented an emerging but powerful force. Although they could not vote, they embodied the concerted moral vision of many of the women in the state. Just as important, they asked assistance in an endeavor that appeared uniquely female. A powerless constituency, Kentucky's illiterates were dependent adults who, as far as the state was concerned, could be cared for by women. Educating them posed no threat to institutionalized male self-interest; therefore, the legislature granted Stewart control of the rural adult education agenda.[60]

Like many women involved in reform efforts, Stewart initially asked for no state funding, intending instead to raise the money herself through donations from public and private organizations and individuals. She expected results strong enough to convince the legislature to appropriate funds and was therefore satisfied with the KIC authority to receive, hold, and disburse donations toward a statewide fight against illiteracy, to organize illiteracy commissions in the counties, and to make surveys for the purpose of collecting information for their own use and the use of the next General Assembly. Governor McCreary named Stewart chairman of the commission, which included her friend John Grant Crabbe, Western State Normal School president H. H. Cherry, Ella Lewis, the superintendent of Grayson schools, and an ex officio member, superintendent of public instruction, Barksdale Hamlett.[61]

Shortly after her speech in Frankfort, Stewart traveled to Washington, D.C., to accept the Clara Barton Medal for her educational efforts in Kentucky and to testify at congressional hearings regarding a $10,000 federal appropriation to support community illiteracy efforts.[62] Presented by the American Red Cross, the Barton award honored Stewart's efforts as founder of the Moonlight Schools, and at the invitation of Commissioner Claxton, she testified before the House Committee on Education. Claxton wanted to expand both the role and the scope of the federal government in educational matters, and in these hearings he hoped to convince legislators to vote an appropriation for local illiteracy programs across the country. In the first of many testimonies before congressional committees on behalf of the nation's unschooled adults, Stewart assured the nation's lawmakers that such support would not be seen as interference; it would be welcomed. The country's illiterates, she insisted, absolutely deserved the assistance. Responding to questions about why people remained illiterate, Stewart attempted to refute the idea that illiteracy was the mark of laziness. Rather, she reminded her audience, many people in rural regions missed schooling as youngsters because geographic isolation and distance from their homes to schools made attendance difficult, if not impossible. Had the opportunity existed and they rejected it, she said, it was still wrong to "deprive them of a chance . . . whenever they awakened to their need." She also spoke in favor of strong compulsory education laws, uniformly enforced, ensuring that no one grew up unable to read and write. She proclaimed it "a shame" that immigrants in cities had night schools while large "native-born" populations lacked such opportunities.[63]

When Stewart returned to Kentucky, the KIC called for one thousand volunteers. Stewart secured a promise from the Kentucky Press Association to conduct a public information campaign and, with John Grant Crabbe's help, put together a roster of 120 speakers to carry the word to educational organizations as well as civic and church groups. In a statewide sweep reminiscent of Crabbe's "Whirlwind Campaign" of 1908, in which he brought the matter of improved public education to public attention, speakers took to the stump, crusading against illiteracy in "old-time revival" style. The press did its part to publicize and inform readers, often giving front-page coverage and bold headlines.

The KIC added legitimacy and the perception of state support to the literacy work at the very time Stewart's vast network of friends, political allies, professional associates, churchmen and churchwomen, and a virtual army of clubwomen took up the cause. Hundreds of supporters kicked off a fundraising drive and public information campaign with "Illiteracy Week" in Louisville in November 1914. The campaign continued the following week in the Lexington district, which included Fayette, Jessamine, Boyle, Mercer, Scott, and Bourbon counties. The first urban drives, the Lexington and Louisville campaigns illustrate the organizational strength of the Moonlight movement, as well as the high level of popular support for the cause.

In both cities, Stewart chose active socialites and clubwomen such as Mrs. Gilmer Speed Adams of Louisville and Mrs. Lyman Chalkley of Lexington, presidents of their districts, to oversee the campaigns. Ella Lyman Chalkley, the sister of Desha and Sophonisba Breckinridge, like others in her family, supported women's rights and other reform movements.[64] Adams in Louisville and Chalkley in Lexington coordinated meetings, parades, and fund-raising campaigns and called together various committees to consider ways and means of raising the $20,000 needed to eliminate illiteracy from their districts. Under the banner of the Woman's Forward Movement (WFM), they planned simultaneous rallies in cities within their districts. Timing and publicity were critical; Stewart orchestrated the campaign so that the day the work ended in Louisville, it began in Lexington, and so on throughout the state as clergymen spread the word from their pulpits, announcing times and places for the meetings and urging their congregations to attend.[65]

Using the tactics of the suffrage movement, young women of the city, "under the direction of Miss Sunshine Sweeney," were asked to "placard the city Monday and decorate all the public buildings with bunting and illiteracy slogans." Posters went up at local theaters, and literature explaining what the illiteracy campaign "means for civic betterment in Kentucky" appeared throughout the city. At every service, volunteers handed out pamphlets and folders explaining the critical need for illiteracy work in the commonwealth.[66]

In November 1914, several days of speeches and lectures by prominent townspeople culminated in a huge rally and speech at the courthouse. In Lexington, suffrage leader Madeline McDowell Breckinridge spoke on behalf of the work at both the State University and Transylvania University. In Louisville, ministers, politicians, and school officials gave speeches and lectures followed by requests for donations, while patriotic songs and hymns rang out as the hat was passed. Campaign workers announced the placement of "contribution boxes" throughout the downtown areas in hopes that "people interested in raising the State from its present low status in the rank of untaught Commonwealths to among the top will give this city's full quota of the $20,000 required."[67]

Both rallies drew huge crowds and earned Stewart's courthouse speech a front-page spread in the *Lexington Herald* on 25 November 1914. Calling illiteracy "the finest problem that has offered itself for solution since the pioneer day," the president of State University, Lexington (now the University of Kentucky), kicked off the rally and expressed his confidence that in the future "Lexington would find education, not tobacco, whiskey and race horses, its greatest asset." After remarks by Lexington ministers, a "male double quartet" offered a rendition of "My Old Kentucky Home," and following Stewart's "eloquent" address, the audience stood and sang "America," after which a benediction was pronounced.[68]

Stewart conducted the literacy crusade much like a traveling evangelist, relying on the same format in city after city. First she identified the great "sin" of the community, the illiteracy that had been allowed to proliferate, then she offered an explication of the necessary remedies, and finally she issued the call for redemption: "Mrs. Stewart was most effective in pointing out the simplicity of the cure," which she illustrated by reading a letter from a fifty-year-old man who had learned to read and write "an intelligent, legible letter in eight evenings." "Think of the waste in that man's life," she said, referring to "his lowered earning capacity, his limited mental horizon, his isolation, which after fifty years was cured in eight sessions of the moonlight school."[69]

At home in the revival atmosphere of the rallies, Stewart moved easily into the rhetoric of Protestant evangelicalism. Motivated as she was by moral fervor and a strong sense of calling, she captivated and inspired audiences with biblical alliteration, casting herself as a Joshua-like figure, marshaling the forces that would bring down the walls of illiteracy: "And, shall we not, by our marching and our shouts and with the blowing of horns and bugles, . . . so advertise the evil and disgrace that all will flee from it, and if one should by chance be left he will call upon the rocks and hills to hide him, and if one should grow up illiterate, so much will his disease be in disfavor that he will seem a thing unclean and as loathsome as a leper."[70]

Stewart knew the inspirational power of evangelical rhetoric, but in order to sustain strong commitment, she believed everyone also had to understand the critical need for literacy and embrace its potential for changing lives. With that goal in mind, she emphasized the economic and social benefits of literacy. Particularly in larger cities like Louisville and Lexington, she linked literacy to productive employment and good citizenship and supplied pamphlets listing the effects of illiteracy, which she said retarded agricultural and economic development, corrupted politics and increased crime, fostered disease and immorality, and prevented development of the child.[71]

At the conclusion of the November rally in Lexington, Stewart articulated a vision for a public education system that served the needs of the entire community, not just its children:

> Hasten the day when the rural dweller, wherever he may be, . . . may have a school that is not only open to his children and his grandchildren by day, but is open to his wife, his grown son and his aged father and his hired man and himself by night. Hasten the day when there shall be no men and women in this country who have eyes to see, but see not the splendid truths which have been written in books, and who have hands to write, but write not the thoughts which, if recorded, might stamp with genius, some one whose wisdom the world, in its urgent need, is seeking.[72]

An ideal educational system cost money, the state illiteracy commission had no operating budget, and no major philanthropy had underwritten the cause, so Stewart directed much of her energy toward fund-raising. Public school authorities had no money to spare, and charging tuition in the Moonlight Schools would have defeated their purpose. Although teachers volunteered their time and classes met in the schoolhouses, materials and supplies, travel expenses for volunteers and speakers, and numerous other costs had to be met. Therefore Stewart, the KIC members, and volunteers, using their well-developed networks to secure moral support, financial assistance, and additional teachers, sought donations from every possible source.

Clubwomen, along with politicians, teachers, and the press, formed the infrastructure of the movement. At its annual meeting in April 1914, the Kentucky Federation of Women's Clubs endorsed the state legislature's creation of the KIC and pledged its "hearty co-operation" in the commission's efforts, largely because Stewart was one of their own: "At the head of the

Commission is a woman; one who is both an officer in the Kentucky Federation of Women's Clubs and a member of its Education Committee—Mrs. Cora Wilson Stewart. For this reason, the Federation is naturally deeply interested and feels that for this, as well as for patriotic reasons it owes its allegiance to the Kentucky Illiteracy Commission and its work."[73]

The support of Kentucky clubwomen not only added the moral and fiscal force of the state's most active group of women but also assured the backing of one of the most powerful and influential instruments of women's involvement in American politics, the General Federation of Women's Clubs.[74] From their origins as self-improvement organizations, women's clubs took on an impressive array of social causes, so literacy seemed a natural addition to their reform agenda. The GFWC sponsored labor and protective legislation of various kinds and founded libraries, trade schools, and university extension courses. Clubwomen pressed for juvenile court reform, lobbied for federal public health legislation, and raised money for parks and playgrounds. But they recognized that their efforts alone could not bring about a progressive transformation of society. Federated women needed the help of the state; thus they sought to pass on to government the work of social policy they found increasingly unmanageable.[75]

Taking advantage of an emerging pattern, Stewart relied heavily on the activism and influence of federated women to generate legislative support. Clubwomen had taken the lead in social welfare politics, and because they acted from a broadly shared, gender-based, maternalist vision, they aimed to extend the domestic morality of their sphere into the nation's public life.[76] After informing themselves about public issues, they used moralistic rhetoric to shape public opinion and the opinions of well-placed males and public officials. They not only lobbied legislators but also dramatized issues in their own communities through churches, schools, and the press. Even though they lacked the vote, this pattern gave them a powerful voice in the formation of social welfare policy.[77]

The KFWC, with a rich history of educational endeavors dating from the establishment of traveling libraries, adopted the illiteracy campaign.[78] The KFWC promoted it statewide by recommending that each club have one program in 1915, preferably the first meeting in January, devoted to the history, methods, and purpose of the Moonlight Schools. Federation and club stationery carried the slogan "No Illiteracy after 1920," and each club member was asked to provide instruction for one illiterate. The state organization also urged each club member to secure a letter from an illiterate who had received instruction and to send the letter to the KIC in Frankfort. In addition, state leaders suggested that each club offer a prize to the Moonlight School in its county that demonstrated the "most pronounced success."[79]

State clubwomen's participation in the literacy movement led to the involvement of the GFWC, and its national magazine printed Stewart's appeal to clubwomen across the country urging them to teach another woman to read and write: "Can we who love books and appreciate the use of the pen, content ourselves while 2,701,213 women in the country are untrained in the art of writing and are blind to the printed page?" The response to Stewart's call was substantial in both individual and chapter donations. Already active in education reform, clubwomen added illiteracy to their list of causes by volunteering in impressive numbers to raise money and to teach in Moonlight Schools across the country.[80] Support for the literacy cause grew naturally out of clubwomen's already well-defined goal of guiding the nation in its appreciation of fine art, literature, music, and the finer points of American culture.[81]

Kentucky clubwomen played a key role in the early efforts of the KIC. They recognized and rewarded the work of the Rowan County Moonlight teachers by sending the group of twenty-one volunteers to Niagara Falls as "just reward for heroic services rendered." The KFWC also underwrote the cost of Stewart's speaking tours and ultimately raised more than $34,000 for the cause.[82]

Kentucky clubwomen joined other clubs and civic organizations in the winter of 1914 to form the Woman's Forward Movement, a coalition of activist women that through its rallies and meetings took the message of social progress through literacy to women across the state.[83] Although it was a temporary coalition group, it served as an organizational and propaganda machine that mobilized many of the state's most wealthy and prominent women, many of whom believed it their civic duty to extend the "benefits of education to the downtrodden," so those "unfortunates" could, in turn, help themselves.[84]

The WFM represented the more secular side of the illiteracy crusade. Stewart's evangelizing played well in most venues, but her work also appealed to female political activists with a more practical agenda. Approximately fifty thousand Kentucky women, all members of organizations such as the Colonial Dames, the Daughters of the American Revolution, and the Federation of Women's Clubs, participated.[85] They took up the literacy cause, but their fund-raisers and rallies featured a strong dose of women's rights sentiment, since many of them were also involved in the suffrage movement. Stewart herself was a suffragist, and although she rarely spoke publicly on the topic, this group appreciated her political activism perhaps more than they valued her missionary spirit and traditional selflessness. Less concerned with the spiritual or religious uses of literacy, they considered it invaluable to the political and economic health of the nation.

Social reform efforts occupied WFM leaders, who used their influence to shape government policies. For example, Mrs. Gilmer Speed Adams, the Louisville campaign leader, kicked off the fund drive in her city by criticizing the state legislature for its failure to appropriate funds for the KIC's work. Illiteracy cost the federal government at least $500 million annually, she maintained, and that figure would be cut significantly when literacy allowed all Americans to work at their full capacity. The government's money would be better spent on programs like the Moonlight Schools, she said. "Mrs. Stewart would have done much more than she has in Rowan County and in other sections of the state," argued Adams, "if money had been available." She told her audience that $20,000 was needed to conduct the schools during the winter, and plans were being made to petition the legislature for that amount.[86]

Reflecting the prevailing distrust of political machines and her hope for meaningful change, Adams stressed the practical value of the schools and the importance of literacy in a democracy. "In the moonlight schools people will be taught not only to read and write, but instruction will be given in agriculture, domestic science, sanitation and other useful things," she said, "and it has been shown in Rowan County of what tremendous benefit this is." The nation would also benefit because "men who now are the prey of designing politicians, and who, in many instances, vote as they are told to vote, will exercise their rights as free citizens and vote for those whom they consider the best men for offices."[87]

A typical WFM rally placed a well-known woman on the program with a prominent male politician, businessman, or educator. At one large gathering, Assistant Attorney General M. M. Logan shared the dais with Mrs. Thomas J. Smith of Ashland, described by the *Ashland Independent* as an active clubwoman, prominently identified with educational interests in the state. The granddaughter of Cassius M. Clay, "a typical Kentucky woman, modest, gracious, and charming," her prominence "insures a large audience." In her address, Smith praised the "much-loved Mrs. Stewart" but criticized both state and federal government and spoke pointedly about women's position in the polity:

> Why cannot Kentucky honor her women as Illinois has her Jane Addams and Ella Flagg Young? A salary of $10,000 a year, the salary that Ella Flagg Young

gets in Chicago, would not be too much value set upon the worth of Mrs. Stewart, but in Kentucky, in order to get an appropriation she must promise to receive no salary whatever. . . . In Washington President Taft placed Julia Lathrop at the head of the Children's Bureau. 'Tis true that Congress did not appropriate much money, only $30,000, while it gladly appropriated $3,000,000 for pigs.[88]

Despite lack of government support for reform initiatives backed by women, Smith said, Stewart deserved high praise for her efforts in organizing women for a common cause. As "a constructive statesman," she said, Stewart possessed great vision. Calling the WFM "the Intellectual Aristocracy of Kentucky women," Smith expressed strong confidence in the ability of the literacy campaigns to improve living and working conditions in every community.[89]

If such rhetoric is any indication of zeal, Stewart perhaps missed a golden opportunity to rally the women of the state into further political action when she insisted that the organization's purpose was strictly fund-raising. The WFM, although it fell short of its $20,000 goal, raised more than $8,000 in the one year of its existence. Stewart disbanded the group at the end of the fund drive, perhaps not realizing its full value in terms of promotion of the cause and reform activism in general.

The WFM drive illustrates the dynamics of progressive reform as nonvoting women attempted to convince reluctant government authorities of the need for state-supported social programs such as literacy. Coming as it did on the heels of public school reform in the commonwealth and throughout much of the South, the illiteracy campaign stressed the timely and important link between literate parents and the education of the child.[90] The editorial support it gained was exactly what Stewart had hoped for, although her success at publicizing and fund-raising may have convinced legislators that the program could and would go forward without the infusion of public dollars.

Stewart knew the state's women could provide more than financial support and a ready supply of volunteers; they could, through letter-writing and public information campaigns, gain political support for their initiatives. Moreover, she expected state legislators to notice the widespread support for her campaign. She fully understood their power and its potential when she enjoined them to "shout it in the gates of the mighty that these people should have a chance. . . . You can bring school authorities to wage war on illiteracy, and can support and encourage teachers as they wrestle with the foe. You can work and hope and pray for the emancipation of these enslaved ones, and can strive that this Nation may become a Nation where all possess knowledge and, therefore, have power, and where all are enlightened and therefore, are free."[91]

Stewart herself had "shouted her cause at the gates of the mighty" with notable results. Her friend Kentucky governor James B. McCreary showed his commitment to the illiteracy cause by issuing a proclamation urging Kentuckians to join the fight. The proclamation stated that instruction should be offered to parents for their own sake and for the sake of their children and the benefit of the state. Literacy, read the proclamation, would increase individual earning capacity, promote "home comforts," and provide for more intelligent exercise of the vote. Instruction should be offered to the young men and young women "who have missed opportunities earlier in life, but may yet take hold of instruction and make achievements."[92] The governor also noted that instruction of illiterates would improve Kentucky's educational ranking among the states and "give her a new and distinct position as the first Commonwealth which has ever attempted to accomplish such a great and important work."[93]

The more cynical observer might note that words such as those in the governor's proclamation are cheap, but reforming women of Stewart's generation often sought a moral commitment from government leaders prior to soliciting actual funding. If initially they had to content themselves with words, most of them expected to capitalize on those expressions of support in other ways. The governor's words represented political capital that could elicit subsequent legislative and bureaucratic support from the legislature.

In fact, McCreary's backing was critical. The elderly governor was both mentor and friend, and his fondness for Stewart led to frequent expressions of faith in her and her work.[94] The governor introduced her at the Frankfort rally on 28 November 1914, when she used the conclusion of her speech to lambaste those who opposed her work. In an "unusually strong address," a confident Stewart, perhaps emboldened by the governor's presence and support, overtly challenged those who questioned the literacy work. She noted that the only opposition to the illiteracy campaign had come from "two ministers, three school officials and a few demagogues." The minister, she noted, declined to join any movement advocated by women. He should, she declared, "to be consistent, . . . turn his back on temperance and missions, exclude women from his Sunday services and from his mid-week prayer-meetings, should disband the Ladies' Aid, and refuse to go to Heaven." The school official had simply missed the point if he believed publication of the statistics on the illiteracy of his county reflected poorly on his administration.

He should, suggested Stewart, "remember that most of the adult illiterates grew up illiterate before his county had the rare good fortune to secure such a broad-minded wide-awake superintendent as himself."[95] Clearly meaning to squelch any opposition to her campaign, not only in Frankfort but throughout the state, she challenged those who would stand in the way of progress and expressed scorn for those who refused to support her crusade: "My heart yearns tonight over every illiterate in the State, and every illiterate in the world, but sad and pathetic as is their plight, I pity but little less that Kentuckian who in this hour of Kentucky's crisis and humanity's need stands idle, scornful or aloof during this valiant fight with folded hands."[96]

With the political pathway at least partially cleared, her traveling expenses underwritten by the GFWC, and an effective fund-raising apparatus set in motion, she carried on rallies in most Kentucky cities, small towns, and rural hamlets. Gathering the faithful in churches, courthouses, town squares, parks, and one-room schoolhouses, Stewart preached a message of social redemption and economic benefit through education. She claimed that the possibility of salvation was closer when men and women could read their Bibles for themselves and earn their own way in the world. Moonlight Schools could do more than teach reading and writing, she said. Her rhetoric soared to new heights as she offered a means of salvation, spiritual and temporal, not only to the illiterates but to those who redeemed them.

In addition to clubwomen and politicians, Stewart's friends and colleagues in the teaching profession assisted in the crusade. Barksdale Hamlett, state superintendent of public instruction, proclaimed a school holiday to support the rallies sponsored by the KIC. He requested that every city and county superintendent close the schools and attend the rallies so they could greet the speakers.[97] His proclamation made it clear that the state superintendent supported Stewart's work and that he expected the state's teachers to do no less. Such official sanction also tied the illiteracy campaign to the more general movement for public school betterment. Hamlett's support legitimized the work for public school administrators and teachers.

Reports of county superintendents for the 1913–15 biennium almost without exception recorded the positive effects of the night schools. The Adair County school superintendent wrote that literacy efforts there had inspired a sense of community spirit. Forty or more teachers had taught Moonlight Schools, with surprising results. The county assessor had informed him "that quite a number of men signed their property lists who had never done so before, and they had learned to write in the moonlight schools." Bath County's superintendent devoted nearly half of his report to the evening schools, using the superlatives, "great, wonderful, and noble." "I have never before seen so much interest and enthusiasm manifested by the people of the rurals in any work." Many illiterates in his community could now read and write "fairly well," he said. He told of the many letters of gratitude he had received and pointed out many benefits of the program in his community, including a renewed civic spirit and a positive effect on day school. In every district, he wrote, "parents were made to see the need of education and through the medium of the moonlight school, became so interested, that they put their children in the day school and insisted on their regular attendance." Clay County reported similar results including enhanced support for the day schools. "The illiterate school enlists the support and cooperation of a class of parents who could never have been reached any other way," he wrote. The top school official in Grayson County, Ella Lewis, reported not only increased enrollment in the day schools but more than double the number of common school graduates over any preceding year. "We also have the largest attendance in the State normal that we have ever had," she added.[98]

The encouragement and support of public school teachers and administrators were critical. Without them Moonlight Schools could not have operated. With these individuals on her side however, Stewart continued to hold not only the moral high ground but also the practical means of implementing a literacy program in every community. Members of the KEA endorsed the work and volunteered in large numbers, primarily because they believed literate parents would enhance the educational opportunities of their children. Although some education professionals believed that adults could not learn, they did not initially oppose the work as long as it did not divert already scarce educational dollars from the common school effort. Most public school officials quickly recognized the potential benefits for the day schools, but others were not comfortable with the message that the schools had somehow failed to educate thousands of people. [99]

Organized by public school officials and local clubwomen, the KIC rallies involved entire communities and took on a festive, county fair atmosphere, complete with competitions and prizes. A good example is Clay County, where organizers posted a notice urging residents to compete for the $100 prize being offered to the program that taught the most illiterates:

Can we win?
Win what?
Win the State Prize.

Of course we can.
Just watch us try.
And watch us win.
The prize is $100.
It would fence our school yard.
It would paint our school house.
It would buy a library.
It would pay our good teacher.
Let us work for the prize.

Since the illiteracy crusade was based on the idea of people helping people, Stewart recommended incentives to help communities establish and attain their goals. Barren County's objective was "500 Illiterates taught . . . during the month of October." Posters read: "Help us, patrons, to get every illiterate in a Moonlight School. No greater opportunity for unselfish service, constructive patriotism, and educational aggressiveness could be offered than to aid in the success of this movement." Huge crowds packed into small school buildings, theaters, and churches to hear Stewart and the others speak. Community organizers advertised her appearance weeks in advance. Notices proclaiming that she would be there to "welcome Moonlighters," give a speech, place a "gold pin on all those who march," or preside at a "Moonlight Supper" in the courthouse yard appeared in small towns and rural communities across the state.[100]

Stewart carefully promoted her cause in the language of the audience she addressed. Just as she had inspired club and church volunteers to unselfish acts of devotion by equating literacy with salvation, she also inspired professional educators and journalists to join in a movement that was sure to bring progress in all its forms. She lavished praise on those who had joined the fight and denounced those who had not.[101]

In three years, Stewart had created a network that included clubwomen, many of her state's political leaders, teachers in the KEA, and the press. Kentucky journalists and editors followed the lead of Desha Breckinridge's *Lexington Herald* and provided extensive coverage of the literacy work. Breckinridge's comments in the Sunday, 22 November 1914, edition of the *Herald* lauded Stewart and the women of Kentucky for their determination to obliterate illiteracy from the state and urged the men of the commonwealth to support their effort "by contributing their money, by projecting themselves and their brains and energy into the movement that the women have organized." The ignorant cannot compete with the educated, he argued, and the untrained cannot lead the trained. We of Kentucky, with a tenth of our citizens ignorant of the rudiments of learning; with a tenth of our voters unable to form judgments except from the spoken word of the politician or the demagogue, are bound to lag in the rear. Let's remove that burden of ignorance; let's give to every man and woman in the State the blessing of education, which we can do if we will all work together in this movement which can be completed so quickly that we will not miss the time nor the money necessary to make it a success.[102]

The editor of the *Lexington Leader,* a Republican newspaper that published a Sunday edition with the *Herald,* also praised literacy volunteers for their humanitarian and patriotic efforts, echoing their challenge to legislators: "In a task affecting so vitally the welfare of the Commonwealth and the individual, it would seem that the work of carrying the lamp of education to the illiterate adults of the State is a responsibility which might be more properly borne by the Commonwealth than by public subscriptions, and the State's inaction makes the whole endeavor wrongfully take on the aspect of a charity rather than a long neglected function of government."[103]

Kentucky journalists welcomed Stewart, as editor of the *Mountaineer,* into the Kentucky Press Association (KPA), lauded her "splendid work," and pledged the association's enthusiastic support.[104] At the group's annual gathering in 1913, Stewart gave the keynote address, in which she stressed the links between education, reform, and economic growth.[105]

With the literacy campaign up and running in her home state, Stewart began to aggressively promote it in other states. Alabama in 1915 became the first to adopt the Kentucky model of a state illiteracy commission, undertaking a program that remained in full operation for many years. Acknowledging the "vision" of "a little woman in a backwoods Kentucky county" and her "remarkable" success in eliminating illiteracy there, Alabama's superintendent of education followed Stewart's instructions to publish the state's illiteracy figures to rally public opinion. The 1910 census revealed that among the state's ten-year-olds, 19 percent of white children and 49 percent of black children could neither read nor write. Alabama's eighteen-year-olds were somewhat better-off, with an illiteracy rate of 4 percent for whites and 19 percent for blacks.[106]

Stewart recommended that states publish their illiteracy statistics as a prelude to a major campaign. Actual figures toppled commonly held beliefs about the uneducated, since most southern states blamed their illiteracy on nonwhites or immigrants. Alabama, for example, characterized illiteracy pri-

marily in terms of race: "Illiteracy in Alabama is excessive, alarmingly excessive, and is due largely to lack of adequate school facilities and the presence
of an unfortunate race which has made progress very difficult indeed for
both races." Illiterates in Arkansas numbered more than one hundred thousand, or roughly 11.8 percent of the state's adult population, and two-thirds
of them were black. Replicated in most southern states, the statistics reflected traditional paternalistic racism and the widespread belief that educating blacks would undermine the status quo.[107]

The education movement throughout the South had, for the most part,
failed to benefit black citizens. For example, South Carolina spent twelve
times as much on its white schoolchildren as on its black students. While the
dollars spent on black schools increased during the Progressive Era, so did
the disparity between expenditures for white and black pupils. Some states
used the distribution of taxes along with the allocation of educational funds
to ensure an inferior public school system for blacks.[108] In Kentucky, incor-
poration laws prohibited separate tax levies based on race; however, local
school boards could, in many districts, levy taxes "for one race to the exclusion of the other," reported the Kentucky Negro Educational Association
(KNEA) in a 1925 resolution urging "Better Negro Education."[109]

In Stewart's vision, Moonlight Schools served blacks and whites, albeit
separately, and several southern states responded to her call to educate rural
illiterates regardless of color. Mississippi opened a campaign in 1916. North
Carolina and Arkansas began statewide programs in 1917. Like Kentucky,
these states created illiteracy commissions but relied primarily on volunteers
for teaching, on private and philanthropic donations for funding, and on the
crusade mechanism for spreading the word. Generally traveling by train and
financing her trips by providing teacher training institutes, Stewart initially
limited her travels to the South, with occasional forays into northeastern states.
In the summer of 1915 she trekked west to introduce the literacy crusade in
Oklahoma, Kansas, and New Mexico. Oklahoma led out in the movement
and made significant progress in reducing the number of illiterates in the
state, but after an auspicious beginning a budget-cutting governor eliminated
its literacy programs.[110] The movement flourished in Kansas and New Mexico,
where Stewart's personal influence was strong. She formed lasting friendships with Governor Henry J. Allen of Kansas and with state superintendent
J. V. Conway of New Mexico, both of whom energetically supported the
literacy campaigns at the state level and later became important allies in the
national illiteracy crusade.[111]

In Minnesota, the campaign opened in the fall of 1915 with a speaking tour by Stewart. Statistics indicated that Minnesota in fact had a net gain in the number of illiterates between 1900 and 1910. The state's educational authorities embarked on a campaign to lower the numbers, but much as southerners had done, Minnesotans blamed their high numbers on Native Americans and the elderly.[112]

As they had in Kentucky, clubwomen in these states took the lead. Federated women in Minnesota engaged Stewart as the keynote speaker for their state meeting in 1916. Stewart also spoke to a gathering of the state's teachers, where she was joined by Florence Kelley of the National Consumer's League. Kelley spoke on behalf of better state and national legislation on child labor and the need to prevent future illiteracy by keeping children in school.[113] This link to other social reform efforts not only helped ensure positive outcomes but also enabled Stewart to broaden her base of support and more firmly establish the need for literacy work. In Wisconsin, Stewart shared the dais with Margaret Woodrow Wilson, the president's daughter, when she addressed that state's education association in November 1915. Wilson, an education activist, frequently spoke on the need to make school buildings "vital centers of our communities," a goal she shared with Stewart. The two women "startled" the state's educators into action with the announcement that Wisconsin ranked thirteenth from the top in the national scale of illiteracy.[114]

An excellent example of a state campaign is the work of Wil Lou Gray, who originated night schools for illiterate adults in Laurens County, South Carolina. After ascertaining that, in 1915, 608 of the county's 4,525 voters could not sign a ballot and voted by making a mark, she established sessions for adults using the Moonlight School model. The schools met on moonlit evenings during December, January, and February when farmers were not as busy with crops and chores. Gray, her state's supervisor of rural schools, encountered strong resistance from state legislators whose fear of educating the masses, especially blacks, kept them from adequately funding adult literacy efforts in South Carolina. Gray, like Stewart, refused to give up.[115] At the urging of the State Federation of Women's Clubs, the South Carolina General Assembly voted a statewide appropriation, and the governor appointed an illiteracy commission in 1916.[116] Called a "closet revolutionary" and public intellectual who challenged the regressive policies of southern politicians, Gray advocated a stronger government role in economic and social welfare and, as Stewart had done, demanded that her state accept financial and moral responsibility for its illiterate working-class population, black and white.[117] South Carolina's first illiteracy commission collapsed from lack of funding, but Gray's subsequent effort resulted in a variety of programs for adults, including the highly successful Lay-By Schools and the Opportunity Schools that still teach out-of-school youth in South Carolina. Wil Lou Gray continued the fight for literacy in her home state until her death in 1984.[118] In 2000, the Opportunity Schools reprinted Stewart's book *Moonlight Schools for the Emancipation of Illiterate Adults*. On the opening page is Stewart's inscription, "To my Valiant Comrade, Wil Lou Gray," signed in Frankfort on 30 January 1923. The cover page calls Stewart the "Inspiration for Wil Lou Gray's Night Schools and Opportunity Schools in South Carolina."[119]

Stewart mailed materials, information, and instructions to the various state governors, campaign leaders, and volunteers, a time-consuming chore that tested her organizational and management ability and that of her office assistant, Lela Mae Stiles. To ease the burden, she approached the National Education Association, which she hoped could serve as a communications link with teachers across the country. In July 1916 Stewart addressed the annual NEA convention, gave a brief history of the movement, and encouraged members and the national organization to get behind the literacy drive. As she always did when addressing educators, Stewart touted voluntary service as the best means of teaching the nation's illiterates, telling the gathering that public school teachers were already "trained, prepared, and stationed for the work." She reemphasized the ideal of teaching as a calling and argued that adults were as worthy and as much in need of teaching as young children.[120] The following year, the NEA announced the creation of an illiteracy commission with Stewart at the helm, making it possible for her to reach educators all across the country through their largest professional organization.

THREE

Moonlight Schools and Progressivism

Kentucky lawmakers had created the Kentucky Illiteracy Commission in 1914 largely because of Stewart's emphasis on voluntarism and the relatively few demands her plan to eliminate illiteracy made on the state. Many of the legislators also supported the ideals of self-improvement, expanded literacy, and its promised economic benefits, although they remained reluctant to finance such gains with public dollars. Therefore, when the KIC opened its doors in Frankfort, it did so with a very small budget. State-authorized fundraising brought in donations a few dollars at a time, and the state picked up the tab for small expenses.

But fighting illiteracy proved an expensive proposition, and even to a skilled fund-raiser like Stewart, the task of securing private financing became increasingly burdensome and the results inadequate. Not only were there more illiterates than she had anticipated, but a large campaign also required dollars to support organization and coordination. Although Stewart had names, literacy workers still needed funds to conduct local campaigns, identify all those in need, and pay for supplies, reading materials, transportation, office help, and publicity. Therefore, in 1916, Stewart decided to petition the Kentucky legislature to fund the agency it had created and the cause it had endorsed two years earlier.

This critical decision brought the crusade squarely into Kentucky party politics, which for the next decade claimed much of Stewart's time, attention, and energy. Her experiences in that arena illustrate the continuities of women's activism in the pre- and postsuffrage years and call attention to the difficulties many Progressive Era women encountered in their quest for state support of their reform initiatives. The politicization of the illiteracy crusade forced the confluence of women's voluntary, interest-based politics and men's traditional, established party politics. Another example of the confrontation between the "the Lady and the Tiger," Stewart's entry into Democratic Party politics points out the ways in which the woman vote influenced male structures of party and power and demonstrates how women and men negotiated new notions of shared access, if not shared authority.[1]

Both Democrats and Republicans had endorsed the literacy work, but Stewart's long-standing affiliation with the Democratic Party and the fractiousness that surrounded reform in Kentucky made a truly nonpartisan effort impossible. As she became more deeply involved in state politics, struggles within her own party crippled the movement. At the state level, Stewart's work had to compete for legislative attention with prohibition, tax reform, woman suffrage, and other issues that divided not only Republicans from Democrats but also Democrats from one another.

In identifying the huge "new" problem of illiteracy and raising public consciousness and outrage to combat it, Stewart had followed a pattern set by moral reformers, male and female, late in the previous century. When she marshaled the forces of women's voluntary associations, churches, professional educators, and the press, she employed the tactics of a second generation of reformers whose entry into the public sphere was marked by coalition building and cooperation, although like party politics, it too suffered from internal division. Those who had gone before perhaps eased the task of securing a state agency to carry on the literacy work, but a pattern had emerged that ultimately had a detrimental effect on the literacy crusade. State lawmakers frequently responded to the petitions of women reformers by allowing themselves to be convinced of the need for social reform, but they followed up by merely debating over and over who had responsibility for the problem and who would pay for it. Debate led to delay, and when appropriations finally passed, they were often pitifully small.

Political scientist and sociologist Theda Skocpol has argued that it was easier for women to extract funding from legislative bodies prior to passage of the Nineteenth Amendment, when it appeared expeditious for politicians to support them and thus win their partisan allegiance once they were enfranchised. Using the example of the Women's Bureau, Skocpol maintains that this circumstance changed after women won the vote, and their "will and capacities" to achieve maternalist politics diminished in the face of powerful backlashes against their policy gains.[2] Although this is a compelling thesis, it presupposes inevitability probably never felt by antisuffrage campaigners or by male politicians who resented and opposed female enfranchisement; historians are still debating whether women's activism in fact diminished in the 1920s. Nancy Cott argues that throughout the 1920s and into the 1930s, women's organizations actually benefited from the new ethos that women were citizens who could and should participate in public life. She insists that the "artificial barrier" of the Nineteenth Amendment obscures the similarities in women's political behavior before and after its passage.[3]

Cora Wilson Stewart's experience in Kentucky politics validates some of Skocpol's arguments and lends credence to Cott's conclusion, but it also appears that male politicians in that state willingly agreed to "support," with largely token appropriations, social welfare issues pushed by women, perhaps to convince them that suffrage was not really necessary. Prior to passage of the suffrage amendment, many male legislators masked their condescension in chivalry; prior to enfranchisement, women's lack of political expertise was charming. It signified true womanhood. Once it appeared that the Nineteenth Amendment would pass, many of the state's politicians treated women in public life with condescension and contempt, promising one thing and delivering quite another. After 1920, whether it was a "backlash" as Skocpol has suggested or simply a parochial "return to normalcy," women's initiatives sparked the same kind of partisan infighting and political chicanery that had marked the state's politics since the turn of the century. Condescension became overt, and as Stewart's experience shows, women's lack of experience was no longer charming. It represented incompetence and signified that women were ill suited to public life.

Stewart's experience in state politics cannot, of course, be separated from the fact that she was a woman, nor can "the great divide" of woman suffrage be ignored, but it reinforces and adds dimension to a point made by historians Arthur S. Link and Richard L. McCormick that too much focus on leadership "conceals more than it discloses" about Progressive Era reform. They note that a crucial dynamic of progressivism was the support of "ordinary people," masses of voters willing to trust a reform candidate, or the "sometimes frenzied mass supporters" of progressive leaders.[4] Cora Wilson Stewart was a hero to many Kentuckians, and their support meant political clout. Like Jane Addams in Illinois, she was the darling of the Kentucky press and enjoyed the full backing of most of the churches in the state, its clubwomen, and its professional organization for teachers. She was, in short, a woman to be taken seriously by the state's politicians, and her cause was one that many Kentuckians upheld with almost religious zeal. Her popularity and celebrity status were especially remarkable in a state that considered politics an art form and "mellifluous oratory" a requirement for leadership.[5]

Hardly a supplicant in her relationship with Kentucky politicians, Stewart represented the potential power of the woman vote in the commonwealth, but, more important, she represented it in a style that party politicians recognized and appreciated. Like many women of her generation, Stewart wanted government to become more responsive to the needs of its citizens, and her literacy crusade came to maturity in a political culture shaped at least in part by women's vision of the role of the state. The literacy crusade followed a pattern set by maternalist reformers agitating for social measures to protect society's weakest members and to address the inequities and inefficiencies of America's developing industrial and urban society. Their strategy of public education and lobbying through networks of voluntary and professional associations was well suited to pressuring legislatures to pass bills along nonpartisan lines, to overcoming opposition from the courts, and to beginning the work that would later occupy vast administrative bureaucracies. These women formed alliances with male leaders that enabled them to largely determine the course of progressive social politics. Their participation in the governing process generally took place outside the polity, but parallel to it. Clubwomen, through their national federations, practiced "a politics of public education," which enabled them to work around party politics and existing bureaucracies. Their tactics included direct lobbying of legislators and formally testifying at legislative hearings. They also engaged in broad letter-writing campaigns for and against pending legislation. Their activities pressured legislators from many localities in a given state, while at the same time lobbying legislatures in many different states at roughly the same time.[6]

This style of politics suited Stewart's reform agenda, which included the belief that every citizen had the right to an education and that full literacy was essential to social progress. Her faith reflected the broader, if somewhat limited, Progressive Era emphasis on social welfare efforts to provide relief to families in poverty. Encouraged by the activities of national organizations and agencies such as the Russell Sage Foundation and the Rockefeller Foundation, to which Stewart appealed as well, these efforts examined individual and environmental improvement as a means of ameliorating poverty, dependency, and disease.[7]

Stewart believed that schooling for nonreading adults could profoundly change their lives and the lives of their children because parents who valued education would keep their children in school. Illiteracy could, she reasoned, be eliminated in the short span of a single generation. However, realizing the full benefit of literacy also required changes in the public schools. Compulsory attendance laws had to be strictly enforced, teacher salaries and standards of teacher training had to be raised, and county school districts had to assume responsibility for illiterate adults as well as children.

This conclusion perhaps put Stewart ahead of her time, but time has validated her analysis. A Kentucky study conducted almost ninety years after she began her work reached similar conclusions. The Task Force on Adult Education reported in August 2000 that low levels of literacy among parents relates directly to the education of their children, who are five times more likely to drop out of school than those reared by literate parents. Moreover, the task force also concluded, much as Stewart did in 1916, that the focus should be on the county as the "unit for improvement and change" and that regional and statewide frameworks were needed to support county-level change.[8]

Stewart requested that the state identify and enumerate all illiterates and make their names available to cities and counties, which would then take responsibility for their education. The state could coordinate instruction, provide books, teaching materials, and supplies, and pay salaries for illiteracy agents assigned to oversee the work in each of the state's 120 counties and assist teachers in organizing and conducting Moonlight Schools. She insisted that the state should also take responsibility for disseminating information so the public could become more aware of illiteracy and its relation to other social problems.[9] The KIC could provide these services, but from its creation in 1914, it had simply coordinated voluntary efforts, since Stewart and other members of the commission served without salary and the agency had no appropriation to carry on its work.

Frustrated by the constant burden of fund-raising and lack of funds and convinced that the commission could fill a void in the state's provision of educational services, Stewart decided to ask the 1916 General Assembly for an appropriation for the KIC. In a move that points up her organizational and public relations skills, she assembled a legislative committee of more than one hundred prominent educators, school superintendents, judges, newspapermen, and clubwomen from across the state to help her lobby for an appropriations bill. On the committee were the heads of both the Democratic and Republican parties, two former governors, including her old friend Democrat James B. McCreary, and the leaders of all the state's labor organizations.[10] The composition of the lobbying group illustrates the breadth of support for the literacy work, but it also points up an important part of her strategy. Like other maternalist reformers, much of her efforts took place outside the official realm of government through lobbying and public education; however, a critical part of the Kentucky crusade, as illustrated by the makeup of the committee, was inextricably linked to state politics.

The legislative committee sponsored a bill, introduced in both the house and the senate, asking for a $20,000 annual appropriation to employ agents in the various counties to direct the work against illiteracy and to enforce the compulsory school attendance law. Committee members had already begun lobbying, and Stewart was scheduled to address a joint session of the legislature on 17 February 1916, in support of the appropriation. In January, however, John C. Duffy, a special assistant attorney general, temporarily derailed their efforts when he reported that an audit ordered by newly sworn Democratic governor Augustus O. Stanley indicated that the KIC had improperly used state money for telephone, telegraph, and mailing expenses. Duffy charged that the commission, "most particularly its head, Mrs. Cora Wilson Stewart, has drawn from the State treasury during the last year the sum of $1,458.82 without license to do so."[11]

Although Duffy stopped short of charging Stewart with corruption, he questioned the propriety of some of her actions. "Mrs. Stewart is not well versed in the ethics of public office," he said. "She has been impetuous in seeking to push her work and has endorsed political office seekers for their friendly attitude toward the illiteracy fight, something that is not proper."[12] Duffy produced no evidence for his allegations but charged that Stewart had mailed "several hundred" letters supporting the candidacy of E. B. McGlone for the Republican nomination for representative from the Seventy-third District. McGlone, who won the election, was married to Stewart's sister, Stella. His opponent was Alexander Stewart, Cora's former husband. Mrs. Stewart vehemently denied having mailed "any letters . . . from any point, or from the office of the Illiteracy Commission" on McGlone's behalf. "It can be proven," she said, "that not so much as a letterhead, stamp or envelope of this commission was ever devoted to that purpose."[13]

Stewart was in Washington when the charges appeared, but she immediately caught the next train to Frankfort, demanding a complete investigation. Denying any wrongdoing whatsoever, she aimed a barb at the Stanley faction, suggesting that the new governor and his administration would do well simply "to keep its own skirts clean." She said the previous attorney general had approved the expenditures, small as they were. Because of the state's parsimony, Stewart often financed the work of the commission with money "from her own pocket . . . in addition to time, thought and labor

without compensation." She called the attack "unwarranted, politically motivated and grossly unfair." "It requires no mathematician to figure that
$1,485.82, covering a period of eighteen months, would not go far in providing stenography, stamps, stationery, printing and telephone to conduct a gigantic campaign such as the Illiteracy Commission is waging."[14]

Stewart maintained that the state authorized payment of the expenses,
and that it was common practice in state government to cover small operational costs from the "sinking fund." She insisted that an official from the
previous administration had ruled that the commission was entitled to "certain small aid," and she had gratefully "picked up the crumbs which thus fall
from the table of the state." Now some new official construed the law to
mean her agency was entitled to nothing. In a prepared statement, she invoked her selfless dedication to her calling and criticized the parsimonious
attitude of the state:

> But to attack a struggling commission, which has existed mainly on public char
> ity, which has handled the smallest amount of money of any commission ever
> created by the state, a commission in which no official receives one dollar for
> service, a commission which has striven to promote the common weal, a com
> mission whose history has been one of great struggle and fearful sacrifice—to
> make such an attack upon it in its crucial hour without even looking for a single
> vestige of proof would be a laughable farce, were it not so serious and so mani
> festly unjust.[15]

The Stanley administration had clearly targeted Stewart in advance of
the vote on the appropriations bill, hoping to discredit her and to justify its
unwillingness to vote money for the cause. Desha Breckinridge, in a scathing
editorial in the *Lexington Herald*, took them to task, noting that, "wonderful
as she is, Mrs. Stewart can not vote. She is without political influence." Therefore, the enlightened citizens of the state would not permit "the humiliation
of this unselfish, dauntless woman, whose life has been given to service too
noble for the comprehension of vote-seeking politicians." The newspaperman challenged the governor, if he wanted to curtail the state's expenses and
"punish the parasites that are preying on the public purse," to go after bigger
game.[16]

Breckinridge's editorial and Stewart's response to the attack illustrate
public discourse concerning women's presuffrage role in politics. Stewart
understood the controversial and tenuous nature of her public role and chose
to defend it by invoking the virtues of selfless womanhood. Her response
demonstrated political acumen and a thorough understanding of her constituency, both outside the polity and within. She allowed herself to be cast as

a victim, so that chivalrous men could come to her defense. Breckinridge, the husband of an active and outspoken suffragist, was one of many who did so. Another, who argued that the state had "never spent money to better advantage," noted that he was one of ten men ready and willing to reimburse the state for the money it begrudged Mrs. Stewart.[17] The editor of the *Owensboro Messenger* also attacked the Stanley administration for its lack of chivalry, noting that

> here in Kentucky . . . it has been our boast and to our credit that women were shielded, protected and honored and to assault a woman's reputation in any way has been regarded as worse than unmanly, it has always been considered contemptible. When the one woman in Kentucky who has stood conspicuous for a great, noble and philanthropic work, giving her time and her brilliant mind without compensation to wipe out the darkest blot upon the state—its illiteracy, is made the target of the common politician, as Mrs. Cora Wilson Stewart has recently been pilloried by alleged reformers, it arouses a storm of protesting indignation from every true Kentuckian.[18]

Interestingly, the article also noted that "Mrs. Stewart wrote and mailed a number of letters in Powell County in a race for the legislature there and used some of the illiteracy commission stationery. She doubtless paid for her own stamps," a charge Stewart had vigorously denied in her public statement. The issue, then, was not whether she had acted improperly. If she had, it was only in minor ways, especially when compared with common political practice in the state. The issue was her womanhood. Tradition and gentlemanly behavior dictated that politicians not treat a woman in public life as they would treat one another. After all, a woman of Stewart's standing might overlook details; she would not deliberately do anything improper or illegal.

Stewart's political friends immediately took her side, writing letters on her behalf and sending letters of encouragement. Judge Allie Young, defending her in response to a financial backer's inquiry about her efforts in Rowan County and her campaign against illiteracy, wrote, "I do know this grand woman gave all her time and money unsparingly for quite a while to bring about the result her untiring efforts accomplished for her people, besides I know her to be the embodiment of truth and the sole [*sic*] of honor, and I cannot imagine why this assault is made upon her." Young, a political boss in eastern Kentucky whose maneuverings earned him the title the "Morehead Manipulator," also expressed his complete confidence that Stewart would be fully vindicated.[19]

Equally confident, former governor McCreary told Stewart he had talked to President Woodrow Wilson about her and "the great work of the Illiteracy

Commission." He reminded her that she had his "sympathy in your great struggle, I thought about you very often but I will talk to you about my thoughts when I see you."[20]

The Duffy crisis was, as the *Owensboro Messenger* had called it, a "small matter," especially when compared with the outrageous scandals involving male politicians of the day, some of which were rehashed in the editorials, arguments, and counterarguments provoked by the attack on Stewart. It may have been a small matter, but this case was different. It involved a woman who had chosen a public life, and her supporters would not have her treated as a "common politician."

In fact, by choosing a public life, Stewart exposed herself to such attacks, some of which were vicious and personal. Much to her chagrin, her carefully guarded private life became a public issue when the *Hopkinsville Kentuckian* ran an editorial that some of her supporters found particularly obnoxious. Giving detailed coverage of Duffy's charges, it implied that Stewart squandered public funds. In what her defenders saw as an obvious attempt to undermine her credibility, it also mentioned her divorce from A. T. Stewart. An anonymous author sprang to her defense in a forcefully written letter to the editor, alleging unfairness both to Alexander Stewart's current wife, "an estimable woman whose happiness cannot be furthered by public notice of former chapters in the life of her husband," and to the first Mrs. Stewart. Writing under the initials M.D. (most likely it was her friend Mattie Dalton), the writer challenged the newspaper to provide more balanced journalism: "Therefore, since you have given some publicity to Mr. Duffy's statement, to Mrs. Stewart's former and most unfortunate matrimonial relations, and to the fact that she has been invited to speak before the Legislature, I am sure you will be glad to show the other side . . . by giving some notice of the report of the Illiteracy Commission, and of the nature of the talk which she will make before the General Assembly."[21]

Dalton wrote her friend a fiery letter, filled with disdain for those who had caused the fuss. "Don't you know, girl, that if they confined themselves to something near the truth, and gave you credit for something near the right attitude of mind, that they would be much harder to disprove?" She encouraged Stewart to persevere: "I have decided that such an attack at this time will make it easier for you to get what you want, and will make friends for you."[22] Dalton's assumption proved correct.

If the Stanley administration had chosen this means of discrediting Stewart prior to refusing an appropriation for her work, it had backfired, a particularly ironic development, since there may have been some validity to the charges. Despite Stewart's own response and that of the many defenders protesting her innocence, a letter from her close friend and associate John Grant Crabbe, a fellow Democrat and secretary-treasurer of the KIC, raised the possibility that Stewart lacked fervor in her attention to detail. In an urgent letter, marked "personal," Crabbe listed five items concerning the budget of the KIC that needed her immediate attention, noting "that these various items are of the utmost importance and that you ought to forget all of the rest of your troubles sending me a special delivery covering all of these points at least at your earliest possible convenience." He urged a prompt reply: "Your courtesy about all of these items will help me a good deal in keeping my treasurer's books in the best of shape." The list included several small checks he had signed at Stewart's request without fully understanding what they covered.[23]

This episode put Stewart's crusade in the limelight, and although members of the Stanley administration counted on strong public reaction, they had not expected it to be directed at them. Neither of the state's major papers gave any credence to the charges and, after their display of outrage at Stanley for the attack on a "blameless woman," allowed the issue to die. Ultimately state inspector and examiner Nat B. Sewell found no evidence that Stewart had acted improperly and even noted the "extreme economy" practiced by the commission in all its endeavors.[24]

Despite the fracas, Governor Stanley and Stewart enjoyed a relatively congenial relationship as fellow Democrats and progressives. Democrats had split over prohibition, however, and the new governor and the literacy crusader took opposite sides of this controversial issue, which had already sapped the party of much of its vitality. The Democratic faithful wrangled among themselves over the existing county unit law, which Stanley supported, and a broader statewide prohibition law favored by much of the party, including Stewart. Despite the fact that he signed more progressive legislation than any other Kentucky governor, Stanley was often criticized as a tool of the liquor interests in the state.[25] Even though his administration besmirched Stewart's name and questioned her integrity, the governor had no personal animosity toward her. In fact, she was on intimate terms with the Stanley family. Amanda Owsley Stanley, the governor's mother, regarded Cora as her "adopted daughter," and the two corresponded often. Mrs. Stanley addressed the younger woman as "My Darling Daughter" and frequently referred to herself as Cora's "Adopted Mother." Mrs. Stanley encouraged Stewart to visit, noting how much she looked forward to seeing her: "I have been looking for you dear. . . . Come to me and give me fresh strength."[26]

The attack no doubt strained their relationship, but Governor Stanley did not oppose the illiteracy work; he actually supported it.[27] He simply did not want the state to pay for it. Elected on a cost-cutting and tax reform platform, he opposed funding the commission because the state could not afford another appropriation that generated no revenue.[28] His cost-cutting talk rang hollow in some parts of the state, as indicated by "The Truth of It," an editorial in the *Elizabethtown News:* "If Mrs. Stewart's $20,000 bill was submitted to the people," attested the author, "it would carry by the highest majority the state ever gave, while Governor Stanley's suggestion of a $50,000 Liquor Commission would not get enough votes to act as pall-bearers for its burial."[29]

The charges against Stewart had, in effect, strengthened her position in the state, but she and members of the legislative committee knew that winning the $20,000 appropriation would still be difficult, given Stanley's position on the budget. Hoping to generate as much public enthusiasm as possible for the bill, they mobilized supporters all over the state in a deluge of proclamations, editorials, and public statements on behalf of the literacy crusade. The County Superintendents' Association of Kentucky, at Crabbe's suggestion, dashed off an endorsement of Stewart's work and urged lawmakers to vote the appropriation on the strength of what it had done to enhance the day schools. Others in the state's education hierarchy asserted their faith in her work and the absolute necessity of state funding to support it. Rice Eubank, of the *Southern School Journal,* praised the Moonlight Schools, noting that the "eradication of illiteracy removes the great drawback of indifference toward schools." State Superintendent of Public Instruction V. O. Gilbert and Western State Normal School president H. H. Cherry also urged passage of the appropriation.[30]

The *Lexington Herald* reported this support and noted that Stewart also enjoyed the "absolute confidence" of both houses of the General Assembly and the support of leaders of both parties.[31] In an earlier editorial, Desha Breckinridge had urged legislators to make a "reasonable appropriation" to carry on the "great work" Cora Wilson Stewart had begun. Calling her the "pet" of the Kentucky Press Association and the educators of the state, he wondered "if the people . . . of Kentucky, or any other state, really appreciate the great work that some women do for education, morality, and religion."[32]

Whether legislators appreciated their efforts, Kentucky women had embraced the literacy cause, and several prominent clubwomen served on the legislative committee. The KFWC urged the legislature to approve the funding measure, noting that the organization had promoted "with earnest endeavor" the illiteracy work in the state "with the expectation that the next general assembly would appropriate funds to place the Illiteracy Commission on as substantial basis of support as are the other commissions of the state." The Kentucky Press Association and the legislative committee of the KEA also endorsed the $20,000 appropriation bill.[33]

Once again, Stewart's network served her well. Professional associates, newspapermen, and clubwomen believed in the literacy work and lobbied their districts for popular support. Several male political allies, including Allie Young and former governor McCreary, also used their leverage to try to drum up the necessary votes. Young wrote state senator Charles Arnett, soliciting his backing for Stewart's appropriation bill: "Your friends in this section, to a man, are for it, and . . . anything you may do in behalf of this bill will be so greatly appreciated, that should you ask assistance from we people [sic] in the near, or far distant future, we will certainly come to your call." Young wrote a personal note to Stewart on a copy of Arnett's letter and sent it to her, along with his promise of assistance: "Call me if I can help you any time. I expect to be in Frankfort Feb. 17 bright and early."[34]

McCreary helped Stewart prepare for her appeal to the joint session of the legislature. Although the former governor could not attend, he helped write her speech and encouraged her to make full use of her oratorical skills. He urged her to write a stronger preamble that showed the significant decrease in the number of illiterates in the state, but he also deferred to her judgment. "I have written at the top of the page the preamble which I prefer but you know best," he wrote. He also told her to request a salary because "the bill will pass easier allowing you a salary than omitting it." Although she took some of McCreary's advice, Stewart declined this suggestion. He recommended strategies for presenting her speech, telling her not to speak until her bill had been reported favorably to one house or the other unless she decided to make two speeches. He thought one speech would make a stronger impression: "Your first speech will carry the members by storm & please & impress them for they have not heard you, but members get accustomed very quickly to even the most . . . magnetic speakers." In the stressful weeks before Stewart's bill came up, McCreary offered words of encouragement and cheer, concluding one note with the promise that he would, "sometime in the future, participate in the dedication of a monument to the champion of the Illiteracy Campaign and the Queen of the Moonlight Schools." He told her support for her bill was "getting stronger all the time, & your eloquence & stirring statement of facts & convincing words will bring you victory."[35]

Allies such as McCreary and Young provided Stewart direct access to the state legislature. With powerful friends, they knew how to get things done. Both considered it morally imperative that they protect and guide Stewart's course in the male world of politics. But in the case of the illiteracy crusade and other reform initiatives led by women, the effect of such southern chivalry was ultimately limiting. Instead of broadening women's opportunity, it perpetuated, even widened, the gap between the public, male sphere of politics and the womanist sphere of voluntarism. Stewart's male allies were in fact escorts. On the arm of a gentleman like McCreary or Young, she could enter the realm of politics, an arena that would not receive her, or do her bidding, unaccompanied.

If McCreary and Young served as figurative escorts, decorum dictated that Stewart be assigned literal ones as well. When she entered the state house on 17 February 1916, a committee of four legislators, including her brother, former representative Bunyan Wilson, escorted her. Four others "appointed" her, and the lieutenant governor introduced her, noting that her name was a "household word in every home in our great and beloved state." Friends and supporters packed the galleries, and many of her female colleagues carried banners as they took their seats for the open session. It was rumored that Stewart intended to attack John C. Duffy, and in her opening words, she acknowledged the gossip. But it was not her purpose, she said "to attack anybody for making a mistake." It was time for serious thought, not for recrimination. Instead, she related the work of the Moonlight Schools and recounted the important accomplishments of the KIC but noted that its "splendid work" could not go forward without state support. She called the appropriation bills "politically wise, economically safe and manifestly just" and told lawmakers not to say they could not afford to spend so much money educating illiterates when in fact, they could ill afford not to. Stewart said illiteracy cost the state thousands of dollars a year. Despite that need, up to half of every $1,000 in school funding was wasted, and at least four of every ten children received no benefit at all. Illiteracy resulted in severe social dislocations, she said. Criminal prosecutions increased, and epidemics of diseases were harder to check. Death rates and infant mortality were higher in illiterate populations, she said, concluding that "illiteracy is the most expensive and extravagant thing a state can have."[36]

She chided Stanley's claim that the state had no funds, noting that there were two ways to increase the state's revenues. One was to readjust the system of taxation and revenues, and the other was to increase the productive power of its citizens. "To remove illiteracy from a citizen increases his productive power 62% per year, say the experts. If one-fourth of Kentucky's 87,000 illiterate males can be taught, it would add a million and a half more annually to their earnings. . . . Better than to reduce the State's debt is to insure such substantial prosperity as will keep it out of debt. Wipe out illiteracy and insure prosperity."[37]

Stewart's speech was designed to appeal to practical politicians who expressed concerns over budgetary problems, but she also appealed to their emotions and love of rhetoric. In closing, she invoked the state's "sainted dead" and her own:

> We often say that we would not call back the dead and when I think of my angel mother, who died so triumphantly with the words on her lips, 'O, this heavenly day,' and of my infant son, who had he lived to manhood's estate or to ripe old age, and suffered all of life's sorrows could have gained no more than he now enjoys. I have never thought that for even a mother's love or a baby's kiss I would call back my sainted dead. But today I could almost call back those matchless and indomitable of Kentuckians gone before to help liberate Kentucky's illiterates.

Her list included Daniel Boone, Theodore O'Hara, Joel T. Hart, William Goebel, and Abraham Lincoln. "If these and all the others of Kentucky's illustrious dead could speak to your souls a message they would say with one voice: 'Wipe out Kentucky's illiteracy; wipe it out; wipe it out.'" [38]

Governor Stanley's forces responded to the thunderous applause following Stewart's oration with a motion to adjourn, a tactical maneuver designed to prevent the passage of the appropriation attached to the bill. Outraged by the strategy used by her fellow Democrats, who reconvened to vote only one-fourth of what she had requested, Stewart was forced to reconcile herself to the fact that $5,000 per year for 1916 and 1917 was better than no appropriation at all.[39]

Anticipating a barrage of criticism in the press, Governor Stanley immediately told reporters he supported Stewart's illiteracy work, which he called "important," but, he said, the state's financial condition made a large appropriation impossible. The state simply could not do everything: "The man or woman who is suffering from tuberculosis and preventable disease, and there is some hope for these if action is taken promptly on their behalf, . . . is in worse condition than one who may be suffering from ignorance." He would not budge from his announced position that any new appropriation had to carry with it the means of raising the money.[40]

Bitterly disappointed with the actions of the Stanley camp, Stewart harbored considerable resentment over their reluctance to fund the illiteracy work at a meaningful level. She had in fact asked for very little compared with the appropriations the state routinely made for other matters. Her frustration only increased when the legislature handed her another setback by passing an act requiring school trustees to take a census of adult illiterates along with the census of schoolchildren but immediately undercut the effectiveness of the law by providing no funds for surveying for adult illiteracy. This time, she openly chastised the state's lawmakers for their shortsightedness: "Only by making provision for a compensation for taking the census will the Kentucky Illiteracy Commission be able in 1918 to take stock of what its volunteer workers have done, and to make intelligent plans for the work yet to be accomplished."[41]

It was one of the ironies of women's activism that lawmakers had become accustomed to voluntary and charitable work on the part of women, and although many supported their work in theory, they refused to accept fiscal responsibility for its implementation, a problem that continues to plague literacy work even today.[42] Like her contemporaries in the Women's Bureau and child labor advocates in the Children's Bureau, Stewart had to content herself with less than she had been promised and considerably less than she needed to do her work. The fact that women's initiatives were often funded at half or lower of the recommended appropriation often actually meant double discrimination, because it generally resulted in lower salaries for female employees.[43] Stewart never asked for a salary for herself, but meager funding meant that census takers and teachers would have to continue on a voluntary basis, a condition likely to severely undermine the effectiveness of the campaign and cripple its potential.

Cora Wilson Stewart's vision included more than just teaching adults to read and write, and she wanted Moonlight Schools to provide more than literacy skills. Public schools of her day routinely taught morals, character, self-discipline, respect for authority, and patriotism along with reading, writing, and arithmetic, and she shared the vision of progressive educators who expected schools to produce citizens uniquely equipped to deal with the challenges of the modern world through the broadened role of schools in their communities.[44] Her vision of progress included better schools, improved roads, sounder nutrition, better health, and cleaner homes with indoor plumbing, all important elements of a more comfortable and productive rural way of life. Securing these improvements required a better educated, more informed, and politically active citizenry.

In this sense, then, Moonlight Schools were liberating agents that could empower the disenfranchised and dispossessed, and framing the literacy crusade in that context allows for a fuller understanding of both Stewart's motives and the widespread support that surfaced for the movement. A number of historians, in studies of women as educational activists, have challenged interpretations of women teachers as passive in the face of educational change and have documented their demands for a greater role in decision making and their resistance to centralization and bureaucratization in both school reform and the professionalization of education. Margaret Smith Crocco, Petra Munro, and Kathleen Weiler, in *Pedagogies of Resistance: Women Educator Activists, 1880–1960*, examine the work of Jane Addams, Ida B. Wells, and others and conclude that many women used their positions in schools and universities, civic and professional organizations, women's clubs, settlement houses, and state departments of education to redefine the purpose, means, and goals of education. Women like Addams, Wells, Wil Lou Gray, and Cora Wilson Stewart played "self-authorized roles" as public intellectuals who shaped public opinion on critical issues such as gender, race, education, and democracy.[45]

Stewart's literacy crusade and the curriculum she designed for the Moonlight Schools illustrate her philosophy and her role as a public intellectual seeking to shape the direction of change in rural America. Confident that people in the southern mountains could have a more comfortable and productive life once they acquired the proper tools, she created a curriculum to enable them to interact with their environment in positive and purposeful ways and to bring about much-needed changes in rural life.

When Stewart began the literacy crusade, there were no experts in the field and no texts or guidebooks to assist her in formulating a plan of attack. Undeterred, she devised a program that adapted the progressive education philosophy of teaching the "whole" child for "real life" to adults—adults with no knowledge of health and sanitation practices, modern farming techniques, or participation in a moneyed economy.[46]

Many families in her county lived in cabins with no electricity or running water. Outdoor privies were common. Most men who earned wages did so in low-paying, unskilled jobs, and many who farmed simply eked out an existence on barren, exhausted land. Women shouldered the burden of housework and child rearing under difficult, even primitive, conditions. All these problems, Stewart believed, could be addressed through the elimination of illiteracy. If she could build literate communities in the rural environs, those newly enlightened communities could then address the various problems of country life.

Historians of education have overlooked the work of community build-ing as a site for educational reforms that sought to address gender, class, and racial inequalities. Limiting definitions of education to schooling marginalizes the collective efforts of activists like Addams, Wells, Gray, and Stewart. Addams and Wells used the settlement house and women's club movements as sites of democratic education where they attempted to ameliorate the growing inequities of urban life.[47] Like her counterparts in Chicago, Cora Wilson Stewart created a site for the education of rural adults in the Moon-light Schools and replaced traditional primers for children with special books for new adult readers. She specifically designed the primers to inform and enlighten new readers to a better life and spur them to community action to secure it.

In her *Country Life Readers,* Stewart used what she called the "realities of country life" to reshape the thinking and behavior of Moonlight pupils. Envisioning the school as a bridge to the home, she sought to create an edu-cated adult community primed to take action to improve schools and homes and enhance country life, making it more attractive and staunching the flow of rural folk from the countryside to the cities. The books would act as cata-lysts for change in a movement that was, therefore, not an end in itself but a vehicle of reform. If adults could be taught to read, they could understand and confront some of the more pressing problems of rural life, including health and sanitation issues, poor schools, bad roads, a poor economy, and the powerlessness of rural voters.

The philosophies, ideals, and goals of the Country Life movement, which began in 1908, shaped much of Stewart's thinking about education reform, constituted an important part of the Moonlight School curriculum, and in-fluenced the content of her primers. That year, President Theodore Roosevelt's Country Life Commission held public hearings throughout the United States, conducted a nationwide survey, and issued a report summa-rizing perceived deficiencies and recommending methods of improvement. The report charged that American agriculture had diminished in importance, and that rural areas were deteriorating as a consequence. It called attention to the generally poor living conditions in rural areas. Poor schools and bad roads existed everywhere, ignorance and poverty resulted in dangerous health and sanitation conditions, household conveniences were virtually nonexist-ent, and credit and banking facilities did not meet the needs of the region. The commission's findings influenced a generation of advocates of rural re-form who focused on the inherent virtues of country life as they sought to relieve the perceived isolation and cultural limitations of the countryside.[48]

Convinced that deficiencies in rural life motivated people to move to the cities, Country Life advocates sought to arrest the process. Some experts believed inadequate farm profits caused out-migration, and they favored the introduction of more efficient farming techniques. Others wanted higher prices for farm products. Many believed that rural education had failed in its proper function and needed to be revamped to include vocational educa-tion, homemaking skills, good health practices, and, above all, a love of coun-try living. Many critics blamed the public schools for the social backwardness, isolation, and poor health conditions they said were plaguing rural America. Most of the movement's adherents revered the agrarian values that supposedly characterized rural life and targeted the schools as a way to retain what re-mained of such values in the countryside. Their aim was to adapt individuals to a more cooperative and community-oriented life built around these traditional values. They sought to improve country conditions and prepare rural people for participation in an industrialized, modernized economy and society, but as Dewey Grantham has pointed out, it was difficult to reconcile their ideas of agrarian progress with the tradition of the independent yeoman farmer.[49]

Convinced that illiteracy in the countryside was a unique problem re-quiring its own set of solutions, Stewart distinguished Moonlight Schools from adult education programs in the cities, most of which were for immi-grants. However, both urban and rural adult education programs stressed the importance of good citizenship and patriotism and preached the virtues of hard work. Whereas educational and informal learning agencies outside the common schools had long existed, dispensing culture and "useful knowl-edge" and relying on America's intrinsic faith in the self-made individual, most served urban constituencies.[50] Their materials and approaches, she believed, were useless to rural people, whose lives, sensibilities, and prob-lems differed from those of city folk.

With all this in mind, Stewart created a series of primers for adult pupils that focused almost exclusively on rural life, emphasizing its peculiarities, problems, and special beauties. The B. F. Johnson Publishing Company pub-lished the first book in 1915, following it with a second in 1916 and a third shortly thereafter. Stewart first chose the name "Rural Life Readers," but editors changed it to *Country Life Readers*, a title that appeared again the following year when Charles Scribner's Sons published a primer under the same name. Angered about the infringement, Johnson's editor, in Stewart's copy, wrote a note that urged her to reciprocate: "Inasmuch as they have seen fit to steal the name of one of our publications, I can see no objection to appropriating some of their ideas, if you can find anything in the book."[51]

To reach as many students as possible, Stewart wanted the books to be affordable, readily available, and meaningful. The first reader sold for twenty cents. When the texts went into a second printing in 1929, the price went up to forty cents for the first book, fifty cents for the second, and sixty cents for the third. The publishers called the books "mature in thought but simple in language," noting that they preached "the gospel of progress" and aimed at "helping the student to have a good life."[52] In a second printing, the publishers abandoned their claim to a rural readership and targeted a broader audience. By then the books had been tried and used by many types of adult learners, including "native-born, foreign-born, negroes, and Indians on the reservations." They were used in classes all over the country, especially in agricultural states such as Maine, Vermont, Iowa, North Dakota, Wisconsin, Washington, Kentucky, Oklahoma, Louisiana, Virginia, and West Virginia.[53] Although designed for rural night schools, the publishers noted, the books also suited adults in the cities, "for they need to become better acquainted with country life and its opportunities." Hoping to expand their readership into the public schools, they noted that the books could also be used by children in both rural and urban districts.[54]

Textbooks in any classroom, including night schools for adults, are important in and of themselves, for they signify through their content and form particular constructions of reality or particular ways of selecting and organizing the world of potential knowledge. They embody the "selective tradition" of legitimate knowledge and culture, one that in the process of enfranchising one group's cultural capital sometimes disenfranchises that of another.[55] Textbooks contain important messages to the students who read them, whether children or adults. As part of a curriculum, they represent society's organized knowledge system and set down what it recognizes as legitimate and truthful. They also help create a major reference point for received knowledge, culture, beliefs, and morality.[56] By their very nature, textbooks dominate what students learn. In day schools as well as night schools for adults, texts are generally the students' first, and occasionally only, exposure to books and to reading.

It cannot as a matter of course be assumed that what is taught is actually learned, since readers do not merely passively receive texts but read them based on their own class, race, gender, and religious experience.[57] Nevertheless, if Moonlight students accepted only a part of what the *Country Life Readers* preached and put it into practice in their daily lives, Stewart expected significant change to take place. That was progress, she thought, and a step toward a better life.

Like the McGuffey readers of the previous century, Stewart's *Country*

Life Readers expressed a conservative persuasion, displayed a social hierarchy largely dependent on providence, and emphasized individual effort and the value of hard work.[58] Their message was clear: God favored the hardworking and moral person with worldly success. The good life as Stewart envisioned it in the *Country Life Readers* pictured scenes from nature, people in family groups, and rural people engaged in the business and work of their lives.

The first reader began with an important message designed to boost self-confidence:

I can read.
I can read a book.
I can read the Bible.
Can you read it?
I will read the news.
I will read many good books.
We will read at home.[59]

A drawing of a family clustered around a kerosene lamp, contentedly listening while the father reads aloud, illustrated the lesson and encouraged families to read together. Stewart considered such traditions important, probably because she had experienced them as a child. The lesson and the picture are simple, but they convey the message to the adult beginner that he or she *can* participate in literate culture. The use of this important introductory lesson became common in other readers for adult students.[60]

Adult students had to believe they could read, maintained Berea College professor Everett L. Dix, who called the printed page an object of awe to the illiterate. "When the printed page tells him that he can learn to read and write, he believes it. When it tells him that he can rise to respectability and perhaps prominence and leadership, that makes it true to him." To be effective, literature for adults who had never learned to read and write had to appeal to their pride, common sense, and desire to be "a man of letters." The first reader, Dix said, should create in the student's imagination "a picture of the man that he would like . . . to be. As he reads his first sentence he should begin to see himself in a new role—as a MAN among the men of the community."[61]

Dix, an influential eastern Kentucky educator and a volunteer teacher in the Moonlight Schools, stressed the importance of the printed text to the unlettered. Although the illiterate had often learned by bitter experience to be suspicious of people, the printed page symbolized authority and reality: "Has he not seen men walk up and pay their taxes in obedience to the printed notice . . . , obeyed that printed page and paid taxes to support the government that taught his neighbor to read and left him illiterate. He has seen a warrant served, he knows the force of a will and a deed. He has heard the Bible read, the words falling from the lips of the reader as the words of one having authority."[62]

Like Dix, Stewart believed texts for the adult beginner not only acquainted the novice with the printed word but also introduced the naive and unlettered to a presumably unimpeachable reality. If it was printed in the book, it must be so! It also made readers part of the hierarchy, bringing them into the social, legal, and economic framework of society. Adults who learned to read could presumably pay their taxes and obey other laws, thus becoming participants in a literate society that had previously excluded them.

In the "reality" of the *Country Life Readers,* Stewart, like other textbook authors, both "created and solidified American traditions." Their choice of what they admired in the past and the present and what they wished to preserve for the future was important because it was often the first exposure for beginning students.[63] Establishing a moral, religious, and patriotic common denominator was a goal of nineteenth-century and early twentieth-century textbook writers. Textbooks could presumably "shape a national character" and define the individual character of pupils, a particularly important goal during the Progressive Era as reformers tried to fit individuals to the peculiar demands of industrialization, Americanization, and, after 1917, war.[64] It was no small task to apply national institutional forces to regional development, and although she cannot be classified as an "industrial Americanizer," Stewart's efforts were informed by that process and indicate, once again, that the isolation of the mountains from larger currents of national thought and activity has been overstated.[65]

In her readers, Stewart carried on the tradition of nineteenth-century textbook authors who idealized the self-made man, emphasized hard work and honesty, created patriotic myths, and "prepared" their readers for citizenship. Historically, American schoolbooks had inculcated patriotic and nationalistic loyalties and sentiments, exalted patriotism, and attempted to define Americanism by creating heroes and myths about those heroes.[66] Stewart saw adult students, like their young day-school counterparts, as fresh minds on which could be inscribed American traditions, culture, and civic responsibilities.

Because citizenship was important for everyone, lessons on the responsibilities of Americans occupy a prominent place in the curriculum. Reading lessons in the *First Book* reflect the Progressive Era view that literacy was critical to the health of the city, state, and nation. A lesson on public revenue, a constant source of dispute and disagreement in the mountains, is representative:

> I shall pay my taxes.
> I pay a tax on my home.
> I pay a tax on my land.
> I pay a tax on my cattle.
> I pay a tax on my money.
> I pay a tax on many other things.
> Where does this money go?
> It goes to keep up the schools.
> It goes to keep up the roads.
> It goes to keep down crime.
> It goes to keep down disease.
> I am glad that I have a home to pay taxes on.[67]

Like other progressives who were concerned about the poor state of schools, roads, and public health in the rural areas, Stewart wanted to acquaint adult new readers with the ideal and spur them to action to improve the reality. Throughout the southern Appalachian region, the tax base was inadequate, the per capita pupil expenditure among the lowest in the nation, roads often impassable or nonexistent, and public health initiatives woefully lacking.[68] Stewart hoped that once introduced to a vision of progress through the *Country Life Readers,* people would begin to work toward it.

The lesson on good roads provides a fine example. Students read that a good road saves time and preserves teams and wagons. They learned penmanship by writing, "The good road is my friend. I will work for the good road" until they mastered the letters. They then wrote, "The bad road is my foe. I will get rid of the bad road."[69] Of this type of learning, Stewart wrote: "When a man has repeatedly written [these sentences], he becomes something of an advocate of good roads through suggestion, if through nothing else. The copying of the script sentences in the book pledged the student to progress and impressed upon him certain evils with fine psychological effect. . . . This type of copy which was carried throughout the book had, like the reading lessons, a double purpose; the necessary practice of writing and the dwelling on and emphasizing of some vital truth."[70] Once literacy had made new readers "intelligent citizens," she expected them to realize that all these things were related, and to pursue progress in all its forms. If adult students had to travel bad roads, ford creeks, and cross worn-out bridges to get to school, they would see the need for improvement and take action.

Stewart's lessons reflect her own activism, for while Moonlight students busied themselves in lessons about ideal rural conditions, Stewart wrote articles about them and looked for practical ways to improve conditions in her home county and all of eastern Kentucky. She joined colleagues in the KEA and NEA in lobbying for state action in the creation of better roads, without which, particularly in rural areas, education reform meant nothing.[71] Kentucky's road conditions were so bad it was nicknamed the "Detour State." In summer roads were hazardous and dusty, in spring they oozed mud, and in winter the ice presented an entirely different hazard. Many counties had no real roads at all.[72] The road issue dominated public discourse to the extent that Democratic governor A. O. Stanley, whose administration secured passage of a bill permitting the use of convict labor in road construction and providing increased state funding for building and improving the highways, remarked in 1915: "To say you are in favor of good roads is like saying you are in favor of good health or good morals."[73]

As Rowan County school superintendent, Stewart often spoke out about the link between good roads and quality schools in the commonwealth. She even secured a promise from Kentucky's commissioner of roads to pave fifty yards of model roadway in front of every schoolhouse in her county.[74] Stewart believed that once rural residents had the opportunity to travel on a good road, even if only for fifty yards, they would demand that officials improve all rural roads. Her close friend and supporter Democratic representative William J. Fields, citing poor conditions in his region and their detrimental effect on the schools, pushed for road improvement when the U.S. House of Representatives considered a bill to provide federal aid to states in the construction and maintenance of rural post roads.[75]

Road improvement concerned educators across the state, and annual reports of county superintendents indicated that Moonlight School attendance actually did help. Several reported that once adults had been forced to traipse over treacherous footpaths, wade creeks, and jump streams to get to the schoolhouse, they took action to correct the problems. A sample report stated, "I am sure that our moonlight schools helped to create such public sentiment for good roads that our county is now building and preparing to build pikes in every section of the county."[76]

Stewart also wanted rural citizens to vote. Her family had long been involved in party politics, and she took voting seriously. Many Progressive Era reformers, whether woman suffragists or urban reformers seeking to clean up machine politics, concerned themselves with this issue, so it is not surprising that several lessons in the *Country Life Readers* emphasized voting. One lesson introduced vocabulary, explained the process, and, following a sample balloting exercise, concluded, "With his vote a man rules. . . . The man who does not vote has no voice in the affairs of his country. He cheats his country, his family, and himself. Every man should make use of his right to vote. He should always vote for the best man or for the one who stands for the best things. . . . The man who sells his vote sells his honor."[77]

Stewart wanted to impress upon students the importance of the vote, a commitment rooted in her region's history and shaped by her times. Rowan County had suffered terribly from the violence of a distant election eve, and vote buying and fraudulent electoral practices often plagued the process. Despite her allegiance to the Democratic Party, there is no evidence that she sought, in subtle or overt fashion, to influence students in their political choices. She simply wanted voters to make informed choices, and the only way they could do that was through education.

Like many of her contemporaries, Stewart believed that only informed and literate citizens of both sexes should vote, but she stopped short of endorsing woman suffrage in her series of readers. Although she supported the movement, given the hostility in the mountain region to the woman vote, she may have thought it best not to mention it in her texts. Whether Moonlight teachers excluded women "voters" from the balloting exercise is open to speculation. Female participation perhaps varied with the teacher's position on the issue, but one of the Moonlight instructors noted the correlation between illiteracy and antisuffrage sentiment. Mrs. Charles G. Firth, secretary of the Kentucky Equal Rights Association and chair of the Kenton County Illiteracy Commission, noted that while traveling in Kentucky in 1914, speaking on suffrage while it was "still unpopular," she learned "at first hand something of the paramount needs of our state." Working for suffrage in the mountain counties, she experienced "difficulties" that led her to "realize the great need for co-operation with Mrs. Cora Wilson Stewart and her staff in an intensive campaign against illiteracy." It was quite surprising, she said, "and humiliating as well, to offer my literature to a man and to have him hold it upside down and blankly stare at it, asking, 'what it was about, anyhow,' and when told it was about 'letting the woman vote,' to have him leer and sneer as he assured me that 'he would do the voting for his womenfolks' and that 'when women got to voting he was going to quit.'"[78]

Voting was becoming an increasingly complex procedure, and many Progressive Era reformers believed that both the process and the issues required an educated and informed electorate. Recent reforms adopting the Australian, or "secret," ballot required the individual voter to read, interpret, and mark choices, while the complexity of some ballots made voting almost impossible for illiterates. Indeed, it is one of the ironies of progressive reform that it reversed the historical trend toward universal suffrage and established a countertrend toward fewer, but presumably "better," voters.[79] Some southern states had amended their constitutions to disenfranchise black voters, and several northern states employed similar tactics to deprive immigrants of the ballot. Moreover, by 1920 nine states outside the South had passed literacy tests for voting, and a number of states had repealed laws that permitted aliens to vote once they had declared their intent to become American citizens.[80] Buying votes in Kentucky was as common as buying groceries, particularly in mountain counties where whiskey and a few dollars could buy most any vote.[81]

In addition to civic responsibility, Stewart wanted to foster an improved standard of living. In successful campaigns to secure pure food and water, eradicate disease through vaccination, and eliminate hookworm and pellagra, Southern progressives had already linked education and health reform.[82] While many education reformers attempted this type of reform in the public schools, Stewart, who was confident that the school could change "the whole attitude" of rural home life, saw an opportunity to take the message directly to parents.[83] Health and cleanliness, child care, scientific farming, and safe and nutritious preparation of food therefore claimed prominent positions in the *Country Life Readers,* all of which contained lessons on good health.

As a teacher, Stewart was woefully familiar with the poor health and sanitation habits of some rural folk. Some poor habits reflected ignorance, others lack of access to indoor plumbing and bathing facilities. Many mountaineers suffered from dental disease; consequently, Stewart, one of whose brothers was a dentist, devoted an entire lesson to the importance of using a toothbrush, telling pupils it would save them money and pain.[84]

Another health lesson stressed the need for regular bathing, reminding readers that if they wished to feel well, their skin must be kept clean. The lesson ended with the phrase "I will take a bath every day."[85] The *Second Book* discussed the advantages of running water and indoor plumbing, encouraging Moonlight pupils to acquire a pump and indoor faucet, which Stewart said was as important on the farm as field machinery.[86]

The *Country Life Readers* also taught nutrition. In one lesson, a wife learned to care for her husband's health by providing healthful foods. Unable to cook, she asked neighbors for help and learned to prepare beef and chicken stock, thirty ways to prepare potatoes, several ways to prepare bread, and the safe method of canning fruits and vegetables. The section concluded with the admonition "No woman ought to marry who cannot cook all kinds of foods."[87]

The careful housewife sometimes had to conserve food, an important resource in the country home. In the *Second Book,* Stewart described how to prepare cornmeal mush when other foods were in short supply. In the illustrated lesson, a woman tells her neighbor: "With corn meal I make mush and serve it with milk for supper. The mush that is left over I put into a dish to mold; I slice and fry it for breakfast. Thin slices of crisp bacon, ham, or chicken served between golden brown slices of mush make a tempting dish." She also noted that fried mush was better for her family than so much meat.[88]

In the context of optimistic progressive uplift rhetoric, the readers offered practical tips that homemakers could use and provided encouraging words like "I will make appetizing dishes of corn meal," or "Any woman can learn to cook vegetables, if she will try."[89] Stewart's readers and the Moonlight School curriculum introduced women at home to new ideas of efficiency and scientific home management and implied that such innovation was not only beneficial but also necessary. Teachers often suggested that homemakers could more efficiently meet the needs of their families by using cookbooks and informational bulletins prepared by county extension agents. Stewart told Moonlight teachers to share these with their students and to encourage their use at home, thus further institutionalizing "progress" and reliance on experts to relieve some of the burdens of the overworked farm wife and free some of her time and energy for other middle-class home-building pursuits. If the quality of life improved substantially, her children might remain in the country. Another important result of agricultural extension and home demonstration work, argues historian Mary S. Hoffschwelle, is that it favorably disposed rural women toward the rural preparedness program of World War I.[90]

Home improvement and beautification, both important elements of the Country Life reform agenda, occupied the attention of home demonstration agents well into the 1920s. Like her contemporaries in southern uplift, Stewart subscribed to the newer standards of living and domestic consumption that would make farm wives more like urban homemakers. Her books urged country people to construct nice, well-built little houses, buy furniture, and plant flower gardens, making the idea more appealing with an illustration of a nice farmhouse surrounded by a picket fence and an orderly row of trees. The message was clear:

This is a nice house.
It is neat and clean.
The yard is clean and has flowers in it.

People that go down this road say: "A nice, neat family lives in this house.
We know the family from the house that it lives in."

On the facing page a run-down house, with crumbling chimney and broken fence posts, provides a stark contrast:

"This place is dirty and ugly.
The house needs paint.
The yard is full of weeds.
A lazy, shiftless family lives here."
"Yes, but how do you know that?"
"I know it from the house. Lazy, shiftless people live in dirty, ugly homes."

The stigmatization of poverty and the characterization of people who live in run-down houses as "lazy and shiftless" attempted to create a value judgment that would push readers of Stewart's books toward an appreciation and emulation of a higher standard of living. Stewart even discussed the appropriate colors of house paint, concluding that "tasteful" houses were painted neutral colors, not gaudy ones.[91]

The First Book also offered practical lessons to improve nutrition and provide higher farm income. One lesson introduced crop rotation, explaining that the uninformed farmer had raised the same crop year after year and ruined his soil. Moonlight teachers were instructed to illustrate lessons on farming techniques in ways that would clearly show the benefits of improved methods. They could display samples of good and bad fruit to show the effects of spraying for insects and disease. A demonstration might accompany the lesson on testing seed corn if a local farmer could be recruited to explain its use and value.[92]

Stewart's *Second Book* provided more advanced reading lessons and began with a poem, "Life in the Country," highlighting the author's views of country life:

Here in the country's heart
Where the grass is green,
Here Life is the same sweet life
As it e'er hath been.
Trust in God still lives,
And the bell at morn
Floats with a thought of God
O'er the rising corn.
God comes down in the rain,
And the crop grows tall—

This is the country faith,
And the best of all![93]

Stewart idealized country life and hoped to keep those tempted by a more comfortable life in the city from leaving. She told Kentucky author James Lane Allen that her purpose in the readers was to show the beauty of country life, asking him to write a lesson on that theme. She reminded him that he would be proud of his home state when it was rid of illiteracy, "and more Kentuckians will be proud of you when they can read the books which you have written."[94]

Although Allen apparently did not write for the series, Berea College president William Goodell Frost contributed "Good Farming Makes Good Folks," a lesson encouraging good farming practices to ensure better crops, which would in turn provide a cash or trade income for the family. "These things mean shoes and stockings for bad weather. They mean newspapers and books for the long winter evenings. They mean a new fence around the yard, better shelter for stock, and thus more money and more comforts later on."[95]

"Care of the Baby" was the topic of one reading lesson enjoining mothers to feed their babies properly: "The baby is fat and it feels well. It will keep well, if care is taken of it. Some mothers kill their babies by feeding them. Some kill them with dirt, which breeds disease. Then the mother cries and says that the Lord has taken her baby." Although this phrasing seems particularly heartless, especially in light of the death of Stewart's own child as an infant, it does point up the intense need for public health information and practice.

Proper care of a child was not simply good for the baby. In Stewart's readers it offered another means of acquiring respectability: "A clean baby makes people think well of the mother."[96] Stewart believed that better-educated mothers would result in healthier, happier children, and like many of her contemporaries in child saving, she sought to transform the child-rearing practices of the uneducated mother.

Stewart's dedication to education and her faith in its ability to transform individuals and lives came second only to her faith in God and in her own calling; therefore, despite their various instructional functions and the information they contained, the readers would have been incomplete without passages from the Bible. Stewart carefully selected the verses she thought most appropriate. The *First Book* related the parable of the sower, which was illustrated with a detail from Millet's famous painting. It also included the parable of the rich fool and the parable of the tares. The *Country Life Readers* related messages country people understood and appreciated, and in various ways glorified agrarian life and equated it with wisdom and virtue. According to Stewart, despite its need for improvement, rural life was superior to city life, and those closest to the soil were closest to God. A psalm taken from the King James Bible and printed under the title "God's Blessings to Country People" relates the rural ideal as Stewart envisioned it: "The pastures are clothed with flocks; the valleys also are covered over with corn; they shout for joy, they also sing."[97]

These selections invoke biblical authority in confirming the virtue of individual achievement through hard work as they idealize and sanctify life spent close to the soil. Stewart's "innovative nostalgia" led her to look backward to agrarian virtue and forward to material progress, social efficiency, and individual productivity, without acknowledging that in an industrialized society the two could coexist only under rare and unlikely circumstances. Like many progressives, she failed to recognize the paradox of attempting to modernize southern agriculture and at the same time preserve the best traditions of the village and countryside. As Dewey Grantham has pointed out, the new agriculture was bound to destroy the yeoman farmer and therefore undermine the very values the reformers treasured most.[98]

Further evidence of Stewart's dedication to traditional values can be seen in her choice of "memory gems" for the Moonlight School curriculum. Although most educators considered memory training in adults extremely difficult, if not wholly impossible, Stewart's experience indicated otherwise. She insisted students memorize Longfellow's "Psalm of Life," a poem that sums up Stewart's view of the rural Eden and perhaps even of her own life:

In the world's broad field of battle,
In the bivouac of life,
Be not like dumb, driven cattle,
Be a hero in the strife.
Let us then be up and doing,
With a heart for any fate,
Still achieving, still pursuing,
Learn to labor and to wait.[99]

Stewart's *Country Life Readers* and the curriculum of the Moonlight Schools reflect her nostalgia for the agrarian ideal, but in Stewart's version, the roads are paved, all children attend school, the postman delivers the mail, telephone and telegraph lines dot the countryside, and farmers live in nice houses, not run-down shanties with outhouses across the yard. Thoroughly convinced of the redemptive powers of education, through her series of readers Stewart attempted to instill her vision of the good life, imbue it with traditional values and morals, teach newer ideals of health and cleanliness, and thus elevate rural living conditions to a modern standard.

Stewart wanted rural Americans to educate not only themselves but also their children so the debilitating cycle of poverty and ignorance could be broken. Her dream was shaped in its early stages by the Country Life movement, and in her vision, Moonlight Schools operated as a bridge to modern life. Through them, Stewart promoted an ideal of improved country life that included good citizenship, good roads, good health, and good schools, which together she believed would stem the tide of out-migration and reinvigorate the rural regions of the South. Despite her good intentions, the books and Stewart's rhetoric promised more than education alone could deliver. "Progress" would come, but it would sweep away the rural ideal with it. Many continued to find a better life not by combining education and reform with traditional values but by abandoning their farms and moving to cities in search of employment in the expanding industrial economy.

Stewart's readers reflect her views on the importance of education as a prerequisite to success in the modern world and her conviction that both education and tradition were inextricably linked to progress and opportunity. Although Stewart held high hopes for her series of adult primers, both in teaching reading and writing and in changing attitudes, it is impossible to gauge with any certainty the actual influence the books had on the students who used them. Correspondence from Moonlight pupils indicates that they shared a proud sense of accomplishment upon completion of each reader and eagerly awaited the arrival of the next. Some reported reading the books a second and even a third time, but these letters were not only solicited; they were selected by Stewart herself, calling into question how widely shared these views were. Nevertheless, Moonlight pupils *did* write letters, something they could not have done prior to their enrollment in the program for adult illiterates, and they considered their ability to do so an improvement over their previous condition.

Although their actual influence cannot be ascertained, Stewart's primers for adult beginners reached thousands of new readers over a period of years; therefore, their widespread use may serve as an indicator of their effectiveness. Early sales were slow, and in response to the publisher's concern Stewart recommended advertising in the *Southern School Journal* and elsewhere. She informed the publishers of developments in the literacy work and often had shipments of books sent in advance of her speaking engagements, where sales were usually brisk. Sales representatives also took her

advice and followed up illiteracy campaigns by visiting county superintendents and school boards, offering the books as "supplementary" readers.[100]

Several states, including Kentucky in 1923, purchased the *Country Life
Readers* for use in their public schools. In addition to purchasing large numbers of books, many school districts supplemented instruction with special
"bulletins" printed for use in the night schools by the Kentucky Illiteracy
Commission, and many of these incorporated Stewart's lessons as well.[101]
South Carolina adopted her series for the Lay-By Schools and the Opportunity Schools. The YMCA purchased sixty thousand of her readers, and the
federal government purchased an additional fifty thousand for teaching draftees. Sale of the books provided much-needed money to finance the work
and to pay Stewart's expenses. Her royalty records indicate that sales ranged
from three or four hundred in a slow quarter to upwards of twelve hundred
in a good one; thus, her 30 percent commission sometimes generated significant income.[102]

Stewart's *Country Life Readers* and the curriculum she developed reveal more than the teaching methods and curriculum of the Moonlight
Schools. They illustrate the inherent tensions in the literacy crusade. Cora
Wilson Stewart was at once committed to the values and traditions of the
agrarian past and to the ideals of modernization and progress. The legacies
of benevolence work and moral reform and Stewart's strongly held views on
the role of the schoolmarm and southern lady in American society shaped
the literacy campaign, giving it a nostalgic dimension that was only partially
offset by her faith in progress and the future. Stewart idealized education as
a kind of magic ingredient, a catalyst that could work miracles, but the Moonlight School curriculum also provided basic literacy skills and some vocational training for adults. Unfortunately, her *Country Life Readers* advocated
a lifestyle that could not be attained simply by creating an awareness of it.
Like other rural reformers of her day, Stewart undertook initiatives that fell
short of their goal because the trappings of middle-class material culture
cost money, a commodity that remained in short supply in much of the rural
South. Had the Moonlight pupils created a product, like the Apison rug makers
of rural Tennessee, who made and marketed hooked rugs and household
linens to generate the cash needed to modernize their lives, perhaps the
kind of changes Stewart envisioned could have taken place.[103]

Cora Wilson Stewart's lessons had relevance to rural people's lives, for
they were rooted in a culture these people knew and understood. Not the
esoteric "book-larnin" many of them disparaged as useless and impractical,
the readers reinforced traditional Protestant beliefs by enabling rural Ameri-

cans to read from their Bibles. The books appealed to their staunch independence by suggesting that education would protect them from both political and economic exploitation. Perhaps more important, the primers introduced them to life beyond the rural environs and to events and circumstances that had always been outside their experience and understanding. To Moonlight pupils and to new readers in rural areas across the nation, they preached a gospel of progress and a message of redemption through education that was both compelling and encouraging. Moreover, most of the lessons had a practical applicability or contained some thought or moral that could be applied to everyday life, thus lighting the spark for lifelong learning.

FOUR

Nationalizing the Illiteracy Campaign

In 1917 the escalating conflict in Europe and U.S. preparedness provided a new focus for the illiteracy work and gave Stewart renewed hope for legislative appropriations in her home state. She turned her attention to the creation of programs for the state's draft-age men, whom she numbered at 30,000, and the patriotic tone of the campaign escalated.[1] In April of that year, when the United States committed itself to war, the federal government called for a general registration of the nation's young men for military service. The nation raised an army of more than 4.5 million men, with just under 2 million posted in the European theater. More than 84,000 Kentuckians served, and almost 2,500 died of injuries sustained in the conflict. At least one-quarter of those called into service could neither read nor write. This startling finding increased public awareness and brought an element of critical need to the rural adult education movement in Kentucky and elsewhere.[2]

Given the immediacy of the crisis, the needs of soldiers and potential draftees took precedence for a while. If literacy and the ability to function in a rapidly changing world were important in peacetime, they took on critical importance in time of war, said Stewart, along with Senator Ollie James and Congressman J. Campbell Cantrill, two Democratic supporters who asked the War Department to institute compulsory literacy training for draftees prior to overseas assignment. Thousands of conscripts received military training at Kentucky's Fort Thomas, Camp Stanley, Camp Knox, and Camp Zachary Taylor. Stewart, James, and Cantrill urged mandatory training for all draftees who needed it, but military authorities denied the request as "impractical" in the current crisis.[3]

Because she believed the war would affect illiterates in ways that it would not affect the rest of the population, Stewart set as a special goal for 1917 the teaching of all the state's illiterate men of draft age before they were called to service, and in a public information campaign designed to drum up support for the intensified effort, noted the particular difficulties they faced. They could not sign their name, read orders, read a manual of arms, or read their Bibles, and just as important in a rural society that valued family closeness, they could not read letters or write home. They could not understand the signals or follow the signal corps in battle, and presumably could not understand the cause for which they were fighting or the principles for which their government stood.[4]

Although soldiers took priority in the 1917 sessions, Stewart also wanted the public to recognize that illiteracy left civilians equally handicapped in their ability to serve the nation in its time of need. Unable to sign food pledge cards, understand bulletins, or read instructions given through the daily press, they could not read the propaganda, could not help their country by signing applications for liberty loan bonds or thrift cards, and presumably could not understand the government's purposes and principles and therefore could not give "intelligent support" to the war cause. Moreover, they could not provide "encouragement and comfort to their boys in service by writing letters from home."[5]

To correct some of these problems, Stewart created a "Course of Study" for 1917 Moonlight Schools that focused on war-related issues and encouraged patriotism. Included were lessons with a clear message urging all Americans to get behind the war effort. A good example dealt with the flag:

> See the flag!
> It is our flag!
> Our flag never knew defeat.
> Why?
> Our flag has always stood for right.[6]

Echoing President Woodrow Wilson's rhetoric on the nation's involvement in the European conflict, Stewart wrote a lesson depicting the nation's honorable and self-sacrificing war aims:

> Why are we at war?
> To keep our country free.
> To make other people free.
> To make the world safe to live in.

To stop the rule of kings.
To put an end to war.[7]

The lessons included a section of drills on European geography, emphasizing the location and names of countries involved in the conflict overseas. The next year's course of study reemphasized the importance of patriotism and service, beginning with a paean to the democratic ideal penned by Kentucky governor A. O. Stanley, who commented on the importance of an enlightened citizenry.[8]

Following American entry into World War I and the general registration of young men for the draft, Cora Wilson Stewart, by then the most experienced person in the country in dealing with illiteracy, accepted a request from the YMCA to write a primer for illiterate draftees. Stewart donated the *Soldier's First Book,* which she specifically designed for training camp use, to the organization, which had also just purchased sixty thousand of her *Country Life Readers* to use in camp schools across the country.[9]

Like the *Country Life Readers,* the lessons in the pamphlets and the *Soldier's First Book* show Stewart's commitment to traditional American values, including patriotism, unquestioning loyalty, and service to the nation, and they highlight her understanding of education as a socializing agent. Several lessons stressed the importance of writing home and cautioned the soldier against straying from the values he learned there. Stewart urged families to write to their soldiers at the front often and to be "especially encouraging in tone." Letter writing also claimed the 1918 campaign focus, in which she urged Moonlight teachers "to teach everybody to write cheerful, encouraging letters to soldiers" and "to bring the whole community into intelligent co-operation with the war activities." General John J. Pershing, commander of the American Expeditionary Force, had issued a "military order" telling the women of America "to write, write, write to the boys in France." Pershing called letter writing a "military necessity and a human need."[10]

Stewart insisted that a "just and honorable nation" would not send its young men into battle so inadequately prepared, saying it was unfair that they "should be torn from their homes and dear ones and sent across the water to fight your battles and mine without being able to read a letter or to write a line back home." The very least Kentucky and the nation could do was to give them the skills to read and write letters from home. "Next to actual engagement in battle," she wrote, "the most momentous event in the life of a soldier is the arrival of a letter from home." Letters provided consolation and assurance on both sides of the water, she said, and "to his anxious mother a letter from her soldier boy is a comfort above price."[11]

Moonlight teachers instructed wives and mothers to write cheerful, upbeat letters to encourage their husbands and sons rather than burden them with petty cares. Stewart provided examples of bad letters to be read aloud in a "whining voice to exaggerate the effect." Good letters were to be read aloud in a "brave and buoyant tone." She instructed teachers to explain that, after reading a depressing letter, a soldier could become depressed and perhaps do something "disgraceful or desperate." A cheerful letter would lift his spirits for days, and if he received the letter before a battle, it might "save his life and the lives of his comrades."[12]

A potent example of "The Kind of Letters Not to Write" was signed "Yours in tears, Sallie." The sample letter was a litany of woes, including sick children longing for their father, hogs getting into the corn, horses dying, and the wife voicing her fear that "if you do get over, I'm afraid the Germans will kill you and I'll never see you again." The lesson made it clear that the selfish woman thought only of herself, while the "devoted" wife was a model of strength and patience, enduring the "small sacrifices of war," and simply smiling "over any inconvenience." Like her husband, she did her part for the war effort and wrote letters telling of the "glorious war conferences" and the thrilling work of saving food, buying liberty bonds, and working for the Red Cross.[13]

The *Soldier's First Book* told men in training for war to remember their mothers. A sentimental poem called "Have You Written to Mother?" reminded busy young soldiers of the one person too important to forget and laid the cold hand of guilt upon those who had done so:

A light, a beacon burning;
Whose beams shall reach you far away.
Shall lure your soul returning.
Tell her you love her dearly still,
Tell her to keep the lamp of prayer,
For fear some sad tomorrow
Shall bear away the listening soul,
And leave you lost in sorrow.
And then, through bitter, falling tears,
And sighs you may not smother,
You will remember when too late
You did not write to mother.[14]

Stewart's lessons for soldiers taught not just reading and writing but right thinking and proper behavior as well. She enjoined young inductees against accepting "dope and smokes" (soft drinks and cigars) and told them to accept instead water and a good book. She urged soldiers to work hard and train earnestly, reinforcing the suggestion in a writing exercise the young men copied over and over, "The army is no place for a slouch." Soldiers had to remain physically fit, since weakness or poor health indicated "that the man or his parents have been very careless." "Lack of frequent bathing, failure to brush the teeth after each meal, the use of other people's towel or comb or drinking cup, sleeping in a room with windows closed, drinking intoxicating liquor, smoking cigarettes, and indulging in vices" constituted the list of behaviors that made a soldier physically unfit.[15]

Through these primers Americans whose illiteracy had isolated them from broad patterns of civic involvement could learn the responsibilities and rights of citizenship, including "intelligent" support of the country's war aims and military service. As they learned to become soldiers and patriots, the values of the village and small town prevented them from forgetting what was right and important. In this series, Stewart's conservative values predominate and, to her consternation, drew the attention of industrial Americanizers and superpatriots who sensed in her rhetoric and approach a kindred spirit.

In addition to creating the need for a specific new curriculum and learning materials, the war, at least temporarily, legitimized a greater governmental role in the welfare of its citizens and created a more favorable climate for the passage of social welfare legislation. Nowhere was this more evident than in public education. Startling illiteracy statistics brought out by the war galvanized educators across the country into action, causing significant reassessment of the role of schools in society, accelerating concern over child health and welfare, and giving broader impetus to the movement to Americanize the immigrant.[16] Stewart's immediate interest centered on illiterate draftees, and her campaign to educate soldiers took place in a climate that was at least for the moment more receptive to women's activism and participation in public life. Determined to do their part on the home front, community leaders mobilized local resources into war work, which provided unprecedented public opportunities for women. They launched campaigns to sell war bonds and conserve food. The American Red Cross, the Committee on Women's Defense Work, and the Food Administration all recruited women for both paid and voluntary work. Although the changes did not last, the war brought women into paid employment in unprecedented numbers as it boosted reform efforts. Prohibition and suffrage amendments gained legislative victories much sooner than expected and gave women the hope of broader involvement in the nation's public life.[17]

Philander P. Claxton, the U.S. commissioner of education and a long-time associate, offered Stewart a job as the nation's "Specialist in Adult Education." A tempting offer, this job in the Bureau of Education would have placed her in a position to push literacy at the national level at a salary of $250 per month, plus expenses. While she considered that offer, her friend A. E. Winship, editor of the New England–based *Journal of Education,* wrote that if she chose not to work for Claxton, he could get her a good job in "war work."[18] In addition, another tempting offer came from the woman's department of War Camp Community Service, an organization that recruited young women "for all kinds of war service to stimulate them to a realizing sense of the splendid part they may play in helping to win the war." Stewart had been recommended to the agency for her ability to organize and field enthusiastic volunteers, and its director wanted her to assist in stimulating community groups to cooperative work in support of the war effort.[19]

Unwilling to abandon the literacy work in her home state just when appropriations were under consideration, Stewart declined these opportunities for paid employment. Nevertheless she accepted the responsibility of "war work," even though it took her away from Kentucky during the critical weeks when the Kentucky General Assembly was considering an appropriations bill for the KIC. She agreed to chair the National Illiteracy Committee (NIC), an advisory group established to help the federal government develop a means of dealing with illiterate recruits. Composed of commissioners of education from several states and NEA president Mary C. C. Bradford, the committee met in Washington, D.C., and recommended to the Joint Congressional Committee on Education that intensive efforts be undertaken to teach draftees as soon as they were inducted. Men who could not read and write had been barred from service in the navy, but the army decided to accept them. Stewart and her committee attempted to convince the army that illiteracy delayed training and hampered the efficiency not only of individual soldiers but of whole companies.[20]

The NIC, in the April 1918 *NEA Bulletin,* published "A Call to the Teachers of America." Calling it "a deplorable thing," the article proclaimed that many volunteers and conscripts who offered their lives in the defense of their nation were doing so "humiliated and handicapped" by illiteracy. Even a simple vision test put them at a disadvantage because the letters of the alphabet could not be recognized by those unable to read. Those who could not write could not sign the payroll or other important records and orders. Military life "was not planned for illiterate men. Life to them in camp is one round of inconvenience and embarrassment," Stewart wrote. The NIC urged

NEA members to lobby their representatives in Congress on behalf of the Bankhead Bill, H.R. 6490, a measure pending in Congress "which looks to the relief of adult illiterates." With typical determination, Stewart told teachers to become political activists, to write their congressional representatives and demand that they use their influence for legislation "which will bring relief to these illiterates, next . . . put on the whole armor of a teacher and . . . enter the ranks of service."[21]

NIC recommendations went into a pamphlet entitled "Illiteracy and the War," which the committee mailed to educational authorities in each state. Noting that military camps were ill equipped for educational work, the committee requested that the school people of the nation take on the task of teaching illiterate draftees. "No more patriotic thing could be done by any school or any community than to locate the illiterate men of draft age in its territory and to teach them to read and write." A six- or eight-week course was "sufficient to redeem any illiterate of average intellect" and enable him to write his own letters and to read simple books, passages from newspapers, and portions of the Bible. Such training would send soldiers off better prepared, with "enlightened minds, patriotic purposes, and eager step to be fighters and not laggards from the moment that they enter the ranks."[22]

Much of the publicity and rhetoric for teaching draftees focused on the social and personal benefits of literacy, especially letter writing, rather than on the need for the soldier to read and write in order to do his job. This illustrates the basic nature of instruction in the night schools. In six or eight weeks, Moonlight teachers could not teach the soldier to read and understand training manuals, but they could help him stay in touch with his family and provide an introduction to written forms of communication. They might also save a proud young soldier the embarrassment of having to admit his "affliction" to strangers: "Shall Kentucky Send Thirty Thousand Illiterates to France? God forbid! Why should she send any? Hasn't she an Illiteracy Commission, 11,000 public school teachers and as patriotic people as ever the sun shone on? To the guns, yes, every man of them—even though with their affliction they might well be exempt from military duty, I believe—but to the books first, and then they'll go to the guns more content and with less embarrassment and less handicap."[23]

Although chairing the NIC required that Stewart attend meetings in the nation's capital, she still found time to mount an intensive public education campaign in her home state, where patriotism was generally strong.[24] The campaign emphasized draft statistics and linked the teaching of potential soldiers and their families to war work and patriotic service. Under her leadership, the KIC set out to identify illiterate draftees from the common-wealth, employing workers in each county to copy names of individuals who had registered by mark. They counted just over thirty thousand young men who had signed with an "X" and were thus presumed illiterate. The commission then printed huge posters that were placed across Kentucky, announcing that the state had fifteen regiments of soldiers that could neither read nor write and asking for contributions from the public to address the situation. The appearance of this new constituency of soldiers gave the work a sense of urgency that brought strong public support. The $5,000 legislative appropriation for the KIC proved inadequate, given the numbers of soldiers in need, so Stewart whipped her fund-raising apparatus into gear and embarked upon the "$30,000 Campaign" to raise money to teach Kentucky's draftees. She devised a new strategy that included sending out hundreds of little banks in which supporters could drop dimes, relying as usual on women to complete the task. In letters to community leaders across the state, she asked for the names of "twenty of the best women" in each town to oversee filling the banks. When she received the names, she mailed the banks, along with a letter of appreciation and instruction. Although the campaign fell short of its goal of $200 in each community, it brought in almost $11,000.[25] That she was able to raise so much through small donations indicates a high level of grassroots support for the push to educate Kentucky's soldiers, but nevertheless, criticism soon developed.

Some community leaders and a few educators questioned the kind of attention the Moonlight Schools had brought to the commonwealth. One group of critics attacked what they called "great flaming posters" that asked for contributions from the public. A letter to the editor of the *Hazard Herald* asserted that Stewart's claim that Kentucky had fifteen regiments of soldiers unable to read or write was patently false. Barely one-eighth that number existed in the entire state, the author argued, charging that Stewart had slandered "Kentucky boys who are making the greatest sacrifice in all history."[26] J. B. Hoge, the local KIC illiteracy agent who had placed the posters in Hazard at Stewart's request, wrote a rebuttal noting that the posters had gone up four months late. Conditions had changed during that time, he said. When the posters should have been placed, Perry County had anticipated sending 1,950 of its men, 350 of whom had registered by mark. In the general call-up, the county actually sent only 145 to army service. Nevertheless, Hoge said, such criticism toward "so important and appealing a condition as helping our illiterate soldier boys—no matter how many of them or how few" was unwarranted. It did not matter "whether there are three hundred, thirty thousand or three million of the boys who cannot read or write; that does not alter our duty to them."[27]

Criticism arose in other parts of the state as well. A letter to the editor of the *Louisville Courier-Journal* challenged Stewart's draft statistics, criticized her for "advertising" the state's illiteracy, and expressed strong reservations about her work. Another noted that since the KIC had begun giving out statements regarding the number of illiterates in various counties, there had been some resentment by school officials "who are somewhat disposed to question the figures."[28] Stewart upheld the accuracy of the KIC's statistics, reiterating her charge that of the 187,573 Kentucky registrants, in fact 30,030 could not write their names and had to make their marks instead. She defended the publicity her campaign had generated, insisting that the notion that Kentucky was "the only state that advertises its illiteracy" was "absurd." "Twenty-two states are engaged in illiteracy campaigns," she wrote, "and in each of these the illiteracy figures have been boldly heralded through the press." She refuted the "pretty but idle compliment" about Kentucky's public school system with a rash of statistics on the state's inadequate per pupil and per capita expenditures, its low teacher salaries, and its inadequate compensation for school administrators. "Our educational conditions are not among the things of which we can boast or of which we are proud," she concluded.[29]

Stewart did not take criticism easily. Although the letter that appeared in the *Courier-Journal* angered her, there is little to suggest that these letters signified a broader disillusionment with her work. Little criticism appeared in the press, and both of the state's major newspapers enthusiastically backed the illiteracy cause. Nevertheless, Stewart did have some opponents, as one short newspaper clipping indicates: "Frequent attempts have been made in Kentucky to discredit Mrs. Stewart and her work, a service which she has always rendered without compensation, but in every instance her critics have gotten the worst of it. The most recent of the moves to discredit her was the action of the state senate when it refused to hear her on the illiteracy work in the state. Her friends throughout the state are pleased to know that, unsolicited, she had received recognition at Washington, which at Frankfort has either been denied her or grudgingly given."[30]

Although this article hints at opposition to her work, Stewart clearly enjoyed more supporters than detractors. The *Courier-Journal* announced, "There is nothing to be gained by debating . . . whether the number of illiterates is one hundred or one thousand. Whatever the number, it is too large and the time that is wasted in discussion could be put to better use. The disgrace of this condition lies not so much in the fact that the illiteracy exists as in the indifference with which it is tolerated."[31]

There was, whatever the cause, a subtle change in Stewart and her attitude in 1917 and 1918. Whether it resulted from criticism of her efforts, frustrations with the legislature, or simple overwork, at age forty-two she felt burdened by "pressing obligations." The death of her father in late spring had left her "saddened," disconsolate, and convinced that 1917 had been "a bad year."[32] Constant pain from a back ailment often left her short-tempered and quick to take offense, and although she had strong political instincts, she was sometimes offended by the rough-and-tumble of Kentucky politics.[33] Although her health was generally robust, it is clear that her work took a physical toll. She had collapsed once in 1914 of apparent exhaustion and in 1916 began to suffer chronic back pain and tense muscles in her neck and shoulders. She endured debilitating headaches and a bout with anemia in 1917. Visits to several physicians left her with no diagnosis, but she finally found treatment at the Mayo Brothers Hospital in Rochester, Minnesota, where she underwent surgery for an illness of the "nervous system."[34] She was also frustrated by her inability to secure a commitment from the War Department to introduce compulsory literacy training at the various army cantonments, despite appeals through Kentucky senators Ollie James and J. C. W. Beckham, and to President Woodrow Wilson himself.[35] She was, however, able to overcome physical discomfort and put worry aside, since her devotion to the new calling of educating soldiers was so intense. Nevertheless, in her memoir and history of the movement, Stewart acknowledged the frustrations she sometimes felt when "not everyone came rushing out" to support the Moonlight Schools: "The right of adult illiterates to learn had been challenged, their ability to do so had been questioned, the advisability of having teachers assume the extra duty of teaching them had been doubted, the statistics . . . had been disputed and resented; demagogues had assumed that any reference to the illiteracy of the state or community meant to traduce it, [and] professional politicians had gloried in holding the purse-strings of the public treasury as tight as possible."[36] Stewart's frustrations were real, and if the soldiers' campaign represents the pinnacle of the Moonlight School work, it also marks the last time her home state would tolerate its depiction as the illiteracy capital of the nation.

Public opinion generally favored the war effort and increased sympathy for draftees, even among budget-conscious legislators. Patriotic sentiment also furthered the literacy work. Stewart used this to good advantage by relating sad or emotional stories to provoke sympathy for those who suffered from illiteracy. One compelling example related the arrest and trial of a "shame-faced" young mountaineer who failed to register for selective service, a story she repeated many times for the press. Upon his arrest, the young mountaineer confessed his "crime" of ignorance, admitting that he could neither read nor write, and that he did not know where or what "Germany" was.[37]

The young man was not alone. Army officers working with recruits at Camp Zachary Taylor reported a "surprisingly" large number of illiterates. Some were "so densely ignorant" that they did not know the names of their home counties and "had no conception of the term county seat."[38] Theirs was a story repeated many times in Kentucky and in other parts of the rural South, and Cora Wilson Stewart played these sad tales for all they were worth, always emphasizing the total willingness of the would-be soldiers to serve their country if they could only be made literate. At the same time, she took offense when the National War Work Council of the YMCA, the agency selected by the U.S. government to coordinate the teaching of draftees, used the term "Blacks and mountain whites" to characterize illiteracy in the South. She said the term "mountain white" was an "insult" to the patriotic young men of that region and to their mothers "who have given them to the country" and a "gross injustice to a part of the country that contributed no more illiterates than New York, Pennsylvania, Massachusetts or other areas in the North." Patriotism knew no regional boundaries, she said. "They are American all—with an American's love of freedom."[39]

Although no reliable statistics attest to the number of potential draftees served by the KIC and other state illiteracy commissions during this time, the war energized the work, boosting both the number of volunteers working in the Moonlight Schools and the number of attendees. Stewart maintained that in Kentucky more than two thousand people learned to read and write in McCreary, Cumberland, Clay, and Leslie counties alone in 1917 and 1918.[40]

Using her figures on the number of illiterates taught, the rhetoric of patriotism and preparedness, and general sympathy for the war effort, Stewart was finally able to wring from the state legislature an appropriations bill, although this time she was not allowed to make the appeal to the legislature in person. Convinced by the war of the urgency and necessity of the literacy effort, members of the 1918 Kentucky General Assembly voted $75,000 to support it; however, Stewart's elation over the funding measure was short lived. In addition to voting $25,000 annually for 1918, 1919, and 1920, when the final appropriations bill was passed, the lawmakers declared that the Kentucky Illiteracy Commission would cease to exist in 1920.[41]

Stewart saw the failure to fund the KIC beyond 1920 as the work of her enemies, but in fact her own rhetoric may have been at least partially responsible. Taking her at her word, state officials could claim that she had promised to eradicate illiteracy from the state by 1920. The commission's slogan, "No Illiteracy in Kentucky by 1920," had set a deadline for success, and parsimonious legislators could simply hold Stewart to it. It is also likely that legislators felt they had spent enough on the problem of illiteracy in the state.

The appropriation enabled the KIC to continue the work on a broader scale. It furnished books and writing tablets for adult students, provided pencils and other materials needed for their classes, and enabled the KIC to employ literacy workers in the field. Stewart wrote and the KIC printed two new courses of study for the Moonlight Schools. She turned out charts and maps showing the location of the state's illiterates, along with pamphlets, posters, and buttons designed to promote the goal of "No Illiteracy by 1920."[42] The KIC employed sixty-two county agents and two district agents in 1918, and the following year it increased county workers to seventy-three and district agents to seven. District agents held supervisory positions, while county agents assisted volunteer teachers in organizing and conducting Moonlight Schools and acted as truant officers for the day schools, with the specific goal of improving school attendance by 20 percent.[43]

In the summer of 1919, Stewart launched the final Kentucky campaign, a massive effort designed to reach the remaining illiterates in the state. In an attempt to meet her goal of no illiteracy by the time census takers canvassed Kentucky in the spring, she put together an array of speakers to take the message into every part of the state. For this final effort Stewart found the perfect spokesman, a war hero whose own experience personified what her crusade was about. She enlisted Sergeant W. H. Sandlin, of Hyden, Kentucky, one of America's most decorated soldiers. Sandlin joined the literacy campaign because he wanted to "do something to make the people of the mountains realize the value of an education." Although qualified by valor on the battlefield in France, Sandlin had been unable to accept a battlefield commission because of his illiteracy. When the war ended, he returned to help "mountain men" as "handicapped" as he was. His simple message, made powerful by his experience, stressed the role of parents in keeping children in school. As a child, Sandlin was allowed to remain home from school, he said, and did not realize the value of an education until it was too late. He urged all Kentuckians to learn to read and write and to send their children to school every day.[44] An effective advocate for the Moonlight Schools, Sandlin drew large crowds and converted many to the cause. The former soldier toured the state with Stewart, speaking in hundreds of small towns and villages and offering prizes for the "best" Moonlight School in the district. His dedication to Stewart and her cause was such that when his first child was born, he named her Cora Wilson Stewart Sandlin.[45]

Although Sandlin was the "star" of the campaign, the roster of speakers included William Jennings Bryan, Champ Clark, several state governors, and many of Kentucky's most prominent educators and politicians. Kentucky's Democratic governor, James D. Black, and Republican gubernatorial candidate Edwin P. Morrow tried to outdo each other with fiery speeches on behalf of Moonlight Schools, while old friends like Rice Eubank and Mattie Dalton took to the stump, along with Judge Robert Bingham and Kentucky senator J. C. W. Beckham.[46] Stewart also enlisted the state banking commissioner, who urged bankers to assist in the campaign to eliminate illiteracy from the commonwealth by 1920 by reporting the names of persons who could not sign their names to checks and notes. Stewart even recruited traveling salesmen in this final effort, appointing a chairman who asked his colleagues to distribute literature to their customers. Jailers across the state also agreed to teach their illiterate inmates.[47]

The 1919 campaign, the largest and richest of Stewart's Kentucky career, was also the last. Although she wanted to believe the KIC would be funded beyond its 1 July 1920, closing date, there was little to sustain her hope. The commission's demise was particularly ironic because the illiteracy work had taken hold in many states across the nation. Following the Kentucky model, eighteen states had formed illiteracy commissions by 1919 and were working toward the elimination of the problem through public information campaigns and adult night schools.[48] Moreover, numerous civic organizations had stepped up their support, including the General Federation of Women's Clubs, which following Stewart's keynote address at its annual convention in Hot Springs, Arkansas, named her chairman of its Educational Committee and endorsed a $100,000 national fund drive to be led by her.[49]

This final campaign also included, for the first time, reform of the public school system, although increased support for day schools had always been a prominent goal of the illiteracy crusade. Stewart combined the issue of adult illiteracy with increased school attendance and better salaries for teachers. Governor Black, who had succeeded to the office when Stanley resigned to take a Senate seat, encouraged public support for "these three paramount educational problems" by proclaiming the week of 25 August "Educational

Week" in Kentucky. In his proclamation, he noted that while redeeming adults, "we must also see to it that our children are kept in school and thus prevent illiterates from coming on in the future."[50] Stewart had long maintained that illiteracy could be eliminated in one generation, but that outcome became more likely with stringent enforcement of compulsory attendance laws.

Seeking to convince their audiences that every child should be kept in school, campaigners decried the lax enforcement of school attendance laws in the commonwealth, arguing that the statutes should be strengthened and enforced "to the letter." If illiteracy was to be prevented, they argued, it was essential that the state appoint truant officers for rural districts to see to it that parents sent their children to school. A complex social problem, school attendance was tied to poverty and child labor. In many rural areas, parents considered their child's work at home more valuable than schoolwork, and in some towns, children worked in flagrant violation of both child labor statutes and compulsory attendance laws.[51]

Stewart had always stressed the potential benefits of Moonlight Schools, particularly in increased day school attendance and individual earning power, and in this final session, all the speakers directly linked improved public education to higher living standards and economic progress. But progress required a more significant investment in its citizenry than the state had made in the past, they said. Audiences across the state were told that Kentucky's $977 per capita income was nearly $1,000 lower than the national figure of $1,965, and that its per pupil expenditure of $9.76 was less than half the nation's average of $22.76. The state's per pupil property investment of $19 also compared poorly to the national average of $55. This had to change, the campaigners said, or Kentucky's schools would remain among the poorest in the nation.[52] Kentucky's exceptionally low teacher salaries were, they said, one result of the underfunding of public education, and citizens were urged to supplement the salaries of teachers "not in the future, but this year," through either local taxation or public subscription.[53]

Most of the speakers also drew strong parallels between literacy, democracy, and patriotism, a popular theme in postwar America. The goal of making the world safe for democracy now seemed threatened by the "red" menace, and throughout the country a reaction had set in that stressed the need for traditional "Americanism." T. J. Coates, president of the Kentucky State Normal School, played to this sentiment, noting that American soldiers had fought and died to secure the blessings of liberty. "You cannot," he said, "have true Democracy when the balance of power is held by people who are unable to read or write," and no democracy "can be considered safe when a large mass of the people are deep in the ignorance of illiteracy." Coates struck a resonant chord when he noted "that illiteracy is a serious menace to the nation, a symptom of a great, dangerous disease. Illiteracy . . . forms a fertile field for the doctrines of Bolshevism and the other doctrines which are a threat to national security."[54] Education had never been more important, he said, but in Kentucky, the system had many "weak points." One of several education insiders on the roster of distinguished speakers, Coates urged school authorities to get behind reform, noting that the nation's public schools would be held accountable for the fact that 10 percent of America's fighting men "had been allowed to remain completely illiterate." They went to Europe "without any knowledge whatever of reading and writing and other fundamental principles of education."[55]

Whether they emphasized improved school attendance, higher salaries for teachers, instruction of illiterates, increased spending for schools, economic progress through education, or the importance of strong public schools in a democracy, at least one of the forty-four speakers Stewart had recruited spoke in every county in the state during the opening of the final campaign, and their efforts were rewarded by strong enrollments in night schools across the state. When the Moonlight terms ended, Stewart noted that although they had not reached their goal of eliminating illiteracy before the 1920 census, they had come a long way. The purpose of setting such a high goal was to stimulate the forces "to the greatest possible endeavor. By setting a high aim, the number taught to read and write has been larger and greater strides have been made than had some goal less worthy been the objective."[56]

Illiteracy agents involved in the final campaign generally reported positive results; some, however, expressed disillusionment. In some districts, public school teachers resented the additional burden on their time and talent, resentment that grew when they learned the illiteracy agents received a "handsome" salary. Some disliked the fact that the local school district was expected to provide local transportation once the agent arrived in their community. Some districts reported an illiterate population that was "indifferent," "slow to respond," and hard to reach. Others called it the "most delightful" work they had ever done and expressed their complete sympathy with those who could not read and write, along with their determination to help remedy their condition. Some, like Stewart, combined a missionary impulse with their educational goals. One dedicated agent wrote of her promise to an elderly woman in her class that if she completed the instruction "Santa Claus would bring her a Bible of the largest print that could be found."[57]

Some of the most positive reports came from agents who served black communities. Ora Pruden reported that her school in the Union Hill district of Barren County was "booming," and agents in several other counties with substantial black populations reported enthusiastic pupils and teachers. Herbert Crick, whose district included Hopkinsville in Christian County, noted that seventeen evening students at "a colored school" seemed to place their "whole soul and mind" into learning to read and write.[58]

Cora Wilson Stewart had done much to create a statewide awareness of the problem of illiteracy, and the KIC had made a significant start toward dealing with it. That the work was slated to end in 1920 reflected not a lack of success but the legislature's reluctance to assume an activist role in educating either the children of the state or its adults. They supported the elimination of illiteracy in theory, along with school reform, but despite widespread ideological support for publicly funded educational initiatives, remained unwilling to vote the necessary appropriations. At the root of the problem of financing was their belief, proven by voting behavior, that communities were generally unwilling to tax themselves heavily to provide for public education.[59] Without money, Stewart could not maintain a statewide adult education program.

The demise of her work in Kentucky also reflected the fact that the war on illiteracy was not an independent reform initiative. Like many Progressive Era efforts, it was tied to other social issues and problems, all of which required solution. Eliminating illiteracy meant not only night schools for adults but also hiring supervisory and instructional personnel; it meant better school facilities to house more students; it necessitated improved roads and bridges so that students could travel to schools; it meant better teacher training and better salaries for teachers—in short, a massive overhaul of the state's provision of public education, an undertaking that legislators in her home state were unwilling to even consider. Their approach remained piecemeal and conservative, fragmented and ineffective. The result was a state education system that by 1920 ranked near the bottom in most national categories.[60]

As Stewart drew public attention to the "evils" of illiteracy, she naturally used Kentucky as an example. She took great pride in her home state's leadership in the illiteracy movement and used the KIC as a model for other states to emulate, but by calling attention to widespread illiteracy in the Kentucky mountains and elsewhere, she held the commonwealth up to a national scrutiny that many politicians and school leaders at home found uncomfortable. Whether her work outside the state, with its emphasis on isolation, poverty, poor roads, and poor schools, "advertised" Kentucky's problems, it called attention to the failures of southern paternalism just as woman suffrage had become a reality and as it appeared that women were about to become a powerful voting bloc. Although many political and educational elites agreed with her, some no doubt felt threatened.

Her own politics linked the crusade to the politically charged issues of woman suffrage and prohibition, two of the most divisive initiatives in state government. Many supporters had linked literacy to the woman vote, noting that if illiteracy was prevalent among men, it was as bad or worse among women. Some advocated instruction for voters, male and female; others favored limiting suffrage for both sexes until literacy requirements were met. Stewart's cause had also been linked to prohibition, which she vigorously supported. Many believed that without education, laws against alcohol could not be enforced.[61] Woman suffrage and prohibition sparked strong feelings, and Stewart could not avoid some fallout from her association with them, especially since Governor Stanley ardently opposed woman suffrage, supporting the amendment only upon intense pressure from the Wilson administration, and then only in a perfunctory fashion. She and the Stanley faction also differed on the best means of implementing prohibition.[62]

In addition, the simple fact that she was a woman in public life may have offended some, although even in conservative eastern Kentucky they may have kept such a sentiment to themselves. Moreover, in Stewart's part of the country, there was a distinctive prohibition against "getting above one's raising," a nebulous and difficult-to-define injunction that did not necessarily preclude success but meant that one should never forget his or her roots. Traveling extensively on behalf of her crusade, she had developed a lifestyle alien to her rural roots and had adopted an outspoken and occasionally even flamboyant public manner. This was brought home to Kentuckians in stories of her "plan" to purchase a fleet of airplanes, a move that many in the state considered not only ostentatious but frivolous and wasteful, and that exposed Stewart to intense criticism.

The *Louisville Courier-Journal* broke the story, noting just under front-page headlines that a "Squad of Airplanes to Help Fight on Illiteracy Is Mrs. Stewart's Plan." From the Waldorf Hotel in New York, the article read, Stewart announced that she was "in town to buy a new sky buggy. It will be the first of a whole fleet, she said." In New York on a fund-raising trip, she also announced her intention to learn to fly so that she could carry on her education work. "We have tried to reach these people, some of whom don't even know of the world war, with automobiles, horses and mules, but the lack of roads and sometimes the lack of even paths, has made the work all but impossible.

With airplanes we can cover the territory in a twentieth of the time it now takes."[63]

Although it is unclear how she intended to pay for it, the Curtiss Aeroplane and Motor Corporation told Stewart the company could furnish a pilot and plane for her contemplated tours in Kentucky at the rate of $500 per week. This price reflected no profit to the company, which, in appreciation and sympathy with the "splendid movement" offered the tours at cost.[64] Stewart had also inquired about the price of new airplanes and learned that the United Aircraft Engineering Corporation could provide a new Canadian training plane for about $3,500.[65] She had even secured the services of a pilot, Samuel B. Skaggs, of Berea, although press reports indicated that she had asked flying ace Eddie Rickenbacker to fly her around the state. Skaggs expressed his eagerness to fly Stewart's "sky buggy," and his hope "that one of your fondest dreams will soon be coming true and that we shall in reality be flying over our state."[66]

The plane-buying episode damaged Stewart's credibility in the state, making her appear flamboyant, even capricious, and undermining her cultivated image as a self-sacrificing schoolmarm. A minor episode, it nevertheless underscored the growing divergence between the rural and urban worlds that to country people meant "gettin' above their raisin'," and stated with compelling clarity the ambivalent public persona of "Miss Cora," a woman caught between two worlds, the modern and the traditional.

The final blow to the illiteracy crusade in Kentucky came with the Republican sweep of the state house in November 1919. Although the Democratic Party traditionally held the governor's chair, two decades of intense factionalism had weakened the party and made it vulnerable to Republican victory. Running on a progressive platform and attacking the alleged corruption and mismanagement of the Stanley-Black administration, Edwin P. Morrow won the election. The Republican majority in the house and the narrow two-vote Democratic margin in the senate assured Morrow's ability to pass his legislative agenda, although the majority went back to the Democrats in the second half of his term.[67] Education lost ground during his administration, as its share of the budget declined from 44.7 percent in 1910 to 38 percent in 1920. It fell to 30 percent by 1927.[68]

Despite difficulties and setbacks, Stewart still anticipated renewal of state appropriations for the KIC. She was on cordial terms with Morrow, a progressive who shared her views on woman suffrage and school reform, and enjoyed the support of many of her party. Morrow had even helped open the 1919 illiteracy campaign. Prior to his election he had solicited

Stewart's advice on educational policy and supported much of her work, but at the urging of George Colvin, Kentucky's new Republican superintendent of public instruction, the governor removed his backing for the continuance of the KIC. His decision turned solely on party politics, and the fact that Stewart and Colvin were enemies. George Colvin's election had weakened her standing among educators in the state, since it was common knowledge that he did not support the literacy work.[69] Colvin's hostility to the literacy work was long-standing and bitter, and he often reiterated his conviction that the "surest way to eradicate illiteracy is to stop making illiterates." The new state superintendent believed that illiterates in his state, like native-born illiterates elsewhere, were illiterates by choice. "One may not sin away his day of opportunity and hope to have it back again," he wrote.[70]

On 2 March 1920, Colvin mailed a questionnaire to all county superintendents, requesting their opinions on the proposed extension of the illiteracy commission and the new appropriation. He then used their negative replies to justify his recommendation against renewal of the appropriation. In stark contrast to the glowing testimonials of previous years, these responses were overwhelmingly unfavorable and differed significantly from reports the superintendents had made to the KIC at the close of the 1919 campaign. For example, Butler County superintendent C. E. Gary reported to the KIC that sixty Moonlight sessions had been taught in his county that year, for a total of ninety-five over the last four years. More than 1,725 illiterates had been taught, and another 1,000 people, not illiterate, had attended the schools. He credited illiteracy agents with "causing much better interest generally with an increased attendance of at least 15 percent. Better educational interest, better roads, better churches, a desire for better school houses and better salaries are other benefits." But to Colvin only a few months later, Gary wrote, "As to the moonlight schools, after careful consideration I am against the appropriation, from the fact that in my opinion we do not get value received from this work, and we need the money for the day schools. My idea is to make the day schools what they should be, and we will not need moonlight schools."[71]

Perry County's superintendent did a similar turnabout. Reporting to the illiteracy commission a "noticeable increase in our day school attendance," he also noted that "Moonlight schools have . . . served as Parent Organizations in which community problems were talked [over] and solved and even Sunday Schools have grown." But to Colvin he wrote, "I do not favor an act of the Legislature appropriating $75,000 for this work. The time to remove illiteracy is in childhood."[72] A similar response came from Henry County, where the superintendent reported to the KIC in 1919 that the county's school attendance was the best it had ever been due to the "splendid work of our County Illiteracy Agent together with my hearty co-operation." The superintendent endorsed the enactment of "such laws as will take care of adult education," but to Colvin she wrote, "The effect in decreasing the number of illiterates in my county has not been great, although the campaign probably increased the attendance at day schools somewhat. I do not believe the movement has done what it has claimed. I am opposed to this bill."[73]

The marked reversal in these assessments regarding the effectiveness of the Moonlight Schools likely turned on where best to place scarce education dollars. Several superintendents expressed the opinion that the money the state planned to spend should be put into teacher salaries, whereas others thought it would be better spent on school-age children. Some also hinted at hard feelings between illiteracy commission agents and teachers because the former were paid more. Money was certainly an issue, as were territory and jurisdiction. Some local authorities resented salaried agents coming in from Frankfort to direct the work of volunteer teachers in the night schools, as indicated by the Boyle County superintendent's response. He disliked officers in Frankfort "sending whom they please into a strange county without conveyance to sit around railroad stations and wait for the county board to haul them around." He called the work in his county "practically valueless." Moreover, teachers had complained because KIC agents typically earned twice as much as teachers.[74]

The profound change in attitudes likely resulted from the application of some pressure, probably from both sides. Stewart had used the 1919 superintendents' reports to justify the KIC's work and therefore perhaps worded questions and selected answers that portrayed that work in the best possible light. Colvin, an outspoken man with ambitions of becoming governor, used his questionnaire to justify the elimination of the KIC. Colvin's stated goal as superintendent was to remove politics from education. Toward that end, he secured legislation that required an elected board of education in each county whose task was to appoint the county superintendent.[75]

Colvin later deliberately attempted to undermine Stewart's efforts outside Kentucky as well. While Stewart was working with school authorities in Georgia on their literacy program, he wrote the state superintendent of schools in Atlanta that her work in Kentucky had been a "dismal failure," adding that "in 1920, the Legislature by practically unanimous vote abandoned the work."[76]

Stewart's request for another three-year $75,000 appropriation to be administered by a department of adult education with her at its head simply did not fit Colvin's plans or Governor Morrow's politics. In an episode that clearly illustrates the degree of resistance to women's political influence in Kentucky at this time, the literacy crusader and her coalition of clubwomen endured a stinging tactical defeat at the hands of the state legislature. Stewart had arranged for the Kentucky Federation of Women's Clubs to rally on 10 March, the day the bill authorizing a separate department of adult education came up in the House of Representatives. Morrow outwitted them by pushing opponents of the bill into calling it up for consideration on 4 March 1920. The Republican majority quickly succeeded in tabling the measure and effectively co-opted the women's march. Incensed at the partisan maneuvering, Mrs. J. C. Layne of the KFWC called it "one of the darkest days in Kentucky's history." When the bill came before the senate, again ahead of schedule, Senator Pleasant Hogue, the first-term "herb and root" doctor from McCreary County, launched a colorful tirade that won detailed accounting in the *Lexington Herald.* Hogue noted his opposition to "wasting" any more of the state's money on "teachin' old people. It ain't no use and furthermore they don't deserve it." As far as clubwomen were concerned, he vowed, "I ain't afeered to vote against this bill, though they's some here that is. They's some weak-kneed politicians that's afeered of the women. I ain't got no use fer these here women that run around with a poodle dog in their arms, and I ain't afeered of 'em." The bill went down to defeat along party lines.[77]

In a fit of pique, Stewart charged Colvin with deliberately misleading the superintendents by suggesting that the bill threatened a proposed salary increase. In fact the bill provided payment for teachers for the night school work. She also embarrassed a number of superintendents by publishing their 1919 reports beside their current ones.[78] The *Lexington Herald's* articles on the fracas indicate that Kentuckians remained somewhat ambivalent about the Moonlight Schools and their cost to the commonwealth. Some resented the attention the illiteracy crusade brought to the state, and some, like Senator Hogue, simply preferred that women stay out of public affairs entirely.[79]

Although much work remained, Kentucky's Moonlight teachers had taught over 130,000 of the state's more than 200,000 illiterates to read and write, according to Stewart, and had enhanced the skills of many who could already read and write a little. In closing the KIC, Mrs. Stewart recommended that the legislature fund a department of adult education to create and standardize a state system of evening schools for adults. She also suggested that the teachers in these schools be paid "reasonable salaries," that the governor appoint a commissioner of adult education and an attendance officer for rural schools as "a preventative" of future illiteracy, and that a superintendent be placed in charge of school work at the state reformatory and penitentiary.[80]

As she ended her work in her home state, Stewart noted that the question of illiteracy had to be dealt with by the two leading Kentucky parties in their platform conventions. Much remained to be done outside the commonwealth as well. "The call to wider service must be answered," she said, and "Kentucky already knows the way."[81]

Stewart considered her options as friends pressured her to prove to Governor Morrow that he "had made a sad mistake" in not passing another appropriations bill. She may have felt some temptation to settle the score with George Colvin, which she could perhaps have done by assuming an active role in the Democratic Party.[82] Since the Republican governor's pro-suffrage stance had attracted many of the state's women, the Democrats felt it necessary to woo them away. As one of the most prominent Democratic women in Kentucky, with powerful connections to churchwomen and clubwomen, professional women and the press, Cora Wilson Stewart was the one woman in the state who could do that. An eastern Kentucky friend who took particular pride in the way Stewart "gave it to the Republicans," cheered her on: "[Governor Morrow] realized you are a woman with a great influence. They had lots of time to think this over before they took the advantage of you."[83]

A humorous piece by Thomas Cromwell, the political editor of the *Cincinnati Enquirer*, illustrates the view many held of Stewart's value to the party. "Colonel Tom" had long admired Stewart and her work, and during the last campaign he made the observation that Governor Stanley and "would-be governor Morrow" should collaborate on a manifesto "to the wild and untamed voters" of their state, promising that the Democratic Party was not out to "hog the universe," since so many seemed to think that the slogan "Buy a Liberty Bond and make the world safe for democracy" meant "safe for the Democratic Party." "If this fails to enlighten the unenlightened," Cromwell concluded, "there is nothing to do but turn loose Sister Cora Wilson Stewart."[84]

"Sister" Stewart was a strong figure in Kentucky politics, having created over the years a distinctive political identity for herself. As early as 1914, she was recognized as a "vital and vibrant force" in Kentucky politics for her ability to rally the women of the state. Party leaders considered her for state superintendent of public instruction that year, when the *Lexington Herald* recommended that the Democratic Party nominate her: "We submit to the Democrats of the Legislature the suggestion that a ticket on which Mrs. Stewart was a nominee, nominated by a party that had given to women the right to vote, would be invincible in the state of Kentucky."[85] Especially once suffrage was attained, she could help bring women into the party. A gifted

rhetorician and fiery stump speaker, she had proved herself capable of rally-
ing the masses. A loyal Democrat, in 1920 and 1921 she served on the three-
member Democratic National Congressional Committee and acted as
vice-chairman for the Kentucky League of Women Voters.[86] Since she and
her popular cause had just been "martyred" by the budget-cutting Republicans, it would be a propitious time to "turn her loose."

Stewart, like many public women of her generation, faced new choices
brought about by passage of the Nineteenth Amendment. She could continue her reform work, following the example of women such as Jane Addams
and Florence Kelley, who had worked to protect women and children in the
workplace and the home, to win prohibition, and to secure peace, and who
were now involved in "cleaning up" the American household. Some women
chose to extend the suffrage fight into one for full equality for women through
an equal rights amendment to the Constitution. Or she could use the vote to
gain access to party politics or elected office.[87]

Stewart did, of course, continue her reform work, but the temptation to
wreak vengeance on the Republicans and strengthen the role of women in
her own party was strong. Always active in Democratic issues, even during
her term as chairman of the KIC, when she preferred to call her efforts
nonpartisan, she also participated in the new interest group politics used by
women to promote their social reform causes outside the realm of party
politics. Moreover, through the National Education Association, the General Federation of Women's Clubs, and the National Congress of Parents
and Teachers, she vigorously advocated passage of "the education bill," so
called because it had so many names and so many sponsors over the years.[88]
The bill, which enjoyed widespread support in the education community,
provided for the creation of a cabinet-level department of education and
called for millions of dollars in federal aid to education, including the elimination of illiteracy.

Stewart was drawn to politics both by personality and by circumstance.
She believed in the absolute equality of rights between men and women,
and she saw the new woman vote as a valuable commodity that would go to
the party that appealed most to the interests of women.[89] But she also considered party politics a two-way street. She had something to give, and the
party had something she wanted and needed. With political power and access to the legislative process, she could address the needs of illiterates everywhere. The Republicans had deprived her of her state agency before the
work in Kentucky was finished, and partisan politics offered the best chance
at redressing that grievance.

Many Americans, convinced that women would vote based on "moral imperatives" instead of party loyalty, expected suffrage to transform politics. Others expected women voters to turn out in blocs to secure their own interests or to "punish" male politicians who had ignored or disparaged those interests. Despite those expectations, the power remained largely where it had always been, in the hands of male politicians. Historian Nancy Cott describes this as the classic "double bind." Had women turned out in blocs, they would have been reviled for selfishly pushing their own agenda. When they did not turn out, they were criticized for their lack of sisterhood and common objectives.[90]

Cora Wilson Stewart took a practical approach to the role of women in party politics. She knew that political offices were too valuable to men for them to give them away to women, but she warned Kentucky's party leaders that women would not be content to simply vote; they would expect to hold office as well:

> I wonder if our men are going to realize that women will now expect to share the offices, and that they will not want the minor offices. I hope to see the Democratic party lead out with some real recognition of its women. A policy of this kind followed for the next few years would settle for all time the question of how Kentucky women will vote. The League of Nations will not always be an issue, and the Negro question will not forever alarm them. The party will have to beat the Republican Party in its recognition of the new voters by giving them more than honorary or secondary positions.[91]

Most party leaders understood or at least gave lip service to such an idea. Some no doubt opposed women holding office but realized the necessity of pulling them into the party. Kentucky's Democratic Campaign Committee hinted broadly that it would reward Stewart if she worked for the party, but it also made it clear that both her service and any subsequent election would be on party terms. The chairman of the speaker's bureau, soliciting her participation in the 1920 campaign wrote:

> I do not know whether you have any political ambition. Whether you have or not, conditions may come about where it would appear perfectly proper for you to have such ambition. If the demand for your services on the stump just now is any indication of the esteem in which you are held by the Democrats of Kentucky, I am sure the time is not far . . . when you have no trouble in gratifying any proper ambition that might arise in your heart, so far as Kentucky's public affairs are concerned. I beg you not to overlook this in deciding just how much of your time you are going to give us in Kentucky.[92]

State party officials, demanding that she not divide her time, wanted her exclusive service. "I am proud, of course, that the National Committee wants your services, but Kentucky needs you and needs you badly, and we are going to be very much disappointed if you give any time outside of the state," wrote State Democratic Party secretary H. M. McChesney.[93]

Stewart's first priority remained the literacy crusade. She was willing, however, to take an active role in the Democratic Party, and few women were more visible than she at the 1920 nominating conventions. Both parties courted women in the 1920 campaign, with the Democrats stressing the fact that women had gained the vote under a Democratic president. They selected a number of female delegates to the nominating conventions, and some women even gained important positions on the national committees. Democrats that year seated 299, and the Republicans 156, up from a total for both parties of only 36 in 1916.[94] Stewart's friend and associate from the National Education Association, Charl Ormond Williams of Tennessee, was the first female to serve as vice-chairman of the Democratic National Committee, and she saw to it that Cora and other women were actively involved.[95]

Stewart served as a delegate-at-large at the nominating convention in San Francisco in July. Her primary role was to convince delegates to insert a suffrage plank in the Democratic platform, acknowledging their enfranchisement and encouraging their loyalty. Given her considerable gift for oratory, one would expect an impassioned plea for the rights of women, but what she delivered was a lecture on civics and common sense. She told party leaders to put aside their antiquated arguments about inequality between the sexes and step into the twentieth century. Women had earned the right to be where they were—in the classrooms, businesses, offices, libraries, and factories of the nation. Their war service was just as exemplary as that of men, she said. They had "helped to raise the money to finance the late world war," worked in the munitions factories and hospitals, "worked as men worked . . . if not actually in the front, . . . just behind the lines," ministering to soldiers and caring for the wounded and dying. The female vote was a reality, she said, and Kentucky had to recognize that or be left behind the times. She told state leaders to "put aside" as out of date their states' rights arguments on the issue. Calling the extension of suffrage a "necessity" and the "withholding of it an absurdity," she said the party that recruited women voters would be assured of their loyalty.[96]

Desha Breckinridge, the editor of the *Lexington Herald,* had asked Stewart to supply her impressions of the platform and candidates, especially her role at the convention and the treatment of women in the platform.[97]

Breckinridge expressed his confidence in Cora's ability to assess the situation: "I realize so keenly how potent an influence you were in the convention and how you grasped the full import of everything done there, that I am anxious to have the readers of the *Herald* get your impressions and the Democratic party get the benefit of your views."[98] She also wrote for the *Louisville Times,* whose managing editor assured her that she had handled the assignment "like a veteran newspaper man."[99]

Stewart also represented the National Education Association, which had just created an illiteracy commission with her at its head. A member of the NEA's Legislative Committee, her task was to secure an illiteracy plank in the Democratic platform and an endorsement of it into the acceptance speeches of the Democratic nominees.[100] The NEA had authorized her to offer assurances of the organization's full support to the candidate who promised the most in terms of education, particularly support for passage of the education bill. It was her job to have her "prominent educator friends wire endorsements" to the chairman of the platform committee.[101]

Stewart was also chosen to second the nomination of Ohio governor James B. Cox for president of the United States. Charl Ormond Williams recommended her, telling the candidate Stewart was the only woman in the country who could do the job.[102] Stewart's popularity among California women, earned two years earlier during the illiteracy crusade in their state, made her an especially good choice. Many of them had also heard her keynote address at the general meeting of the Federation of Women's Clubs of California in 1918. Stewart's presence served Cox well. When it was rumored at the convention that he might be "wet," female delegates gave him the benefit of the doubt, noting that "Cora Wilson Stewart would not have nominated a man whose ideals in this respect and all others were not of the highest."[103]

The nominating convention represented a golden moment in Stewart's career. In a gesture toward women voters, her fellow Kentuckians honored her service by casting one vote for Mrs. Stewart for president of the United States and extended the same tribute to Kentucky suffragist Laura Clay.[104]

Before leaving San Francisco, Stewart arranged for the presidential and vice presidential candidates to prepare statements regarding their positions on education for the NEA. Both supported educational issues, and she expected their statements to win votes from professional educators across the country. Cox's running mate, Franklin Delano Roosevelt, calling public attention to the nation's five million illiterates, made his position clear in his acceptance speech. In a letter to Stewart, Roosevelt apologized that he could not "expand much on the subject as my speech was so short."[105] Cox wrote a statement in September, in which he promised to give serious attention to the necessary reorganization of the executive departments in the federal government. He offered a somewhat vague promise to "favor the effective administration of affairs relating directly to all matters of human welfare, including education." But Cox considered federal aid to education appropriate and necessary and said he would give particular attention to the removal of illiteracy, the Americanization of immigrants, the preparation and proper compensation of teachers, and the equalization of opportunity to secure a "complete practical education."[106] Stewart campaigned for Cox not only because he was a Democrat but also because she believed he had taken a stronger stand on education than had Warren Harding.[107]

Stewart's performance at the convention in San Francisco not only strengthened her standing among Democrats in her state and gave her an opportunity to lobby educational special interests at the national level but also led to a role in the 1920 presidential campaign. Governor Cox wrote to thank her for "the most excellent speech" on his behalf and asked her to speak for him in the West. He complimented her vision and competence, noting that she had "a glimpse of what progress means in government and after all, that is one of the basic things in this campaign."[108] Cox's request put her at odds with Kentucky Democrats who wanted to keep her at home, but she took to the national campaign trail with great enthusiasm, giving fifty-three speeches across the country.[109]

Cox's support on education issues was worth anything the Kentucky Democrats could offer, but Stewart could not forget her home state. True to her word, she stumped on behalf of her friends, campaigning with special enthusiasm for Congressman William J. Fields, who won by a large majority, giving much of the credit for his victory to Stewart. Given the Republican landslide, he said, his victory was particularly noteworthy.[110] The Republicans countered Stewart's efforts by assigning George Colvin to "follow" her over the state. Within a day or two of each of Stewart's engagements, Colvin appeared to champion the Republicans.[111]

The Republican victory in 1920, at both the state and the national level, was a setback, but Stewart did not see it as a permanent one. She remained hopeful that the literacy work in Kentucky would be revived, but she had already begun to focus more intently on the national arena, where she was already actively involved in coordinating state-level campaigns, as her strongest hope. Of the political situation in Kentucky, she remarked to a friend, "You didn't expect me to stop when Kentucky did—did you?" She believed the Republican opposition there lacked the vision to deal with the problem of adult illiteracy, and she would simply have to be patient: "Though I regret the delay," she wrote to a friend, "I am not discouraged. The illiterates will have their chance."[112]

For Cora Wilson Stewart, political access, before suffrage and after, required male conduits. She relied on newspapermen such as Colonel Tom Cromwell and Desha Breckinridge, who urged her on, cheering her from their editorial pages and chiding those who stood in her way. She used her brothers Homer Lee and Bunyan, who could put the local Democratic party apparatus at her disposal. Although her old mentor, Governor McCreary, died the year before the suffrage amendment passed, many others, including William Fields, "Honest Bill from Olive Hill," a longtime friend and the next governor of Kentucky, offered to take his place. Most of them did so out of genuine affection for Stewart and respect for both her cause and her ability to pursue it with such single-minded vigor and enthusiasm. That she enjoyed broad-based support from the people of the state was, of course, another important consideration.

Breckinridge may have been the only one who supported Stewart out of any sense that women had a "place" in the polity. Cromwell thought her an interesting and charismatic anomaly who added dimension to Kentucky politics. It is difficult to assess with any certainty the motives of the others. McCreary was simply quite fond of her. He found her charming and delightful, but he probably also recognized her value to the party. She and Fields shared a common moral zeal; both were ardent prohibitionists with strong religious convictions, and they shared many of the same practical reform goals, including improved schools and better rural roads.

One important male supporter remains obscure. It is impossible to gauge either his motives or his intentions, but William Purcell Dennis Haly was an important influence on Stewart's party career. "The General," as he preferred to be called, was the power behind the throne in Kentucky Democratic politics. Since his days as the primary strategist for the ill-fated William Goebel, Haley had built a powerful machine that secured the elections of J. C. W. Beckham to the governor's chair and to the U.S. Senate. He also engineered the return of McCreary to the governorship in 1911. His opponents, who included A. O. Stanley, reviled him as a tyrannical boss and political fixer, but his friends loved him. The General drafted campaign platforms and gave sage advice on winning and holding public office.[113] His interest in Stewart was intense, and he often sent messages through her KIC secretary, Lela Mae Stiles, whose office was at the capital in Frankfort.

In 1922, Haly chose Stewart to run for state superintendent of public instruction and asked several people to try to convince her to do so.[114] A former colleague on the KIC, Woodson May, of Somerset made the official offer, asking her to accept the Democratic nomination for this position, "the nomination, as you will concede, . . . this time being equivalent to an election." May proffered his services as campaign manager and assured Stewart of "a success that will be convincing evidence of the desire of the people of this State to place its educational affairs in competent hands and at the same time show an appreciation for a most wonderful work already accomplished."[115]

Although initially favorable to it, Stewart ultimately withdrew from consideration for the state superintendency, and the party nomination (and election) went to Democrat McHenry Rhodes. It is likely that she did so in anticipation of winning another, more prestigious office. Later that same year, General Haly sent an urgent message through Lela Mae that Stewart was to attend "a big Democratic conference of men and women and legislators" and that it was "most necessary" for her to be there three or four days beforehand.[116] Leaders in her congressional district, including her brother Homer Lee, were pushing her to succeed to William J. Field's congressional seat when he attained the governorship in the 1923 election. Rowan County judge J. W. Riley assured her that Fields would be elected, but if he were not, he would of course, "want to hold on to his job" but would be so weakened by his gubernatorial defeat that Stewart could easily beat him.[117]

Initial strategy called for a resolution from district leaders on behalf of both Fields and Stewart, but after conferring with Haly and her brother Homer, Stewart informed Riley that it would be best to wait until the election to announce her candidacy. She feared a split in the party, since she had "learned definitely" that Fields would not resign unless he won the election. "I feel confident that Fields will be elected," she wrote, "and we could then count on his support which, of course, would be a big factor in winning the race."[118]

Stewart was in Washington during this time, organizing and streamlining the state illiteracy efforts through regional and national illiteracy conferences, but she returned to Kentucky to campaign for Field's election, once again stumping the state on his behalf. But the election of her old friend to the governorship proved a profound disappointment, and her hopes of winning his seat in Congress evaporated as well. Fields had solicited Stewart's advice on educational matters, going so far as to have her draft a proposed education platform and to suggest that she would have an important role in its implementation, but after his election, the new governor refused to commit himself to appropriations for a revival of the literacy work in the state. In an interview with the chairman of the illiteracy division of the KFWC, arranged by Stewart, Fields revealed his reluctance, noting that the illiteracy work had "suffered a reaction" and that he would not suggest reintroducing it unless he was sure the people wanted it. When she reminded him that she represented more than one thousand of the state's women, his response was, "Yes, but how many votes do they control at home?"[119]

Stewart could barely contain her anger. In a handwritten letter, she expressed disbelief that Fields could ask her to prepare an educational program and expect her to leave out the illiterates. "You have withdrawn yourself from my counsel and shown that you are offended because I have urged certain relief measures for the illiterates of our State as part of your program for governor." There was no longer any basis for cooperation between them, she said, and "I shall desist from efforts to thrust the banner into unwilling hands. My presence at your inaugural I judge shall not be necessary."[120]

In addition to his default on the illiteracy issue, she learned that her former friend had also failed to support her as a candidate for his congressional seat. Although she still stood some chance of winning, she told her brother to withdraw her name from the race. Writing from Washington, D.C., where she was overseeing the National Illiteracy Conference, she told Lela Mae that the race for the governor's vacated seat "would be decided by the nineteen county chairmen." With the nominee being decided in the proverbial smoke-filled room, Stewart concluded that a woman would have no chance, although she remained convinced that in a primary she might prevail. "I know the inside of the congressional matter, and where the nomination will go. We could not have both this and a revival of our work, so I decided to stand by the work."[121] The lesson Stewart learned from Kentucky Democratic politics was that she could have neither.

The *Woman Citizen,* then the official journal of the National League of Women Voters, had warned women in 1920 that joining a party did not admit them to the inner circles that made policy and urged them "to keep their conscience" when they entered.[122] Belle Moskowitz, the influential adviser to future New York governor Al Smith, had noted that "the major political parties are still man-made and man-controlled. Few of their leaders can work with women on a basis of equality."[123] Another woman disillusioned by party politics wrote that in the postsuffrage age, "Political offices are the assets of the political machine. In general, they are too valuable to give to women."[124] All these observations are borne out by Cora Wilson Stewart's experience in Kentucky politics.

But there were other avenues to power. Historians now see women as pioneers in interest group politics.[125] Many activist women rejected party politics as a means of gaining access to the power of the state, accepting in whole or in part the telling analysis made by Winifred Starr Dobyns in the *Woman Citizen.* Applying the analogy of "The Lady and the Tiger" to the woman voter and the political machine, she concluded that reform could not be brought about by women from the inside. She noted that the aim of most political organizations was not good government, public welfare, or even patriotic service. Although politicians gave lip service to these goals, their primary interest was in filling their pockets at public expense, giving "jobs to thousands who find politics an easy way to make a living," maintaining themselves and others in office so that they could trade favors with business, and giving protection to "evaders of the law."[126]

Although Stewart's assessment of state party politics may not have been as harsh as Dobyns's, she came away from her experience convinced that there was little she could do for the Democrats, and even less that they could do for her. That women across the country reached the same conclusion is not surprising. Certainly women came to party politics as outsiders, and since their arrival coincided with their determination to "clean house" in postsuffrage America, politicians of all stripes felt their single-sex domain threatened. They were willing to admit women, but on male terms. In fact, males as politicians reacted much as males as legislators did, since they were one and the same. Happy to give lip service to the role of the "New Woman" in politics, they "escorted" her into their realm and dictated the terms on which she could stay, while from their legislative offices, they praised her maternalist reform initiatives but declined to foot the bill.

Cora Wilson Stewart's experience in Democratic politics altered her course but did not change her goals. Buoyed by public opinion, supported by a network of clubwomen and school professionals, and assisted by a cadre of male backers, she took advantage of American involvement in World War I and the changing role of women in the polity to further her efforts on behalf of illiterates. The creation and funding of a state illiteracy commission politicized her crusade and tied her to Democratic politicians who supported her work, but her experience in party politics, though exhilarating at times, ultimately disappointed her. It enhanced neither her personal ambition nor her crusade. In that sense, then, her confrontation with "the tiger" was typical. She accomplished little through Democratic Party politics. Despite woman suffrage, access was limited and conditional, and the results were meager. Stewart's activism continued across the "great divide" of the Nineteenth Amendment, but because of her experience in party politics, she decided to rely instead on the more effective politics of issues and interest groups. Governmental backing remained critical to the success of her crusade, and Stewart began in earnest to gain it at the national level.

Cora Wilson epitomizes the southern lady in this
formal portrait taken at the turn of the twentieth
century. Like most of her contemporaries in uplift
work, she accepted many of the class-based
assumptions of her time and place.

Volunteers in Rowan County's first Moonlight Schools were given a trip to
Niagara Falls as a reward for their efforts.

Moonlight Schools met in the evenings in schoolhouses lit by kerosene lamps
and heated by wood- or coal-burning stoves. Claude Turner, a local teacher,
taught one of the larger sessions in Morehead in 1911 and 1912.

Moonlight Schools caught on quickly. This photograph shows a group of adult pupils in Elliott County, Kentucky, in 1914.

Roads were poor in eastern Kentucky, making travel to and from schools difficult. Stewart championed the cause of improved roads and secured help from the state in building a stretch of model road in front of several county schoolhouses. Shown in this photograph are mule-drawn wagons hauling gravel to a new roadbed in Morehead.

"Jolt wagons," like the one shown here, were common in rural eastern Kentucky. In front is Kentucky governor James B. McCreary, traveling in support of a public school rally. McCreary's backing of Moonlight Schools resulted in the creation of the Kentucky Illiteracy Commission.

Volunteers at the Normal School in Castleton, Vermont, provided instruction for black female inmates at a nearby prison.

The Moonlight School idea expanded to include adults in towns and cities across the country. Shown here is a class of beginners in Philadelphia in 1930. Stewart insisted on programs for blacks, and although they were generally segregated, they employed both black and white instructors.

The illiteracy crusade served as a catalyst for a number of adult education programs like this one for mill workers in Columbus, Georgia, in 1930.

American participation in World War I revealed a large number of draftees who could neither read nor write. They became the focus of the literacy campaign in 1917 and 1918, leading Stewart to create the *Soldier's First Book* and to demand that no soldier who lacked the ability to read and write be sent into service overseas.

Stewart also focused attention on illiterate parents. Those who learned to read and write would gain a new appreciation for education and, she hoped, ensure that their children attended school. Mothers were especially important in this process, and in 1929, Stewart created a special primer just for them. Shown here is a young mother holding the *Mother's First Book*.

Stewart was appalled at the high illiteracy rates on Indian reservations
and took her campaign to them in the 1920s. Women's Club
volunteers in Washington, Oregon, the Dakotas, and other western
states provided instruction for both children and adults.

(Above) In March 1931, Stewart held an illiteracy clinic on the Blackfoot Indian Reservation near Glacier Park, Washington. (Right) Stewart had to contend with societal misperceptions regarding the ability to learn. For example, many education professionals believed that adults lost aptitude for learning as they aged. This North Carolina couple and many others like them disproved that theory by learning to read and write when they were well into their eighties.

Racial stereotypes provided the misperception that
blacks typically failed to learn, even in the best of
circumstances. Moonlight Schools reached out to blacks
in rural areas and small towns across the country and
produced many "star pupils." This middle-aged man
won the top prize in his class in Bullock County,
Kentucky, in 1922.

Stewart chaired the illiteracy section of several international education meetings. Shown here are delegates to the 1923 International Conference on Education, held in San Francisco in June and July. Stewart is in the front row, seventh from left.

As head of the National Advisory Committee in Illiteracy, Stewart welcomed a delegation of Tennessee mountain Moonlight students to a White House gathering hosted by President Herbert Hoover. The group brought letters and handicrafts, along with a box of sweet potatoes, which was presented to the president. Stewart is shown looking on from the second row, third from Hoover's left.

Stewart relied on legislators for support and found party politics both stimulating and frustrating. She is shown here in the center of the Kentucky delegation at the Democratic National Convention in 1920. At left is Kentucky suffragist Laura Clay. Atop the donkey is Alben Barkley.

Cora Wilson Stewart in her later years. Stewart retired to Tryon, North Carolina, where she died at age eighty-three.

FIVE

The National Crusade against Illiteracy

Progressive Era reformers often began their campaigns in their own communities, frequently through voluntary associations, and public roles for women enlarged as these groups consolidated, federated, and became increasingly adept at influencing politics at local, state, and national levels. Through their organizational networks, women could spread a policy idea quickly across the states and down to local communities, thus influencing the formulation of legislation at all levels. Using national organizations such as the General Federation of Women's Clubs, the Women's Trade Union League, the National Consumers' League, the Women's Joint Congressional Committee, the League of Women Voters, and hundreds of special interest and professional groups, they mounted nationwide campaigns and secured passage of state and federal legislation in support of their social welfare causes. The creation of federal agencies such as the Women's Bureau and Children's Bureau institutionalized their reforms and involved federal and state bureaucracies in the welfare of "deserving" and needy citizens.[1]

Cora Wilson Stewart's work followed this pattern. After her 1920 defeat in Kentucky, she turned her full attention to the states and to the creation of a national illiteracy movement, hoping to mount a nationwide crusade and create Moonlight Schools in communities across the country. She continued to rely on organized women and professional educators for moral and financial support; therefore, much of her work in the states took place outside political channels.

Although Stewart's generation of optimistic and idealistic

women found their disenchantment with the political system sometimes acute and painful, many continued to believe that the nation and the world could be changed for the better. Laboring for disarmament and world peace, they espoused progressivism as intently during the 1920s as they did in the previous decade.[2] But in addition to a more conservative political climate, this generation of women also faced challenges to their values and ideals as a new generation of professionals in education and social work sought to wrest control of their professions from volunteers, poorly trained practitioners, moral reformers, and crusaders like Cora Wilson Stewart.[3]

Whether it required the efforts of volunteers or professionally trained experts, Stewart's mission field remained fertile. Illiteracy in the United States stayed high, and with 4,931,905 illiterates in 1920, the United States ranked ninth among industrialized nations. Illiteracy rates had dropped from 20 percent in 1870 to 6 percent in 1920, or from one illiterate in every five Americans to one in seventeen, but because of population growth, the real number of illiterates decreased by only three-quarters of a million. Concentrations of illiteracy were highest in the South, with Louisiana, Mississippi, South Carolina, and Alabama heading the list. By 1920 these states, each of which operated adult literacy programs patterned after the Moonlight School model, had seen an average drop of just under 7 percent. According to the 1910 census, Louisiana had topped the nation at 29 percent, followed by Alabama at 22.9, Mississippi at 22.4, and New Mexico at 20.2.[4] The reduction in Stewart's home state of Kentucky had been 3.7 percent.[5]

Illiteracy existed everywhere, not just in the South. According to a 1921 NEA study, 389,000 illiterates lived in Georgia, but New York recorded 406,000. Pennsylvania, at 354,000, had more illiterates than Alabama with 352,000, and illiterates in Illinois, Ohio, and New Jersey exceeded the numbers in Louisiana, Mississippi, and Texas.[6] But rural illiteracy at 7.7 percent surpassed urban at 4.4, with only 25.7 percent of rural youth aged fifteen to eighteen enrolled in high schools. In cities 71.1 percent of that age-group remained in high school. The highest rates of adult illiteracy existed among Native Americans, with percentages of 45.3 in 1910 and 34.9 in 1920. Among immigrant whites, the percentage rose from 12.7 in 1910 to 13.1 in 1920. The rate for blacks dropped from 30.4 percent in 1910 to 22.9 percent in 1920, and among native whites from 5 to 2 percent.[7]

Based on admitted inability to read and write, these figures masked an even larger problem, and NEA researchers charged that a careful study based on reading and writing a simple paragraph would double the numbers, bringing the total closer to ten million than the five identified by the Census Bureau. Using draft statistics to back their claim, they recommended immediate action, calling it "unsafe" to disregard the number of "absolute and confessed illiterates" so limited in their command of the English language that they could not read and understand newspapers and write letters home.[8]

Changing these statistics required a huge campaign, similar to those in Kentucky and other states but carried out on a national scale. Toward that end, Cora Wilson Stewart built a broad coalition, bringing a network of national organizations together in common cause. Under her tutelage, an NEA committee studied illiteracy for two years and in 1918 created an illiteracy commission to act as a central information center and clearinghouse in a new national movement to confront the problem. In addition to providing a much-needed morale boost for the crusade, the NEA Illiteracy Commission connected Stewart to teachers in each state, provided financial resources for researching and publicizing illiteracy in the states, partially underwrote the expense of her travels, and brought to bear the strength and influence of the nation's largest professional association for educators.[9] The commission put her in touch with other departments, committees, and individuals within the NEA and supplied a forum for drawing attention to the problem of illiteracy among native-born Americans living in small towns and rural communities. Although it operated on an annual budget of only $1,000, the NEA commission nevertheless enabled Stewart to sponsor regional and national conferences and to participate in international gatherings that brought illiteracy workers together to focus public attention on the problem as never before. Coordination of the work in the states would have been much more difficult, if not impossible, without the commission, which included six state superintendents of public instruction, two specialists in adult education, a state college president, and the editor of the *New York Times*. This highly capable and well-connected group could reach every influential educational organization in the nation. Stewart began by having it analyze the statistical reports of the U.S. Census Bureau to develop figures to arouse public awareness of the extent of adult illiteracy in each state.[10]

Success depended on broad public understanding and involvement. Pleased with its effectiveness in the state campaigns, Stewart once again turned to the General Federation of Women's Clubs, which, like the NEA, created an illiteracy commission with her at the helm. The GFWC appropriated no funds for the commission, but it underwrote Stewart's travel expenses and, like the NEA, allotted illiteracy broad coverage in its publications and assigned Stewart a prominent position on national programs. The GFWC could field an almost endless supply of ready, willing, and able volunteers, the crucial element in the literacy coalition. Stewart also tapped the resources of the Women's Christian Temperance Union, which formed a similar commission under her direction, and in 1921 she secured the creation of yet another commission under the auspices of the National Council of Education, a subsidiary of the NEA. Although she did not head it, she also organized and served as advisory chairperson of an illiteracy council sponsored by the National Congress of Parents and Teachers.[11] She also rallied unaffiliated volunteers through an intense public education campaign in newspapers, magazines, and radio.[12] Her coalition linked professional and lay efforts within a huge network that brought thousands of people into the fight against illiteracy, enabling Stewart to tap both public and private resources.

Stewart's experience in Kentucky had taught her the critical importance of executive backing; therefore, she established partnerships between state governors and the NEA commission. In letters to the governors of each state, she requested their support and urged them to mention illiteracy in their inaugural addresses, to keep the issue before the state legislatures, to create or revitalize their state commissions, and to appoint both men and women to the commissions. In some letters, she provided names of potential appointees. With each letter, she enclosed a newspaper clipping of a speech by prominent New York churchman Rev. Newell Dwight Hillis, decrying America's standing at ninth place in literacy among the industrialized nations of the world. Stewart also reminded the governors that the GFWC, the National Council of Education, the WCTU, and other national organizations had already established committees to work with the state commissions in removing illiteracy from their communities. She informed them about the work of governors in other states, including figures and target dates, and sent each governor a breakdown of illiteracy statistics in his state, categorized by sex, race, and national origin. The statistics included a list of the ten counties with the most illiterates and gave figures for at least two major cities in each state. A critical link in the national infrastructure, state illiteracy commissions rounded out the coalitions by facilitating communication among state leaders and providing the necessary supplies, training, and information to workers in the field.[13]

To further secure the support of educators, Stewart contacted state superintendents of public instruction and offered the NEA Illiteracy Commission's assistance in compiling and distributing illiteracy statistics. In a letter to Will C. Wood, California's school chief, Stewart stressed the importance of publishing illiteracy statistics and breaking the numbers down by counties and cities. Presented this way, she said, they became "an indictment," and people began to take responsibility for their local illiterates. She offered to provide copies of the statistics for every newspaper in their states if the superintendents would see to their release.[14] Stewart also sent letters to American Legion commanders, asking them to include illiteracy in all their public addresses and to place it on the agenda at their annual meetings. In addition, she enlisted presidents of state teachers' associations, press organizations, and women's civic clubs.[15]

Like southerners who had blamed their illiteracy on blacks, many state leaders attributed their problem to immigrants, and some western states claimed that most of their illiterates lived on reservations. These attitudes necessitated what Stewart called "the battle of statistics," in which city, county, and state figures were "hurled at every school official and headlined in the press." This tactic gave illiterates a face, she said. They were no longer "far away, somewhere, up in the mountains, or, anywhere, other than next door."[16] Once people acknowledged the existence of illiteracy in their own communities, it could be eradicated, particularly if local and state governments backed the cause. Public information, then, became an important function of the national campaign.

While it was important that the public recognize illiteracy as a major social problem, crusade rhetoric masked the fact that illiteracy lacked a public policy definition and that no one had identified the stage at which an individual passed from illiteracy into literacy. The standard varied from state to state. Kentucky set it at completion of the second grade, while other states established the bar at the third or fourth grade. California set completion of the sixth grade as a criterion for literacy and required that all individuals under the age of twenty-one complete it. Difficult to enforce, standards could not be measured, since sole responsibility for taking the census resided with the federal government, which simply classified individuals on the basis of admitted inability to write in English.[17] Stewart set her own criteria at completion of the second *Country Life Reader*, the Kentucky standard. Because that could be achieved in two six-week sessions of night school, it ensured a rapid decline in illiteracy statistics, but whether this standard reflected a substantial decline in illiteracy is open to interpretation. Stewart believed it did because it "opened the door" to further learning. She chose, however, not to quibble over definitions and, in the absence of any widely accepted standard, pushed the national crusade forward with the specific goal of eliminating illiteracy in the United States by 1930.

Stewart preferred a community-based approach in which volunteers taught illiterates in their own Moonlight Schools, using her *Country Life*

Readers and other locally chosen materials. She extended the "each one teach one" model to the national campaign, but for it to be successful, Stewart had to take her message of redemption through literacy directly to the people and arouse both the illiterates and those who would teach them. Hence her role as crusader was a pivotal one.

In 1921 and 1922 she traveled constantly, visiting nearly every state in the union. Calling on her extensive network of professional colleagues and clubwomen, Stewart developed an exhausting itinerary that took her into schools, churches, civic and social clubs, private gatherings, and public assemblies. She spoke to hundreds of county superintendents and conducted institutes for their teachers and then met with governors and state officials, urging them to take up the cause. Stewart stressed to her audiences the urgent need of the illiterates and assured them that victory could be achieved only through concerted action. Like her work in Kentucky, the national crusade took on the tone of a religious revival. It also added Native Americans and the prison population to the list of those particularly in need of literacy training. Visits to several reservations inspired her to work with tribal leaders and reservation officials to reduce their exceptionally high illiteracy rates and prompted her to write a special primer for Native Americans, the *Indian's First Book*. She also convinced prison authorities in several states to begin educational programs for their inmates.[18]

Her efforts drew positive results. Iowa's governor wrote to offer his support for the movement in his state, indicating that he intended to "proceed vigorously" with the organization of a statewide campaign. He told Stewart he had enlisted the state teachers' association, several fraternal societies, the Farm Bureau, the Federation of Labor, clubwomen, and "indeed every civic and social organization in the state."[19] Stewart had campaigned for the governors of Kansas and New Mexico in 1920, and the two of them had appointed illiteracy commissions that were already up and running. However, they also issued proclamations designating an "Illiteracy Eradication Week" and urged their counterparts in other states to support the cause.[20] Arizona's governor named a commission in his state and at the suggestion of the U.S. commissioner of education, John J. Tigert, asked Stewart to come and whip up public enthusiasm.[21] North Dakota pledged to wipe out illiteracy within two years, and California planned on "knocking the 'il' out of illiteracy" in three. Pennsylvania's governor signed an annual appropriations bill for $125,000 to combat the problem in his state.[22]

Most states followed Stewart's suggestions, creating illiteracy commissions, and relying on her advice once they were established. She urged the president of Arizona's commission to secure a proclamation from the governor and gave him some practical lessons on securing volunteers, telling him to involve the clubwomen of the community as fund-raisers and teachers and suggesting institutes to recruit and train teachers. She even mailed sample pledge cards.[23] Stewart recommended her *Country Life Readers,* already in use in many states, and suggested ways of identifying and contacting local illiterates. Names could be secured, she said, from bankers, city or county officials, employers, election officers, and others "who have occasion to ask men to sign records, checks, [or] payrolls."[24]

Stewart constantly communicated with coalition leaders, assisting and offering advice and information. The NEA commission put together a directory of educational leaders for use in the states and provided maps and statistics on demand. She corresponded with organizers and teachers, offering guidance and encouragement to those opening night schools in their own communities.

In early summer of 1921, she completed the manuscript for *Moonlight Schools for the Emancipation of Adult Illiterates,* which she touted as the "lamp of experience" for everyone engaged in the literacy work. The book, published by E. P. Dutton in 1922, reflected Stewart's faith in the community-based approach and offered a "message to the teachers of every land," including those "who have had little preparation for teaching."[25]

The National Education Association, the GFWC, the WCTU, and other national professional and volunteer organizations staffed and underwrote the literacy crusade at the national level. Their role was critical to the successful operation of the campaigns and cannot be overstated. However, equally important were individual members of Stewart's network of professionals and volunteers. Without their loyalty and dedication, constant nurturing, and occasional intervention, the work would have been not just lonely and frustrating; it also might have been impossible. Stewart's personal identity centered on her work, which was, quite literally, her life. She developed lasting friendships with several clubwomen and educators who served as links in her chain of networks and coalitions, shared her enthusiasm for the literacy crusade, and eased the burden of life on the road. In addition, lifelong Kentucky friends assisted Stewart's work from home, as did her brothers and sisters.

Stewart employed Lela Mae Stiles, a friend and confidante, as her administrative assistant at the Kentucky Illiteracy Commission and the NEA Illiteracy Commission. Stiles ran the office from Frankfort and served as her employer's link to the commonwealth. Familiar with Stewart's history and acquainted with most of her friends and family, the loyal Stiles was an astute observer of both people and politics and kept Stewart informed by relaying gossip, sending newspaper clippings, and forwarding mail. Using materials sent to her by Stewart, Stiles compiled statistics, made maps and charts, sent out correspondence, booked train and hotel reservations, and otherwise attended to the needs of her friend as she traveled the country. When Mrs. Stewart's health or spirits flagged, Lela Mae sent a little gift, a special card, or a memento to cheer her. For example, when Stewart traveled to Maine and encountered an early cold spell, Stiles had her employer's fur coat cleaned and shipped to her. Without Lela Mae, Stewart's work could not have gone forward with any degree of efficiency, and they both knew it.

Lela Mae understood Stewart's almost paranoid fear of bad press and zealously guarded her public and private image. When she first left Kentucky to work on the national campaign, Stewart wanted only positive reports to reach the home folks and instructed Lela Mae to manage the information as best she could, even in the home Lela Mae shared with Stewart's closest friend, Mattie Dalton, and her longtime colleague and mentor, Frank Button, and his wife. Stewart frequently sent greetings through Lela Mae to "the household," but on more than one occasion cautioned her about making injudicious comments, even in this intimate setting. "You will need to keep your own counsel," she wrote, "for some chum evidently leaks out things not thinking that I am the one affected at last."[26] At a low point in her crusade, Stewart wrote to Lela Mae asking her not to "discuss these difficult times with the household. It would not add to our prestige."[27]

Despite the fact that she often concealed professional disappointments and criticism of her work from close friends, Stewart shared both triumph and defeat with Lela Mae, who gloried in the victories as if they were own. Responding to the news that Stewart had been elected to the executive committee of the NEA in 1923, the secretary wrote, "I am so proud of you I don't know what to do. I think your election to the Executive Committee is just *wonderful*." Both women understood what such an appointment could mean, especially for the future, and Lela Mae wrote, "You will get to go to Washington at the expense of the N.E.A. [and] you are in direct line for the presidency."[28]

Stewart valued Lela Mae's judgment and frequently asked her opinion on important matters. In 1923, when Stewart considered resurrecting the work in Kentucky, Lela Mae wrote, "Of course I'd love to start the book soon—but if anything can be done in Kentucky it should *be done*. The work is rapidly assuming such vast significance and recognition that I don't see how we can continue to reconcile the fact that Kentucky—where it all started—has ceased to be interested. . . . If Kentucky people are ever going to be awakened again on the illiteracy question we shall have to work out some plan to get better publicity."[29]

Lela Mae also shared Stewart's disappointments, and while the older woman rarely gave in to thoughts of vengeance, her secretary often dreamed of it. She particularly disliked Stewart's old political nemesis George Colvin and rejoiced openly when he "fell from power" in 1923. Writing to Stewart in Omaha, she noted that "Colvin was defeated so overwhelmingly Saturday that I don't see how he can hold up his head again. . . . Isn't this great, I wonder if Colvin feels as much like a czar as he did."[30] A few days later, she was still enjoying his defeat. "Shorn of what little power he has now I can't see him getting anywhere in the future. It pleases me to know that the majority of people have found him out just as we did long ago," she gloated.[31]

Lela Mae shared the ups and downs of the illiteracy crusade, and without a regular salary, finances presented a problem for both women. Stiles operated the office on a shoestring budget, counting every penny. On one of the many occasions when money was tight, Stewart wrote, "You have been put out about your fall shopping, and I am so sorry. I sometimes think I should not be attempting to keep an office with these delays and disappointments. It distresses me more than you know."[32] During the campaign in the Northwest, Stewart ran short of money when NEA and GFWC checks failed to arrive as anticipated. "If nothing comes," she wrote, "then I will go ahead and budget it some way. It usually turns out that I have to make up all deficits. I cannot see where I have altered my situation much over the Kentucky campaign. If I cannot pay my own personal debts, where am I getting? I assume entirely too much for one person, and that has been the quarrel of my family all along."[33]

Both women tried to make the best of vexing financial problems. Stewart told her secretary to "try to make your ink, paste and all go a long ways and leave all buying possible until we get out of debt for the last year's work." She apologized for "sending you that miserly $2. . . . So often I have run short at hotels that I was afraid to let a $20 go just then." At the end of 1922, Stewart recorded an outstanding debt of $75 to Lela Mae and listed her own income for the year at $2,750, "earned in about four months employment." That represented a handsome sum for the time, but even so, it only enabled her "to reduce her indebtedness by half."[34] Driven by the service ideal and committed to taking no salary for the literacy work, Stewart extended her own selflessness to Lela Mae, although she rewarded her when finances allowed. In a letter extending a raise to her helper, Stewart noted that she could only pay Stiles about half what she was worth, "but our work being one of pure patriotism, we cherish the hope that you will get much satisfaction out of your large share in it."[35]

Public campaigns like suffrage and school reform provided outlets for many women whether they served as paid employees or as volunteers. Common causes brought women together and sometimes served as the foundation for enduring friendships. Especially in teaching, where white career women often remained unmarried, their work provided purpose and direction for lives that did not center on home, husband, and children.[36] Stewart's work connected her to like-minded women across the country, several of whom became close friends.

One important associate was Mrs. Alfred (Zugie) Zuger, an outspoken and loyal literacy volunteer who represented the women's clubs of North Dakota on her state illiteracy commission. She also chaired the Club Women for Illiteracy Campaign and organized much of Stewart's crusade in the West.[37] The two formed an intense personal bond that lasted many years. Zugie wrote long, adoring letters and frequently sent packages to Stewart as she traveled. Thoroughly dedicated to the illiteracy cause, she worked with the prison population and with Native Americans on reservations in her state. She enjoyed her role in the campaigns and exuded enthusiasm: "I love the work, and I am so so interested in it! I dream about my illiterates! I love and bless the day I MET YOU!"[38] To her long, newsy letters, she added extensive postscripts. "Oh, I do want to help you in every way I possibly can," she wrote, "because you have worked so hard for this splendid field of work." She eagerly anticipated Stewart's arrival in the Dakotas and made elaborate plans to visit "the pen" and travel to the Black Hills to see her Indian friends. "Oh, to be with you," she wrote. "I hope and pray dear, that you will never be disappointed in me, and that God will give me health and strength to live up to all your expectations!" She kept several photographs of Stewart close by, one on her dresser, another on the flyleaf of her letter file, and a large one in a "fine frame" in the living room, "where I can feast my optics on you at all times! I LOVE YOU Mrs. Stewart, and I think you knew this long ago!!!!"[39] Stewart was not generally given to such ebullient expression, but Mrs. Zuger described her letters as "dear" and "sweet" and wondered "how could anyone HELP but love and adore you!"[40] Zuger's love for Stewart more than likely reflected her immersion in Stewart's cause and the joy she took in teaching. The written evidence might reflect a physical as well as an intellectual and emotional attachment, but it is more likely that the romantic language reflects simple affection and the conventions of written communication among women of their generation.[41]

Stewart's network included both clubwomen and members of professional organizations, and since the GFWC worked closely with the NEA as a "staunch supporter" of the association's legislative program, many of her colleagues played active roles in both.[42] Stewart's charismatic personality and organizational skills enabled her to effectively use these networks to advance the work she loved while supporting and encouraging other women in their causes. The committee structure of both organizations facilitated such interaction. An excellent example is Administrative Women in Education (AWE), an important organizational link for women educators like Stewart. In its ranks she found close companionship, professional advice, and assistance in extending the literacy work. Organized at the 1915 NEA annual convention, the association planned to unify the activities of school women holding administrative positions and bring them into closer cooperation as they investigated and sought solutions for the nation's educational problems.[43] By the mid-1920s, AWE leadership rested with several of Stewart's closest friends and associates. Josephine Corliss Preston, Washington's state superintendent of public instruction, and Minnie Jean Neilson, North Dakota's school chief, took active roles in this group, facilitated Stewart's visits to their states, and worked to extend the benefits of public education to rural adults in their home states. Sharing common goals and ideals, these women dedicated their lives to education and, in the course of their work, found ways to support and encourage each other. They also formed alliances to further leadership skills and ambitions of their own. For example, Josephine Preston rose to the 1919 presidency of the NEA with assistance from this group, as did Charl Ormond Williams, the superintendent of schools of Shelby County in Memphis, Tennessee, and a powerful force among Democratic women in the South, in 1922. Neilson served as a vice president. When Stewart became a member of the NEA's five-person Executive Committee in 1923, her own presidency appeared certain.[44]

Although many of Stewart's relationships enriched her professional and personal life, gossip and infighting occasionally marred both. As she mastered the intricacies of the female professional and reform culture, she understood, but had difficulty accepting, the power structures of both the GFWC and the NEA. She found their bureaucratic structures confining and their fiscal procedures disappointing and inadequate. Moreover, jealousy and mistrust characterized some of her relationships with women in both groups. For example, one North Dakota clubwoman took it upon herself to chastise Stewart for "dancing with the Indians," an event the crusader had cheerfully reported to Lela Mae and the eastern press.[45] The Dakota woman resented an "outsider" meddling in Indian affairs and reminded Stewart that the "Red

Man" had a "reactionary tendency"; if the authorities relaxed their vigilance, she opined, "the Indians would ever more wander from point to point leaving domestic animals to perish and crops to spoil while they themselves danced, feasted, . . . and kept their children out of school."[46]

In addition to occasional tempests over territory and influence, some unpleasant experiences with reimbursements undermined Stewart's affiliation with both the GFWC and the NEA. Stewart's relatively constant frustration with delayed expense checks erupted in a confrontation with Helen T. Hixson, director of NEA accounts and treasurer. Impatient with one particularly long delay, she wrote NEA secretary Agnes Winn, asking that she request Hixson to send her check "at once." Stewart received a lengthy description of the maze of approvals required for each request, and although she appeared somewhat mollified by the apology, reported to Lela Mae that Hixson was "ugly" to her. "She knows she has been very contrary and discourteous with me," she wrote. "I shall not retaliate, however."[47] Stewart seemed less upset over a scolding she received from an NEA official who lectured her about her accounts and "the unbusiness-like way" she handled them. Instead, she "took it amiably and promised to reform, saying not a word about [her] life of travel and rush which reduces efficiency." In a 1927 letter to her colleague and friend Josephine Preston, the superintendent of schools for the state of Washington, Stewart criticized NEA colleague Olive Jones. Stewart alleged that Jones had made "dark hints" against her, although she did not specify the nature of the "hints." Stewart's correspondence is typically straightforward and businesslike, but in this letter she charges that Jones needlessly came to Washington, D.C., from New York "every week" at NEA expense. Without repeating what Jones said about her, Stewart told Josephine Preston there was no truth to Jones's remarks and assured her friend that she had been "childishly careful" in her financial dealings with both the NEA and the GFWC. Stewart noted that fiscal officers in both organizations were her "most ardent admirers," a fact that made her "proud indeed." The "dark hints" perhaps suggested fiscal irresponsibility on Stewart's part, for in the same letter the literacy crusader went on to defend her handling of the affairs of the Kentucky Illiteracy Commission during its six years of operation as a "monument to women," since she was the "first and only woman chairman of a Commission in our state." "I have said little about these things," she averred, "but they are in shape for use when I need them."[48]

Cora Wilson Stewart had grown accustomed to hero status in her home state, and when the demise of her work in Kentucky led her into the broader world of the NEA and the GFWC, she found it difficult adapting to relative anonymity. She could not abide challenges to her authority or having her knowledge of what was best for the nation's illiterates questioned. Despite this relatively thin-skinned reaction to any criticism of her work, she typically faced challenges with optimism and good cheer. She now approached the move as simply a new phase of her life. Writing to her friend Lida Hafford, an influential Kentucky clubwoman who had assumed the directorship at the GFWC headquarters in Washington, D.C., she remarked, "Dear Lady, you must not be under the impression that I have given up my work. I am only enlarging it." When the KIC ceased to exist in 1920, Stewart wrote, "I go on forever. My aim of ten years service to my State, ten to my nation and ten to the world is now entering upon the second chapter." She told Hafford that her work, "like suffrage and prohibition, has reached the stage where it must go through national politics, and I must go with it wherever it leads."[49]

For several years Stewart had advocated passage of the so-called education bill, legislation providing for the creation of a cabinet-level department of education with generous federal funding for the illiteracy work. Backed by the NEA since 1858 in one form or another, such a measure received its greatest support in the 1920s, when many educators sought federal aid to boost a "waning profession" and bolster lagging and inadequate public schools. Taking advantage of strong national sentiment for education reform, in 1918 the NEA's Joint Commission on the Emergency in Education drafted and introduced a bill proposing a department of education with a secretary in the president's cabinet and offering matching funds to the states. The NEA, anticipating opposition from those who feared that federal aid led to federal control of education, launched a massive campaign to rally support among educators and the public. Long disgruntled with a bureau of education under a commissioner, the NEA argued that education had become a national responsibility requiring powerful national oversight. The bill, which became closely tied to lobbies for higher teacher salaries and the Americanization of immigrants, occupied legislative attention for almost three decades. Pervasive suspicions of encroaching federal power ultimately defeated it.[50] Based on the idea of government beneficence, the bill pledged federal aid for removing illiteracy, and Stewart spent much of the 1920s lobbying for its passage. For example, on behalf of a version of the bill called Towner-Sterling in 1921, she lobbied Congress as a representative of the Kentucky League of Women Voters and the Kentucky Federation of Women's Clubs, blanketed her home state with letters urging support of the bill, and used her political influence to secure support from Kentucky's congressional delegation.[51] The

Kentucky Federation of Women's Clubs, at Stewart's urging, adopted a resolution supporting the bill.[52] Supporters of the bill included activists in other education reform campaigns who, like Stewart, believed that federal aid and oversight would require recalcitrant local authorities to improve the quality of public schooling. Professional educators had already made great strides in the reorganization and bureaucratization of public education, but they were determined to create an efficient education bureaucracy following the corporate model, a goal that Stewart did not embrace. Far from monolithic in their goals and ideals, supporters of the bill included progressives of all stripes, including NEA president Olive Jones, who couched her advocacy in patriotic terms.[53]

Confident the legislation would pass, Stewart intensified her commitment to eradicating illiteracy as her national movement and the bill gained momentum, infusing her work with renewed zeal and hope for federal funding. Beginning in November 1921, Stewart organized and hosted four regional conferences on illiteracy. Each attracted prominent speakers and won press coverage in several major papers.[54] Held in New York City in November 1921, the eastern conference featured as keynote speaker Carrie Chapman Catt, president of the National American Woman Suffrage Association, who pronounced the literacy campaign second in importance only to the work of the world disarmament conference. The following year, illiteracy workers from western states met in San Francisco, where Stewart's old friend David Starr Jordan, president emeritus of Stanford University, urged delegates to work hard so the illiterates in their region could, like Abraham Lincoln, extricate themselves from their predicament. When representatives of northern and midwestern states convened under Stewart's leadership in Chicago in February 1922, Jane Addams closed the program with a tea at Hull House.[55]

The regional conferences helped organize and give direction to the growing movement, and their work reflected an increased tendency toward national solutions for social problems. They also reflected the trend toward institutional, standardized, "professional" solutions, which unfortunately was the very opposite of Stewart's philosophy. Delegates at the regional conferences formalized the work being done in the states and formulated a national agenda for dealing with illiteracy. Although they respected Stewart's work and without fail adopted resolutions praising her and the NEA commission for the national campaign against illiteracy and endorsing the education bill, many of their recommendations conflicted with her vision for the work. For example, delegates to the Chicago convention, representing several states with high urban and immigrant populations, proposed measures to combat "foreign illiteracy." They endorsed congressional restrictions on immigration and supported the imposition of literacy tests for voting. Moreover, they applauded the "fine work being done by the Federal Government and the states in Americanization" and recommended an increase in such programs. To prevent "native illiteracy," the Chicago group urged "strict compulsory school attendance laws with county, municipal, and state enforcement provisions in each state." For adult illiterates of all types the group advised expanding evening, continuation, and special courses, and training special teachers for adult education. As an incentive, and "for the protection of the sacred right of franchise," they suggested that "no person be permitted to vote in the United States who is unable to read and write in English."[56]

Their proposals represented strong national trends concerning the role of education in society. Public education played an ameliorative role; it could provide access to a better life. But it also served a coercive function, training citizens in patriotic thinking and instructing them in moral behavior. Implementation of their recommendations would extend the reach of public education in the United States, a goal long advocated by the NEA. Not only young citizens but also adults would be "schooled to order" in classes that were the training ground for democracy. Certain that the nation had to protect itself from the dangers of radicalism whether in the voting booth or the factory, the delegates saw compulsory schooling and Americanization as the best means of achieving that goal.[57]

In a series of resolutions, delegates at each convention voiced support for the pending education bill, currently called Towner-Sterling, an outcome Stewart considered essential and one of the chief purposes of the conferences. Convinced that broad systemic change in education provision held the only hope for the nation's illiterates, she labored to "bring the Education Bill prominently before a large, representative group of people, influential laymen . . . and educators." She mailed copies of the resolutions to newspapers in the home states of participants and sent copies to their members of Congress.[58]

Delegates at all four conferences emphasized the economic benefits of literacy to the individual and to the nation and affirmed their belief that poverty resulted not from laziness but from environmental causes. Delegates to the northern and eastern regional conference in Detroit in May 1923 focused on the workplace. They resolved to appeal to all "employers of labor" to adopt rules requiring their laborers to possess some education "to the end that the common man be fitted for greater economic service and better and more intelligent citizenship." The Detroit group also demanded a link between the franchise and literacy, commending "the sixteen states requiring qualifications for voters" and strongly urging the rest of the states to follow suit. Their resolutions also urged lawmakers in every state to fund the literacy work and encouraged state departments of education to formulate courses of study for the training of night school teachers.[59]

Ironically, the regional conferences produced a set of goals that, following a national trend, sought to remove the volunteer and place the literacy work in the hands of trained professionals. It was time, many of these educators believed, to replace the crusader with the expert. Stewart followed trends in education and certainly valued professional training for teachers; however, she remained convinced that coalitions fueled the success of the national crusade, and she hoped volunteers could continue to work with the adult education professionals toward their common goal. The coalitions not only supplied the individual contact between illiterates and their instructors that Stewart thought essential to the development of literacy but also provided the crusade with local organizational structures, books and other teaching materials, and moral support. An important part of her job was to maintain these alliances and promote enthusiasm and dedication among volunteers. As the literacy campaign reached national proportions, Stewart took on the additional role of liaison between the various public and private organizations, grassroots supporters, and volunteers in the field.

Cognizant of the fact that volunteers would always be necessary and anxious to keep organized women actively involved, Stewart gave the keynote address at the May 1923 meeting of the GFWC in Atlanta, where she stressed the importance of literacy to maintaining a free society. The NEA afforded yet another important opportunity to expand the work when it convened the World Conference on Education in San Francisco on 28 June through 6 July of that year. The goal of this conference was to promote international cooperation by extending the benefits of education around the world. Its organizers wanted teachers everywhere to "inculcate in the minds of their pupils ideals of peace and friendship toward all peoples" and to extend the benefits of universal education to children and adults.[60] Symbolic of the drive for peace during the interwar years, the conference promoted world cooperation in educational affairs. Asked by the sponsor of the conference, her friend Augustus O. Thomas, who chaired the NEA Foreign Relations Committee, to chair an illiteracy group, Stewart put together a program examining current standards of illiteracy and scheduled lectures by representatives from Scotland, Italy, and Japan. The group, which included delegates from those three countries and Ireland, China, Canada, and Honduras, agreed to form an international commission on illiteracy to meet as a permanent section of the world conference.[61]

The extension of the literacy crusade to the national level fulfilled Stewart's hopes and dreams for the work, and its popularity seemed to ensure a steady stream of volunteers. In addition, the Towner-Sterling Education Bill gained presidential endorsement to reorganize the executive branch to include a Department of Education and Welfare. Cabinet status and the appointment of a secretary of education symbolized the importance of education to the nation and enhanced the prestige of teachers and the profession as a whole.[62] Stewart's friend Charl O. Williams directed much of the NEA's efforts in favor of the bill. Joining the NEA to lobby in its favor were the National League of Women Voters, the GFWC, the National Committee for a Department of Education, the American Federation of Labor, the Daughters of the American Revolution, the National Congress of Parent-Teachers' Associations, and other citizen groups across the country. In its various forms, the bill specified a significant role for the federal government in the elimination of illiteracy, a provision that would have institutionalized the literacy work and assured appropriate funding.[63]

Sustained by the hope of a significant infusion of federal aid to her cause, Stewart's sense of calling intensified as the movement gained momentum, infusing her work with renewed zeal. Her successes had, over the years, kindled the missionary spirit sparked at age seven in her prayers for her dying baby brother, Cleveland.[64] She believed that illiteracy was the nation's most pressing problem and that the Moonlight Schools offered the most practical solution. Moreover, she believed her experience in developing the latter left her uniquely qualified to expand the literacy work.

Confident of success and secure in her leadership, Stewart set in motion a plan for the first national illiteracy conference to be jointly sponsored by the NEA and the GFWC coalition. She first secured the GFWC's approval and financial support in the amount of $500. She then traveled to Washington, D.C., to request approval from the NEA and from fellow Kentuckian Dr. John Tigert, U.S. commissioner of education. Tigert agreed that the Bureau of Education, which he headed, would participate and promised the support of the American Legion as well. The NEA authorized Stewart to use half of the NEA Illiteracy Commission's $1,000 annual appropriation to finance the undertaking.[65] The Americanism Commission of the American Legion, true to Tigert's promise, agreed to support the conference as well. In fact, Garland Powell, the Legion's national director, noted that his organization was willing to go to "most any limit within our power to foster and perpetuate this work," although he also noted that the commission was "in very hard straits" financially.[66] Stewart scheduled the conference for 11 through 14 January 1924, under the joint sponsorship of the NEA, the American Legion, the GFWC, and the Bureau of Education.

Although she had arranged joint sponsorship, Stewart saw the national conference as her meeting, the logical culmination of the regional conferences, and the beginning of an effective national organization to combat illiteracy. She believed she had earned the right to take the initiative, and the positive responses to her idea delighted her. Following an organizational meeting in September, Stewart decided that she, Powell, and Mrs. Sherman Adams of the GFWC would be the principal speakers. She also hoped that President Calvin Coolidge, Secretary of Commerce Herbert Hoover, and labor leader Samuel Gompers would speak. She invited several governors to speak as well and suggested that the president of the World Federation of Education Associations, Dr. A. O. Thomas, also address the gathering.

After arranging for speakers, Stewart settled on tasks for the delegates. She wanted them to hammer out a legislative agenda complete with recommendations for funding. Delegates to the regional conferences had shown overwhelming support for restricting the ballot to literate voters, an initiative that had taken hold in a number of states and that reflected the prevailing fear of radicalism. In words that suggest her conceptualization of voting legislation as incentive rather than restriction, she noted that national delegates should examine whether laws depriving the uneducated of the ballot would really "hasten their opportunity." Powell suggested that delegates determine whether to create a national organization to direct the activities of various agencies and groups involved in the literacy work.[67] Finally, she expected delegates to endorse the education bill, now called Sterling-Reed, with its proposed appropriation of $7.5 million to combat illiteracy. In early October, Stewart sent letters to governors (omitting outgoing governors Morrow of Kentucky and Walton of Oklahoma, both known enemies of the work), all state superintendents, each state illiteracy chairman, each GFWC president, and other supporters of the cause. About 250 letters went out announcing the joint conference sponsored by "four great organizations," the NEA, the American Legion, the GFWC, and the U.S. Bureau of Education.[68]

Stewart's actions provoked an immediate and unpleasant response. GFWC president Alice Winter telegraphed that the Bureau of Education should announce the meeting. Stewart's reply opened with a question regarding funding, noting that nothing had been appropriated except $500 from the NEA. She lamented having to "expend from personal funds." As to sponsorship of the meeting, Stewart wrote, "conference was called by me weeks ago in the name of the four organizations and therefore cannot be called by Bureau of Education or headed by same."[69] Attempting to smooth things over, Winter wrote a joint letter to Stewart and Tigert recommending that "the rest of us could gracefully and wisely fall behind the Bureau of Education, such position not indicating inferiority or subservience, but only . . . friendly cooperation, along lines that would make for maximum efficiency." Winter agreed, she said, with the president's argument that the government could not take part in a conference over which it had no control, and which might "go off on some tangent through resolutions" advocating legislation that might embarrass the administration. Since she was in San Francisco, Winter designated a representative to "assist the two in finding a way out of the misunderstanding."[70]

The situation deteriorated. During the next week, representatives of the sponsoring agencies met several times, and Stewart's leadership of the conference disintegrated. In a private meeting with Stewart, Tigert agreed to send out a printed call that did not conflict with previous mailings, but he designated his assistant, Mrs. Cook, to represent him in further talks. Stewart considered Cook "hard to handle" and after their second meeting characterized her as "a woman who will challenge your plans with some appearance of questioning both your judgment and your motives." Tigert's assistant immediately attacked Stewart's list of proposed speakers, calling them "unknown" at the national level and insisting that the list include more prominent individuals. She also questioned Stewart's assumption that she would preside over the meeting, suggesting instead that Commissioner Tigert open the meeting and that rather than designating a chairperson before the meeting, they should allow the delegates to select one. Although this appeared to be a concession, Stewart saw it as the end of her hopes of chairing the conference, since "she had never in history known anybody to call a meeting to order that they were not then made the chairman."[71]

Incensed, Stewart considered resigning over what she considered a rude affront. She felt "like starting for Kentucky tonight," she said, but took Lela Mae's advice and remained in Washington. Stewart poured out her frustration to her secretary, sending copies of memos and letters and asking for Stiles's "unbiased opinion." She claimed Cook opposed her list of speakers because she was "a Catholic," and Winter "cut the ground from under" her because she was "a Republican, first, last and all the time." Stewart discounted Powell and Tigert as "weak" and incapable of making decisions, judgments that Lela Mae energetically seconded. From Frankfort, Lela Mae offered encouragement, urging Stewart to stick it out and "devise some plan to get yourself made Chairman." She echoed her employer's concern that the conference would be "wrecked" if Tigert presided.[72] In an angry letter, Stiles observed that the popularity of the literacy movement had attracted vultures. "Who made the illiteracy work popular? They need somebody to tell them a few plain truths. Ten years ago they wouldn't have cared who held an Illiteracy Conference and probably would have been glad to shirk any responsibility." Now they were quite eager "to rush in and claim the glory and shove you aside."[73]

A major sticking point was the education bill. Stewart did not want to damage its chances of passage. The bill was moving through committee and appeared certain of passage in the next congressional session, but she realized she could not afford to alienate the Bureau of Education by insisting that the conference endorse the measure. Although his predecessor, Warren G. Harding, had approved of the bill, President Coolidge had recently gone on record opposing it. Stewart learned that presidential aide Garland Powell had assured Coolidge that if he granted executive support to the national illiteracy meeting, Powell would see to it that the conference took no action on "any pending bill which has been or may be introduced into Congress."[74] Lacking another choice, Stewart took the advice of friends in the NEA and surrendered leadership of the conference.[75]

The education bill ultimately failed passage, at least temporarily, falling victim to the growing fear of federal power in the wake of the Red Scare. Its defeat may have been the death knell of the literacy crusade. In the wake of presidential opposition, many of the bill's early supporters fell away, including NEA president Olive Jones, who refrained from speaking in favor of the bill out of deference to President Coolidge. Jones had already questioned Stewart's judgment on several issues. She told Stewart that Tigert believed her purpose in holding the conference was to boost the education bill and to "gain personal glory." An outspoken woman whose grim manner had already made enemies of a number of women in Stewart's circle, including Charl O. Williams, Jones accused Stewart of "terrible bungling." Jones's remarks enraged Stewart. She was upset because the bill not only represented funding and real hope for the illiteracy cause but also meant a permanent partnership with the Bureau of Education, the GFWC, and the NEA. Stewart now feared she had lost the respect of all three. Confiding to Lela Mae, Stewart said she "would not have much self respect left" if she associated much with Jones. "I do not think she would care if I got in bad with the N.E.A. and missed the presidency," wrote Stewart. Entirely demoralized by the incident, Stewart morosely concluded, "This is the grimmest business I ever dealt with."[76]

Stewart did not preside over the general session. Instead, the four "cooperating" agencies were represented by their national officers, each of whom spoke at the opening session and presided over a session. Stewart received most of the credit for organizing the gathering, and the conference resolutions reflected her input; however, the delegates unanimously agreed that it was time for the illiteracy crusade to move beyond the stage of voluntarism toward government-supported action centered in the public schools. In a series of resolutions, the group recommended lifting the age limit for free public education, requiring school boards to organize day or night classes for adults once a minimum number of citizens had applied for instruction, and making mandatory an annual illiteracy census in each state. In addition, the group followed the Americanization trend and recommended that in order to raise "the level of citizenship, and safeguard the ballot against the evils and dangers that are inherent in an illiterate electorate," states should implement literacy tests for voting. Commissioner Tigert agreed to appoint a nine-person committee to review the recommendations of the conference and to forward the results of their work to illiteracy workers throughout the country. He also asked Stewart to serve on this panel. [77]

Following the conference, resentment over the criticism and the challenge to her leadership festered and ultimately led Stewart to sever her ties with the GFWC and, to some degree, the NEA. Before the conference ended, she notified Adams that she intended to resign the chairmanship of the federation's illiteracy division as soon as a replacement could be found.[78] Already disillusioned with the NEA and convinced that her hopes for the presidency had been lost, she considered resigning from the illiteracy commission as well. She did resign in the summer of 1925 when the organization shifted her illiteracy commission to the Department of Adult Education, an administrative move that limited both her autonomy and the direction of her crusade.[79] Stewart's resignations from the GFWC and NEA illiteracy commissions reflected her fear that her movement was losing ground to adult and immigrant education and that her personal leadership had been impaired, but they did not actually end her affiliation with either the NEA or the GFWC. Certainly the episode wounded her pride, and she perhaps felt it necessary to make the gesture, but Stewart remained an adviser to the GFWC in its illiteracy work and continued to chair the National Council of Education's commission, thus retaining some ties to the NEA.

Some of the problems could perhaps have been avoided. Stewart could have anticipated and possibly deflected the personality conflicts, since it was common knowledge in her circle that Olive Jones was difficult to get along

with and that Winter could be imperious and overbearing. She had enough
experience with bureaucrats to know that they often did what was expedient,
and she was well acquainted with Tigert's low-key management style. It is
possible that the break came because Stewart saw the attack on her leadership of the illiteracy conference as an affront to her leadership of the entire
movement, and that rather than risk such challenges from the organizations
that had assisted her, she would set her own course, independent of their
support. Neither her diaries nor her correspondence reveals her feelings in
detail, but it is reasonable to assume that she harbored some anger and resentment, especially since she had already had several unpleasant encoun-
ters with Olive Jones. This last one had ruined any chance she had of attaining
the NEA presidency, which no doubt offended Stewart's pride and disappointed her deeply. It also made the association less useful to her. With typical determination and willpower, she ultimately decided to simply put the
matter behind her. Stewart believed she had been called by God to lead the
movement, and her confidence in that calling gave her the resolve not only
to distance herself from those who might not fall in line but also to plan a
course that did not include them.

Stewart did, however, continue to do her part in pushing what was now
simply labeled the Education Bill. The organizations that supported her work,
including the GFWC, the NEA, and the WCTU, all officially backed the bill
and lobbied Congress on its behalf. Stewart joined a group of educators who
testified before the House Committee on Education during hearings on the
bill in February and March 1924. Along with colleagues George D. Strayer,
chairman of NEA's Legislative Commission, and A. E. Winship, editor of the
Journal of Education, Stewart attended the hearings and attested to the spirit
and determination of illiterates "trying to make up for time they have lost."
Boston clubwoman Mrs. Frederick Bagley joined their delegation and advised the legislators to carefully consider the difference the federal government could make in the lives of the 1.4 million school-age children whose
lack of "educational opportunity" kept them from attending schools "of any
type."[80] Stewart's South Carolina counterpart, Wil Lou Gray, also presented a
compelling argument for federal aid to education. Recalling a literacy map she
had just seen depicting one southern Ohio county entirely in black, she said, "I
naturally was interested in knowing why it was black and found that it was
shown in that color because the people who settled in the county came from
the South and that they were quite illiterate. It seems that we do not stay put.
We move around which indicates that illiteracy is a national question."[81]

Although the national illiteracy conference resulted in the first major challenge to Cora Wilson Stewart's direction and leadership of the adult literacy movement, it was not the last. Leaders in educational programs for urban adults and immigrants approached the work differently, and these professional educators began to see the grassroots literacy crusade as a threat to their own efforts. They agreed with Stewart on the importance of full literacy in a democracy but saw no role for the volunteer or the crusader in the educational process. These educators promised similar, if slightly more modest, outcomes than Stewart's Moonlight Schools, and their programs required longer enrollments. But they stressed education as a continuing process requiring new or expanded institutions such as community colleges and university extension services staffed by professionals specially trained to deal with adult pupils. Stewart saw the work as a "campaign" with a definite objective and time limit. Whereas Moonlight programs promoted middle-class values and the acquisition of consumer goods to enhance rural life, schools for immigrants and urban illiterates had a different focus. Their efforts combined social justice and social control. Literate citizens would have more opportunity, but they would also be trained to right thinking and moral order. If they did not acquire reading and writing skills, they would have to forgo some of the benefits of citizenship, including the right to vote. Literacy became an instrument of social control that when combined with fear of immigrants resulted in immigration restriction laws like those passed in 1917, 1921, and 1924.[82]

Although the nation was home to three times more native-born than foreign-born illiterates, most adult education programs focused on immigrants. World War I had brought a new urgency to public education, and subsequent calls for 100 percent Americanism swept the country, intensifying efforts to Americanize the immigrant, ensure rapid naturalization and citizenship, and cement loyalty to the United States.[83] Citizenship training took on a national security dimension, and the public schools became important instruments of immigrant education. Prior to 1916, few public school systems had programs for adult immigrants, but by 1921, thirty-one had created such programs. Despite this trend, no materials or pedagogy existed for teaching adult immigrants.[84]

Wartime Americanization further institutionalized adult education. Through the Smith-Hughes Act of 1917, the government acted to provide resources for it, but support turned to control in the wake of the Red Scare of 1919–20. Several groups, including the National Security League and the American Defense Society, established themselves as guardians of national orthodoxy and pledged themselves to active roles in educating and Americanizing the immigrant. The American Legion, created in 1919, became a bastion of narrowly defined patriotism and 100 percent Americanism, the GFWC got on the bandwagon, the Daughters of the American Revolution took an increasingly hard-line posture, and fraternal organizations embraced "patriotic service" as their primary mission. Campaigns to educate immigrants occasionally turned coercive as many states restricted the vote to individuals who could read and write.[85]

Americanizers saw Stewart as a potential ally, but she avoided joining forces with them. Since she had publicized the existence of illiteracy among the country's native-born citizens, and since they were significantly more numerous and their absolute illiteracy more compelling than the need of some immigrants who could at least read and write in their own language, she preferred to keep the Moonlight School movement separate. Moreover, Stewart's crusade operated under extreme financial difficulties, and she resented the attention and resources expended to aid immigrants. She also disliked the term "Americanization" and what it stood for. She preferred to call it "immigrant education."[86] Stewart disagreed with those who were hostile to immigrants and wanted to limit their access to this country. In fact, she had supported President Wilson's 1916 veto of a bill restricting immigration, noting that "the United States of America is a place where illiterates should meet with instruction, not exclusion." She was not averse to coercion, however, and suggested that the federal government actually require adult education. "Not only should [education] be proffered," she said, "if necessary, it should be pressed upon them, immigrants and native alike."[87] Stewart also thought the federal government should take responsibility for educating both the native and foreign born. In testimony before Congress during hearings on the federal education bill in 1924, she lambasted federal lawmakers for "permitting about 1,700,000 foreign-born illiterates to come to this country and to be scattered over the States." Without the consent of the states, she said, the illiterates had been "foisted upon them."[88]

Despite Stewart's aversion to it, Americanization shaped adult education in several ways and also influenced the illiteracy work at the national level. It not only offered a compelling rationale for teaching all Americans, regardless of age or national origin, but also increased federal and state support for such efforts. Government support, in turn, emphasized professional standards and training for teachers and often meant licensure or official sanction of programs that met certain standards. Professionals therefore came to have little tolerance for untrained volunteers like those who taught Moonlight Schools.

Many educators, like social workers, had by the 1920s become convinced that their skill, acquired by formal education, fitted them to deal with the complex problems of the modern world. If the poor were victims of a hostile environment, alleviating their condition required more than the ministrations of the "born teacher"; it required professional expertise. If the Republic was in danger, it required a public school system that could reach most of its citizens, expose them to a common educational experience, inculcate middle-class values and norms of behavior, and nurture law-abiding, respectable, patriotic citizens. This was particularly true in adult education, where the task of using formal schooling as a primary means of absorbing European immigrants into American society was too serious to be entrusted to amateurs. This was a job for professional educators, not volunteers, social reformers, or crusaders. [89]

Although Stewart drew a strong distinction between programs to educate immigrants and those for native-born adults, educators in the cities had long been concerned with teaching both and had adopted from the public schools the task of breaking down immigrant cultures and traditions and promoting adherence to the dominant culture's habits and ideas.[90] They extended their reach when Americanization and the Red Scare resulted in increased state and federal funding and the creation in most states of departments of adult and immigrant education. Many of them were also affiliated with the NEA's Department of Immigrant Education, which in 1924 became the Department of Adult Education.[91] Their emphasis on professional training as a prerequisite to teaching adults, their desire to standardize the curriculum and materials used in teaching adult students, and their reliance on state funding to accomplish their goals brought them into direct conflict with Stewart, who saw them as a threat to her leadership of the adult literacy movement.

Cora Wilson Stewart welcomed assistance in the illiteracy crusade, but she wanted it on her own terms. She was anxious to protect her leadership of the cause and conscientious in her efforts to maintain its crusading character and emphasis on voluntarism. Merging the literacy campaigns with the adult education movement may have appeared both practical and necessary to some, but it represented the surrender of an older, more traditional approach to social reform to the innovations of a new generation of education practitioners. Stewart was not ready to surrender. When they gathered at the conferences sponsored by the NEA Illiteracy Commission, she questioned their methods, particularly their apparent lack of regard for illiterates as individuals. She feared they would ignore those with no skills and concentrate on adults who had already acquired the ability to read and write, and she was certain that the length of their program and the lack of specific "milestones" would discourage and frustrate older learners who wanted to see immediate results. She shared their emphasis on education as a means of inspiring co-operation and thereby securing social progress, but harbored intense reservations about their methods.[92]

Several organizations already involved in adult education wanted to combine their efforts in a national assault on illiteracy, but they did not ask to join Stewart; they asked her to join them. She refused. Robert C. Deming, president of Connecticut's state board of education and chairman of the NEA's Department of Adult Education, invited Stewart to work with him, asking her to "drop him a line" telling him of her interest in his department and how she could best serve it. "We need your energy and enthusiasm and counsel," he wrote, "and we want you to realize that this department represents a national instrument for great national good fashioned to the hand of those who want to see a literate nation and an intelligent citizenry everywhere."[93] Stewart promptly declined his offer, noting that although she had a "sincere interest" in adult education, and felt very "sympathetic" toward his depart-ment, "the friends of the illiteracy crusade, at least those who have been with it from the beginning, are unwilling to dissipate their energies in the various phases of adult education." She noted that she had given her life to the cam-paign, and that the illiteracy work claimed all her energy.[94] Astonished at her refusal to join him in the work, Deming reminded her that they labored for the same cause. "Our job too is to remove illiteracy. . . . Your job is our job, we are covering the same fields and on our roster are all the heads of state de-partments in the south and elsewhere doing the same work in which you are engaged." Chastising her for so narrowly defining her cause, he admonished, "By all means, as you say, give all your time and energy to your chosen life work, but in so doing give it so that every minute and ounce will count to the uttermost through the inspiration and help you can give others and they can give you for concerted attack."[95]

Despite their similarity in goals, Stewart saw profound differences be-tween her work and Deming's. The illiteracy crusade was temporary, she thought, but the nation would always attract immigrants. She expected to "cure" illiteracy in a single generation by teaching illiterate parents who would not allow their children to grow up unschooled. Moreover, absolute illiter-ates claimed her attention, while Deming's programs served adults with some training. Just as important, adult education programs had, with rare excep-tion, never served rural populations. Had they done so, she would have had no work! Stewart articulated her position to her longtime friend and colleague A. E. Winship, editor of the Boston-based *Journal of Education,* whom she consulted before replying to Deming. "Some folks are about to confuse the issues," she wrote. Illiteracy leaders should not involve themselves in more extensive programs "than they have funds or energy to carry on, which means that the illiterates will be neglected just as much as they were before the illiteracy crusade began." Because her program took in everyone over the age of ten and included many young people, it could hardly be consistently called adult education, she added. But terminology was not the only problem. "I have made a hard fight to keep the illiteracy crusade from being confused with immigrant education and other things. We have a very definite proposition—it is simply to teach five million people to read and write and to do it in a given time."[96]

Deming considered Stewart's desire to keep the illiteracy crusade independent of the adult education movement an affront. Although she had always placed adult and immigrant education on the programs for all the conferences sponsored by the NEA commission and included its leaders as speakers, there was a fundamental and apparently irreconcilable difference between the two over approach, technique, and leadership. Stewart therefore expended some of the energy needed to wage war on illiteracy in a war with adult education professionals over the best methods for teaching adults. The conflict was ultimately resolved in favor of the "professionals," as Stewart's community-based, voluntary movement fell increasingly behind the times.

In a speech at the 1927 NEA annual conference, Deming made clear the extent of the controversy and the divergence over methods. Discussing the status and future of the association's Department of Adult Education, he noted that it would soon include all public education for adults. Aiming a barb in Stewart's direction, he remarked, "You may not believe that this type of instruction requires trained leadership . . . and a special technic and special courses of study. Above all you may not believe that after flag-raisings and political oratory and 'reduce illiteracy by 1930' campaigns that state and local laws and appropriations are essential if anything is actually to be done."[97]

Stewart had never disputed the need for special techniques in educating adults, and had in fact pioneered some. She fully agreed that special courses of study were necessary for adult learners. She also supported Deming's contention that laws and appropriations were essential and had long promoted legislation establishing federal aid to education. Those were not the real issues. She and Deming differed over who would design the curriculum and teach the classes. Stewart thought her own materials quite good enough and believed that communities should care for their own illiterates through individual instruction by day school teachers and volunteers. Deming and his associates saw it as a task for specially trained teachers whose work would be overseen and directed by specialists such as himself. The dispute was also about leadership. In fact, the real issue was whether professional educators such as Deming or reformers such as Stewart would prevail as the purveyors of adult literacy.

Stewart vigorously defended her approach. She claimed responsibility for having made the public aware of illiteracy in the first place, and in a speech at the NEA convention in 1928 charged Deming and his associates with looking backward instead of forward, following their "pioneer grandfathers, who developed the elementary school for children, rather than their pioneer fathers, who blazed the trail for the education of illiterate adults." The real sticking point for Stewart was that adult education programs attracted a majority of semieducated adults and a minority of illiterates. They also established no clear and immediately achievable goals, she said, and adult pupils lost interest. Overwhelmed by what appeared to be an endless process, they abandoned education altogether.[98]

Deming may have feared that the move to institutionalize the literacy movement bypassed the education establishment. Certainly, through information campaigns, the recruitment of volunteers, the creation of state commissions, and proposed federal funding and oversight, Stewart and her supporters appeared to have neglected the public school systems except as sources of volunteer instruction. This came as a particular affront at a time when the professionalization of their vocation and the extension of its power and influence in society profoundly concerned educators all across the country. Deming and others like him expected the literacy work to be done by professionals, many of whom had come to disparage and devalue the work of volunteers and organized women.[99] In part they were reclaiming control of the teaching responsibility from untrained women, but in part they were asserting the primacy of the professionally trained individual, whether male or female, not only to conduct the work but also to be paid for it. Stewart sought to reconcile her independence with their misgivings, reminding the NEA membership that "it should be a matter of pride to educators that public school teachers first answered the challenge" to illiteracy.[100]

Stewart understood that the debate was about professionalism, which she supported. Nevertheless, she held fast to her belief that the methods she had developed were the most effective ones. Calling the literacy movement a reform that "could so easily have started from the outside rather than from inside the profession," she noted that two distinct methods or schools of thought had developed in the field she opened. One group wanted to eliminate the "crude pioneer methods with their spectacular and vociferous campaigning" and wanted schools with paid teachers specially trained for teaching adults. This group's method aimed at stability, thoroughness, and standardization. It would turn out fewer but better-trained students through longer periods of school attendance. Teachers would be professionals rather than volunteers. But, said Stewart, this technique simply emulated the methods of the evening schools of the cities, a process that had been going on for more than fifty years and that remained ineffective and inadequate. With attention always focused on pupils with some degree of education, they ignored those who were truly illiterate.[101]

The crusade remained the best method, she said. "There is need of beating the drum, hence a vociferous outcry against illiteracy and a spectacular campaign to bring everybody to the rescue." A crusade focused on those in real need and aroused public support for the work. Although Stewart welcomed trained teachers and was glad to see them paid, she thought that process too cumbersome. It took valuable time, she said, while crusaders and volunteers were already available "to help a brother out of the ditch." Calling her efforts the "Red Cross work of education," and literacy training "first aid and rescue work," she urged "immediate succor rather than leisurely training." It would take years to train special teachers, design special programs, and secure public funding, years that would be lost to those in immediate need.[102] Moreover, her instincts told her that illiterates responded to informal networks of instruction, perhaps directed by teachers and professionals, but overseen in the field by volunteers whose human commitment to the cause defused potential resistance and resentment and focused on immediate results.

However, immediacy was not the only problem. Important differences in method existed between her and the adult educators. The professionals first grounded the adult illiterate in penmanship, "by teaching principles and movements before introducing sentences or words." Her method emphasized the immediate achievement necessary for success with adult illiterates. Moonlight teachers began by teaching students to write their names. Using individual instruction, they set immediate goals and used practical lessons about everyday life. Whether farmers, Native Americans, prisoners, soldiers, or mothers, students learned from reading materials that had relevance to their lives.

The crusading method was "dramatic," Stewart said. It went forward with "wartime intensity," using slogans, campaign songs, posters, parades, and prizes as "the munitions of war." Professionals, Stewart charged, simply "plaster[ed] a certain selected group of a thousand words onto the minds of the illiterates," using sterile methods destined to fail.[103]

The struggle with the adult education professionals illustrates the widening gulf between an older generation of educators like Stewart, the "born teacher" who believed that anyone could teach given the right spirit, and the newer generation who believed that training and expertise, not calling, prepared teachers. Her own experience, gained from years of teaching adult illiterates, joined with her ego and determination to maintain control of the illiteracy crusade, making it impossible for her to merge her work with theirs.

Stewart no doubt sensed she was losing ground, and she must have felt a great deal of frustration. She had dedicated her life to the literacy cause, and to her, education was an end in itself. She believed it could change the world. It certainly changed lives. The newly literate were capable of better, more productive employment; they were better citizens and more devout Christians. She had made illiteracy a prominent national cause, but the regional and national conferences she sponsored had attracted more and more delegates who listened to prestigious speakers and discussed strategies for extending the work and then passed resolutions emphasizing professional instruction rather than voluntary action and institutions rather than individuals as the carriers. Stirring crusades and marches, revival-style oratory, and the voluntary services of organized women symbolized a bygone era, as a new generation eschewed voluntarism and placed its faith in the university-trained educator and the state-supported school as the most effective means of abolishing illiteracy. Stewart had to either reconcile herself and her work to this trend or distance herself from it completely.

SIX

A New Vision

Suspicious of the motives and methods of the adult education "technique people" whose power and influence in the U.S. Department of Education and the NEA were beginning to exceed her own, and disillusioned and angered by attacks on her leadership of the literacy work, Cora Wilson Stewart decided to create a new organization to wipe out illiteracy. Domineering personalities like Olive Jones, of the NEA, and Alice Winter, of the GFWC, had tried her patience. In addition to the philosophical difference with Jones, the bureaucratic red tape and cumbersome operating procedures of both groups slowed progress and weighted Stewart down with paperwork, while the protocol and glacial pace of the federal education bureaucracy stalled necessary action. Weary of the challenges and infighting that had sapped her energy and confidence, Stewart decided that in an independent organization, she could escape assaults on her leadership, set her own course, pick her own associates, and therefore determine policy and outcomes. Toward that end, she created the National Illiteracy Crusade to assure continued help for the nation's absolute illiterates. She had learned from experience that programs for immigrants and native adults with some literacy skills existed, if not in abundance, at least with enough frequency to meet demand. Largely absent, however, were programs for adults who possessed no reading and writing skills, and this group claimed her primary attention.

Interest in reform was beginning to wane, and professionals rather than crusaders had prevailed. A more systematic approach to

reform now emphasized professional expertise and methodology and preferred the bureaucrat to the volunteer. Whether politicians or professionals,
men reasserted their role in the reform arena, where they intensified the
focus on legislative solutions to social problems and further altered mecha-
nisms of reform.

Convinced that it meant the end of rapid assistance to rural illiterates in
favor of systematic, long-term city programs, Stewart feared an institutional
approach would interrupt the crusade's momentum and undermine its emphasis on quick statistical results; therefore, she simply decided to keep her
work separate from that of the recently formed American Association of Adult
Education and the National Association of Public School Adult Educators,
an NEA group that had grown out of the Adult Education Committee. Writing to her friend Sally Lucas Jean, whom she enlisted as the organizational
consultant to the NIC, Stewart noted that these groups preferred courses of
study, trained teachers, "and other processes of a complete system. The trouble
is that they want to do this in places where there is not even a campaign
being carried on." Their method was, she said, like putting electric light fix-
tures in places where there was no powerhouse and where not even a torch
had been carried.[1] Her new organization would carry the torch.

Stung by criticism at the NEA's annual meeting in 1925 when Willie
Lawson, assistant superintendent of public instruction in Arkansas, remarked
on the danger of permitting "untrained individuals" to undertake the teaching of adults, Stewart hardened her resolve. Lawson pointed out the pitfalls
of allowing a "sob section" of "howling reformers . . . to take the job away
from us. Theirs is no standardized plan but a missionary 'labor of love' with a
huge enthusiasm to begin the work but no contract signed to complete it."
She acknowledged "Mrs. Stewart's inspiration" and called her work "abso-
lutely invaluable and almost necessary." Lawson conceded Stewart's contribution in examining conditions, informing public opinion, and arousing
citizens to their responsibility but said it was now time for the professionals
to take over and the crusaders to stand aside.[2]

Cora Wilson Stewart had no intention of standing aside; instead, she
intended to reinvigorate the crusade and eliminate illiteracy by 1930. And
she intended to do it her way. The Moonlight campaigns had already taught
thousands to read and write. Whether they learned only to write their names
and read a few simple sentences or developed the ability to write simple
letters and read the Bible, Moonlight School students acquired basic literacy
skills that enhanced their everyday life. The literacy crusade had also made
Stewart a popular and sought-after expert, admired by many for her work

with the nation's illiterates. Selected by *Pictorial Review* in 1925 as the "American woman who had made the greatest contribution to the advancement of human welfare during the previous year," Stewart received a $5,000 prize for her work with illiterates. The selection panel included William Allen White, Charlotte Perkins Gilman, Ida Tarbell, Sophonisba Breckinridge, and Maud Wood Park. The prize money seemed an answer to her prayers and a validation of her decision to renew the crusade.[3]

A sense of energy and excitement characterized Stewart's personal and professional outlook as she "consecrated" herself anew to the task of wiping out illiteracy. At age fifty, this new chance meant, she said, "more humility, more system, a balance between work and play, and the elimination of all false trappings in mind and in dress." Always a spiritual person who considered herself a servant of God's will, at the New Year she once again focused herself on her cause as she vowed to live a simple but busy life, enjoying the "day's great adventure" and living and acting "more after the spiritual and more for the cause."[4] After a brief trip, she returned to Washington reinvigorated, with a clean slate, ready to begin again. With a new assistant, Evelyn Williams,

> I shall enter a new office and make a new start. . . . Thanks for such a faithful helper as Evelyn who has moved and furnished my offices during my absence. Thanks for the counsel of . . . wise friends. . . . Thanks for reasonable health and strength—another ten years will see illiteracy much reduced and I hope will enable me to make a real contribution. Today is a new day—a beautiful sunny day—and I am a renewed creature in Jesus Christ our Lord under whose banner I march and who is my leader and captain.[5]

With Williams's help, Stewart spent the winter of 1925 creating the new organization, which she first named the National Illiteracy Committee. Her former assistant, Lela Mae Stiles, had found new employment when the campaign faltered in their home state. For the board of directors Stewart selected only individuals with national reputations and a great deal of life experience gained in the public eye. She chose the three "greatest women" she knew: Carrie Chapman Catt, Ida Tarbell, and Jane Addams. Stewart visited Catt, whom she called "a female Moses" for her crusade for suffrage and for her leadership of the current campaign for world peace.[6] Catt initially declined to serve, but Stewart reminded her of the encouragement she had offered four years earlier, telling Catt that if she did not serve "it would weaken the cause and discourage me to death." Catt agreed that Stewart could use her name and promised to offer counsel occasionally, since "advice is the thing we have most of to give."[7] Stewart also recruited one of her heroes, Ida Tarbell, and enlisted Jane Addams, whom she considered the "most Christ-like woman in America," as vice president of the organization.[8] She respected these leaders, valued their opinions and ideas, and demonstrated no hint of worry that their stars would outshine her own. Indeed, she may have selected them, at least in part, because she knew neither could take an active role in the running of the organization or undermine her leadership in any way.

Stewart chose board members carefully. She knew their names lent legitimacy and prestige to her cause and could possibly attract additional philanthropic and popular support. But her choice also says something about her own status as a reformer. She aspired to greatness herself and believed these women had much to teach her. She admired Catt's outspoken nature, calling her "frank, honest and fearless—not afraid to express her opinion." She admired similar traits in Ida Tarbell, especially her ability to "search for and bring out truth." Jane Addams, Stewart's "model in graciousness," was a woman of "child-like simplicity," a "saint" to be emulated. Moreover, she and the settlement workers at Hull House had responded to the needs they saw around them. In doing so, they had already made an important contribution to the development of progressive education. As they labored to tailor schools to the needs of students, they attempted to make the student the center of the school and the school the center of the community, using education as a means of social reform.[9] Stewart's work with rural illiterates shared those goals and embraced the same ideals.

Stewart actually shared several traits with her heroes, including stubbornness, determination, remarkable drive, and consummate organizational skills, and like each of them, she had enjoyed public acclaim and endured public criticism. Also on the board were her old friends from the NEA and Administrative Women in Education, Charl Ormond Williams and Josephine Preston, along with Florida congresswoman Ruth Bryan Owen, the daughter of William Jennings Bryan.[10]

If the new organization was to make any political headway, Stewart needed powerful men in leadership roles. Although initially reluctant to accept, Kansas journalist William Allen White, whom she met while living at the National Arts Club in Washington, D.C., agreed to serve as president of the group.[11] John Finley of the *New York Times,* and University of Wisconsin president Glenn Frank, who also edited *Century* magazine, agreed to serve. And Stewart convinced several old friends, including Senator Henry J. Allen of Kansas, Herbert Houston of the Cosmos Broadcasting Company, A. O.

Thomas of the NEA's World Conference on Education, and Dr. A. E. Winship to add their names to the growing list.[12]

A few declined her invitation. At White's suggestion, Stewart visited Lillian Wald of the Henry Street settlement but found her advice unhelpful. "The most that Lillian Wald had to say to me," Stewart wrote, "was what I already knew and was doing—that those who were in the organization had to put up the money first to advertise it." She visited John Dewey to ask for his support. But his refusal was, she concluded, "a blessing," since she had already told prominent artist and board member Lorado Taft, who had suggested Dewey, not to "get too many old people." Political activist Maude Wood Park also declined, which proved fortunate, Stewart concluded, since "she went out as President of the League of Women Voters and the League has never done anything very constructive."[13] Stewart's acerbic comments reflected her growing disappointment and fear that "her illiterates" were doomed to remain such.

Much to Stewart's surprise, the NIC's board of directors came under immediate attack. In an episode that illustrates the hysteria that had overtaken some Americans in the postwar years and points up how vulnerable women in public life were to criticism, the president general of the Daughters of the American Revolution charged that some of Stewart's board members were "Reds."

In the first two decades of the twentieth century, women's social work and welfare advocacy had gone forward in a relatively supportive environment, shaped by a belief that the United States was in a social crisis created at least in part by the new immigration. Survival of the Republic seemed to depend upon turning the new immigrants into educated, self-controlled, disciplined democratic citizens, and those engaged in that work were relatively immune from public criticism.[14] But the DAR had recently undertaken a program of patriotic education as part of the Americanization effort, and some of its members had grown intense in their pursuit of "patriotic service."[15] Because of its past support of her work, Stewart had approached the organization as "a group of women of patriotism, loyalty, and idealism," and asked its members to join the NIC. They responded with "arrogance, suspicion, and intrigue." Stewart related her encounter with the group, which included representatives of the American Legion, to William Allen White, telling him she had been "summoned" to a meeting, only to find herself "facing six lusty defenders of the flag, who branded five members of our Board as Reds:—Jane Addams, Glenn Frank, Carrie Chapman Catt, Ida Clyde Clarke, and Ida Tarbell—and who advised that we should ask these people to resign." The group particularly disparaged Jane Addams, who, although a member of the DAR, drew fire in their infamous "Spiderweb Chart" exposing putative conspiracies against the U.S. government. Although Addams later regained some of the acclaim and public adoration that had been hers before the war, throughout the twenties she focused most of her efforts on the Women's International League for Peace and Freedom and on internationalist and pacifist efforts in general, activities that did not set well with the DAR or the American Legion.[16]

Stewart described a "grilling fire of questions" about who authorized the work and why it had been undertaken without their "advice, approval, or consent." "They demanded to know," she wrote, "if I was an 'internationalist.'" Stewart described her "inquisitor," John Thomas Taylor, of the American Legion, as "offensive" in manner and imagined his response "when he put this question to me in thumb-screw tones, if I had pulled out my Little Bible and flashed on him the American flag pasted inside the front cover, which goes with me wherever I go, all up and down this broad land of ours." Although she described the encounter in mock-sinister tones, noting that each member of the committee "grabbed one of our letterheads, folded, and transferred it to his pocket," she was put off by the episode and feared it would hurt their cause. She told White, who was touring in Russia, to "hurry back . . . and tell me if they do anything worse there than this. If I'm in prison when you return, be Christian and come and see me, please."[17] White responded directly, calling them "hate-peddlers." He told her the DAR was a "funny bunch—people who are Ku Kluxers at heart and just have too much money to put on a sheet and pillow case." But he urged her not to "stir them up." "A row with them would only hurt the Illiteracy Cause, but we can always remember what sort they are."[18]

Stewart had enjoyed a long and fruitful relationship with both the DAR and the American Legion. Volunteers from both organizations acted as literacy volunteers, and many contributed money to the cause. Although Stewart had not changed, the superpatriots questioned her loyalty because of the associates she had chosen, and the mudslinging continued. Had Stewart lacked backbone, or had she shared the narrow views of her detractors, she could have put an end to the attacks by making the changes they suggested and publicly embracing the Americanization goals they espoused, but when White took the DAR to task for its 1927 blacklist, Stewart applauded. She particularly resented the attacks on Addams, and although she did not share Addams's pacifist views, Stewart respected and defended the older woman's position.[19]

Cora Wilson Stewart was no radical. Although she had broadened the literacy work to a national scope, it remained an essentially conservative endeavor designed simply to improve choices for illiterates by better equipping them for life in the modern world. Higher living standards and more fulfilling lives for the nation's illiterates were her goals. She envisioned education as the catalyst for broader reforms that could extend the benefits of modern industrial society to Americans in the countryside and in small towns and villages, without fundamentally altering its values and traditions. Although her work straddles a thin line between paternalism and empowerment, occasionally making inroads in each direction, she saw literacy as a force for positive change. That the fundamental nature of the literacy work did not change is evidenced by the reader Stewart prepared for women at home.

Stewart's travels and experiences with illiterates enabled her to see the particular needs of groups of people, and like many of the "child-savers" of her day, she sought to transform the child-rearing practices of the uneducated poor. In most working-class families, child-rearing responsibilities fell primarily to women, and with this in mind, Stewart created a primer for mothers. Published in 1929 by the NIC, *Mother's First Book: A First Reader for Home Women* presented lessons centered on the home and daily activities. Constructed around everyday tasks such as care of the baby, cleanliness, and proper foods for the family, the lessons and exercises also emphasized the importance of education and cooperation with the school and idealized the role of the mother in the home. Like the *Country Life Readers,* their aim was not only to teach reading and writing but also to lead women "to better home practices and higher ideals in their home and community life" through education.[20]

Like her other readers, the mother's book encouraged hard work and the adoption of middle-class values and material culture. Although the primary burden of child care fell to the mother, both parents shared the obligation of keeping their children in school, and in this reader, Stewart sought to fully impress upon her students the gravity of that responsibility and its long-term consequences. Several of the lessons emphasized the changes education could bring and recommended that parents and teachers work together in the Parent-Teacher Association. One reading lesson featured a sample letter from a homemaker to her sister, telling of her new literacy and the transformations it had wrought in her life:

These are happy days for me. I feel as if I have taken a new lease on life. I have learned to write my own letters and to read those that come to me. You should see the pride I take in my work. We have put running water into our house and we are now about the cleanest people you ever saw. John will be home from college soon and Mary is coming from Kentucky for a visit. We plan to show those older children of ours one of the neatest homes in the world.[21]

The Victorian ideal of the "angel of the house" permeates the primer for mothers. For example, Stewart encouraged women at home to think of life as a garden where flowers and fruits flourished or where weeds and thorns took over. "It takes work and thought to make the home like a lovely garden," read one lesson. "It takes smiles to make home like a pleasant garden. It takes kind words, kind thoughts, and kind deeds to make home as fragrant as a rose garden."[22] Doubtless the positive memories of her own mother, long cherished and idealized, served as a model, although the readers do not encourage women to work outside the home as Annie Halley and Cora Wilson Stewart did.

Mothers took priority in 1928 as Stewart launched a special campaign to bring literacy to the nation's homemakers. She chose Mother's Day for the opening and enlisted Mrs. James J. Davis, the wife of the U.S. secretary of labor and mother of five, to offer the first lesson.[23] Like soldiers in 1917, mothers were called to special duties and responsibilities and would be better prepared to carry out those tasks if they could read and write. They could keep clean, neat homes. They could feed their families fresh fruits and vegetables and lots of milk to keep them healthy. They could use lots of soap to keep the family members and the home clean at all times. They could learn to read and write and thus keep in touch with children as they left home. The *Mother's First Book* encouraged women to join the Red Cross, attend lectures by nurses and nutritionists, and, in a short piece written by Frances E. Willard, to practice "The Kindness Habit."[24]

The values-based, personal approach set out in the *Mother's First Book* represented Stewart's preferred method and defined her divergence from adult education professionals. It began with individual instruction and women learning to write their names. It also incorporated practical knowledge and everyday information previously inaccessible to those who could not read and write. Although many women could not attend classes, they could learn at home using this new reader brought to them by local literacy volunteers, a process that would end if Stewart gave in and joined the "technique people."

Although maintaining an independent campaign enabled her to implement her own philosophies and approach to teaching the nation's illiterates, Cora Wilson Stewart soon discovered that waging such a campaign carried built-in frustrations. Without the financial backing of the NEA and GFWC,

money remained the most pressing problem, and even sixteen months of
fund-raising resulted in only a handful of individual donations. Stewart had,
however, begun to tap into corporate resources, especially those with a vested
interest in literacy, and their support enabled her to carry out a number of
well-publicized literacy drives. Hoping to profit from its emphasis on daily
bathing and careful washing of clothes and bed linens, the Association of
American Soap and Glycerine Producers' Cleanliness Institute underwrote
the cost of the *Mother's First Book*. The largest corporate donation came
from Theodore Ahrens, owner of the American Radiator Corporation in
Louisville, Kentucky.[25] Early in 1929, Stewart also persuaded Metropolitan
Life Insurance Company to provide information on illiteracy to its twenty
million policyholders nationwide. The company carried out a $50,000 adver-
tising campaign in the nation's major magazines, encouraging people all across
the nation to teach one illiterate to read and write. Metropolitan also furnished grooved writing pads for teaching penmanship, while the NIC supplied readers to those who requested them. Stewart's records indicate that
more than six thousand letters came from all over the United States and
from eleven countries in response to the Metropolitan campaign. She answered most of them with some kind of personal note or encouraging word.[26]

Accustomed to doing a lot with only a little money, Stewart secured for
the NIC office space at no cost. Red Cross director Judge John Barton Payne
donated a suite in the Red Cross building in Washington, D.C., and also
arranged for the Washington Loan and Trust Company to handle NIC funds
without charge. Despite some corporate assistance and Barton's generosity,
the organization desperately needed substantial financial backing.[27] Hoping
to ease the burden on Stewart and secure backing from some large philanthropy, the NIC commissioned a professional fund-raiser, Burr Price, who
had collected more than $35,000 for the Woodrow Wilson Foundation, but
his efforts proved no more successful than Stewart's.[28]

In an attempt to draw public and media attention to the work of the
new organization, Stewart used the familiar tactic of securing a proclamation
of support from the male political establishment. Calvin Coolidge answered
her request for presidential support in a letter acknowledging the literacy
work and affirming its importance. Characterizing the eradication of illiteracy as "a national responsibility," he called service to that cause "a community privilege." "When it can be said that every community is a literate
community, the United States will have become a literate nation. Your organization, and others that may cooperate in the movement, will be useful, I
trust, in stimulating in every community a desire to show a record of com-

plete literacy in 1930, and in bringing the United States to rank first in this respect among the nations."[29] Stewart appreciated the president's kindness in sending the letter, but she chose to keep her distance from the Bureau of Education and Secretary Tigert. Although the two had met cordially since the national illiteracy conference, she believed that the bureau could be of little future use to the crusade.[30]

Stewart traveled extensively, always looking for ways to expand her network and draw more people into the crusade. She did find that attitudes about illiteracy had definitely changed since the early days of the campaign, when many professional educators had maintained that adults could not learn. In a profound reversal the University of Alabama hosted an illiteracy conference in 1926, prompting her to write to William Allen White about the time "when university people felt it their sacred duty to dispute our claims that grown men and women had learned to read and write." That summer, she traveled the Midwest and returned to the Northwest, where she visited Josephine Preston, Minnie Neilson, and Zugie Zuger. She shared a draft of her reader for Native Americans, the *Indian's First Book*, and attended the Northwest Indian Congress.[31] In addition to Moonlight Schools taught by local clubwomen, later, in 1931, Stewart provided a fifteen-day residential session on the Blackfoot Indian Reservation. The session included three class periods daily and provided seventy-two lessons for more than two hundred Indians. Stewart particularly loved the residential setting and the contact with the Indians. She saved stacks of letters written by the Native American students along with poems, photographs, and various other mementos of the experience. Members of the Blackfoot tribe developed their own newsletter, similar to the *Mountaineer*, which they filled with local news and events. The teachers received Indian names, and Stewart was called "Chief Woman," which must have given her enormous pleasure. Stewart dedicated this reader to Josephine Preston, who had called the very first Conference on Indian Education.[32]

In 1925 and 1926, Stewart stepped up her efforts to eliminate illiteracy in the nation's prisons. Certain that lack of education contributed to recidivism, she convinced prison authorities in Kentucky, Virginia, and Florida to offer classes for inmates. Virginia made the classes mandatory for parole.[33]

Despite Stewart's dedication to the cause and the president's proclamation, the NIC never became the viable and vibrant organization she envisioned. She had difficulty getting people interested in the cause. A decided change in public response to Stewart's appeals may have been the result of poor booking practices for her public appearances and speeches, as she suspected, or it might have been a general decline in interest in progressive topics in the postwar years. Wracked by financial problems and hoping to drum up public support, Stewart contracted with several booking agencies to secure speaking venues. One agency failed to book any engagements and even asked that she reimburse the company for its expenses. The Alkahest agency, which had arranged a few lectures, wrote her asking for leads and noting its inability to secure audiences for her topic. Stewart also traveled on the Chautauqua circuit, attempting to spread the message that way, but this too proved disappointing. Writing to William Allen White in the fall of 1928, she noted that she had covered the states from Maine to Minnesota and traveled almost as far south as the gulf, with "good results" only in Maine, Alabama, and Texas.[34]

Discouraged by her lack of progress but still determined to wage a national campaign, in the fall of 1929, Stewart decided to approach Republican president Herbert Hoover to request presidential backing for a national organization to combat illiteracy. As secretary of commerce, Hoover had supported the literacy work by releasing census data, including the names and addresses of illiterates, to state illiteracy commissions.[35] Stewart had met Hoover on a number of occasions and, although she was a Democrat, supported his election by speaking privately to groups of literacy volunteers about his support for the work.[36] In a letter dated 2 March 1933, the president acknowledged his gratitude, telling Stewart he had been "deeply gratified to have had during the past four years your unfailing support in projects of social betterment." Stewart gained access to President Hoover through her friend Senator Henry J. Allen, formerly the governor of Kansas. Desperately anxious to secure presidential endorsement and backing of what she hoped would be a final national push to eliminate illiteracy, she met several times with Secretary of the Interior Ray Lyman Wilbur but was disturbed by his tendency to want to "study" illiteracy. She asked Allen to show his "active interest" to help "start things off right with Wilbur." Stewart preferred the crusading, active campaign and feared that Wilbur's academic approach might "anesthetize" the already lagging movement. A research commission would simply slow down the "present enthusiastic effort" and dishearten volunteers everywhere. Stewart hoped Allen could help her bring the secretary "to our view." "He mentioned that I knew the methods, and seemed unaware of my other activities. He is judging me by some few little readers—our tools for illiterates to dig out with—the humblest service that I have rendered. I am no maker of text-books, but filled the need because no other way had opened up to get it done."[37]

Stewart wanted the Interior Department's backing, but she wanted it without any controls. Using the strategy that for her was most effective, she asked her male associates to prevail upon the Hoover administration to appoint a presidential commission not to study illiteracy but to wipe it out. Such a commission, she believed, "would put power into the movement at this time and help us in a big, final battle before the census in May 1930."[38] Her push for quick action indicated both her frustration with bureaucratic machinery and her desire to fulfill the goal she had set for herself when she began the national campaign. She had learned in years of campaigning that the short, determined drive was best, and a dramatic decrease in illiteracy statistics would prove her work successful.

A new campaign in Louisiana, begun in 1929 and funded at $100,000 by newly elected governor Huey P. Long, provided the administration with a current example of a successful statewide campaign. With his state leading the nation in the number of illiterates, Long commissioned T. H. Harris, the state's superintendent of public schools, to organize night schools following the Moonlight model. Stewart traveled to the state three times at Harris's request and met with Dr. M. S. Robertson, who oversaw the effort in Louisiana. Calling it one of the "most dramatic" attempts to eliminate illiteracy the "world had ever seen," Stewart marveled at the number of whites who attended but noted that the state's blacks were "simply stampeding" the schools. The NIC provided twenty-five hundred books to Louisiana at no cost, and Stewart assisted Harris in a fund-raising drive to secure an additional $100,000 to meet the huge demand. *New York Times* editor Dr. John Finley had accepted the office of president of the NIC when William Allen White resigned, and he wrote an editorial for his newspaper urging support for the Louisiana movement.[39]

Much-needed financial assistance came to the NIC and the Louisiana campaign through a fortuitous meeting of a group of powerful male supporters of Stewart's work. French Strother, Herbert Hoover's administrative assistant, was a former staff writer for *World's Work* magazine and knew the early history of the Moonlight Schools in Kentucky. His close friend and associate Herbert Houston, the current editor of the magazine, now served on the NIC board. The two men met at the White House with philanthropist Julius Rosenwald, and Strother urged the Rosenwald Fund to support the literacy work. In a subsequent meeting with Rosenwald Fund director Alfred K. Stern at Hull House in Chicago, Jane Addams joined Cora Wilson Stewart in appealing to the foundation for aid. Stern pledged $235,000 to the cause and earmarked $50,000 in matching funds specifically for the Louisiana effort. Other state illiteracy commissions could also apply for that amount in matching funds.[40] Wil Lou Gray in South Carolina and Clutie Bloodworth in Alabama both secured grants for programs in their state.[41]

While this was taking place, Stewart traveled to Geneva, Switzerland, to attend the World Conference on Education, where she presided over the Illiteracy Section. This was the largest international literacy conference ever, and delegates passed resolutions urging governments to take responsibility for illiterates within their borders. They specifically urged Stewart to recommend that the U.S. government take the lead and thus serve as an example to the rest of the world.[42]

When Stewart returned to the United States, she learned that despite the efforts of Senator Allen, Herbert Houston, and William Allen White, she had to content herself with the National Advisory Commission on Illiteracy (NACI), appointed by the Department of the Interior rather than directly by President Hoover. French Strother wrote Stewart that the president was reluctant to "multiply" the number of national commissions, fearing that "unless he holds these down to those dealing with the most pressing problems of major importance, that their numbers will so increase that they will lose significance in the mind of the public."[43]

Stewart expressed strong reservations about the federal commission as it emerged. She feared that it would become solely a research body, which to her meant certain death for the movement. She needed a viable organization capable of mounting a last energizing crusade to stimulate states to action, coordinate their efforts, and provide funding, information, and guidance. Stewart also worried about the relationship of the NIC to the federal commission, and although she initially favored merging the two, she soon decided such a course was unwise. Given her reservations about the commission's emphasis on research instead of action, it is likely that she wanted to preserve the NIC as a potential fallback position. Experience had also taught her to be wary of sharing authority with the federal government.[44] She did, at Secretary Wilbur's request, turn over $1,200 in NIC funds to the advisory committee.[45] In fact, there was little else to turn over. Her crusade had compiled some statistics and maps, and she had written a primer for Native Americans for use in literacy programs on the reservations, but there was little besides the name to merge.

Stewart's apprehension proved valid, but not for the reasons she anticipated. Instead, the composition and leadership of the commission became an immediate problem. Houston and Finley, along with Ruth Bryan Owen, former governor R. A. Nestos of North Dakota, and T. H. Harris of Louisiana, served on the board, but so did a number of prominent professionals in the field of adult education. Her friends shared Stewart's concern over the direction the group might take, and Herbert Houston immediately wrote presidential assistant French Strother with his recommendations. Houston wanted to see that Stewart got the credit she deserved for the work and that the administration understood her role in the movement. "I wish you . . . to see that [a press release announcing the creation of the commission] develops the fact that this Commission is a natural and inevitable outgrowth of the National Illiteracy Crusade, which Mrs. Stewart organized and has led with great power and courage from the beginning." He noted that such an announcement would please "all the education people, among whom Mrs. Stewart has been a leader for years." It would also show that the movement had popular support and "that the President has simply given governmental sanction to a broad movement already under way."[46]

Houston also wrote to Wilbur to let him know that when he had accepted appointment to the commission, he had assumed that Stewart would chair it. "She is an extraordinary woman, with an absolute singleness of purpose in relationship to the Illiteracy Crusade," he noted. He told Wilbur of his long association with Stewart, which began through his "old partner," Walter Hines Page, when he was on the Southern Education Board. "From that initial interest I have gone forward and helped this great movement whenever I had an opportunity to do so."[47] This early intervention by a powerful man secured leadership of the commission for Stewart, but only temporarily.

Houston, Allen, Finley, Harris, and Nestos, all of whom shared Stewart's vision for the commission, together formed a powerful bloc that, for a time, was able to protect Stewart's leadership and set the course for the agency. Unlike the adult education professionals on the commission who believed that the work should be done exclusively by specially trained teachers working from the public schools, they remained convinced that a community-based crusade represented the best chance for success. Stewart wanted the NACI to cultivate connections with voluntary associations and individuals because she thought them quicker, more effective, and less expensive than specially trained teachers. There was no time for training special teachers if they were to make a big push before the 1930 census and have a dramatic effect on the number of illiterates in the nation. Stewart also wanted the commission to proceed carefully because she sensed that some states would not cooperate because they feared or resented federal control.[48] While they would respond to a crusade, they might be put off by a government directive on how to teach illiterates in their own state. With these goals in mind, she carried on an extensive correspondence with her friends on the board, keeping them constantly apprised of developments, planning strategies, and calling for help whenever she needed it.

Stewart believed her goals differed from those of Secretary Wilbur and the adult educators on the commission, whom she called the "Technique People" because of their emphasis on method and approach. Her apprehension grew when they secured a grant from the Julius Rosenwald Fund for $15,000 to finance a study and publish a manual for educators involved in the eradication of illiteracy. She suspected that the group was "about to run away with the committee and its work" and decided to call a series of meetings of the executive board in order to define and establish the direction of the commission before it could be preempted by the adult education professionals.[49] Even if it meant constant struggle, Cora Wilson Stewart intended to run the organization her own way. Although the first few meetings went well, largely due to the presence of powerful men on the board who used their influence to her advantage, the leadership and direction of the NACI never rested securely in her hands. It soon became evident that the adult education faction intended to ignore her leadership to pursue a separate project, the compilation of an extensive manual on adult education. The resulting showdown made it clear that Stewart's power to influence the direction of "her" commission rested solely in the hands of her male supporters. She held no authority of her own and was obliged to work almost exclusively through them.

The problem developed when the director of the NACI, whom Stewart had recruited and hired, went over to the "other side." Dr. M. S. Robertson, the leader of Louisiana's literacy effort, joined the commission on loan from his home state. Stewart had become acquainted with him during her work there, and through her friend A. H. Harris, Louisiana's state superintendent and a NACI board member, secured his services for a year. Robertson's program in his home state was one of the most progressive and successful in the nation, and Stewart thought him a dynamic and energetic "crusader." Secretary Wilbur, in announcing the appointment, explained to Stewart that as chairman of the executive committee, she would meet with Robertson weekly and "provide guidance on the general aspects of the work, but not on the educational."[50]

Stewart had secured a private donation from friends to ensure Robertson a generous salary, and had anticipated a cordial working relationship, but within a few weeks, the two clashed. Wilbur's description of her role offended her, and she took particular exception to an incident in which the new director left Washington on business and instructed his secretary that Stewart was not to have access to any of the agency papers or reports in his absence.[51] Other disagreements occurred, and by late August she sought Harris's intervention, asking him, as Robertson's former supervisor, to "stir him in the right way." She told Harris that instead of bringing the constructive plans and enthusiasm of the Louisiana campaign, Robertson had raised "absurd issues," including a supposed rivalry between herself and Secretary Wilbur. She assured Harris that no such rivalry existed. "Naturally, after all these years of waiting and working for some participation in the illiteracy movement by the Government, I would seek above everything else now, to make that participation effective."[52]

If Harris intervened, his influence had little effect, for the situation soon deteriorated. The commission had undertaken the publication of the instruction manual financed by the Rosenwald Fund, and the debate over the content and approach grew heated. Robertson "went over" to the position of the men on the technique committee whose job it was to compile and edit the work. They had created a lengthy and comprehensive manual that Stewart thought favored foreign-born illiterates and focused too heavily on adult education rather than illiteracy. Once again, she feared that the native-born rural illiterates would receive short shrift. After revising the first eight chapters of the manual and sending it back to the editors for further revisions, she argued that the book, which advocated twice the number of instructional hours offered in the Moonlight Schools, encroached on and overlapped with the work of other agencies that could carry out the adult education mission far better than the NACI. The NACI's job was simply to "concentrate on our task and first get the millions of illiterates taught to read and write." Stewart's concerns were real. Certainly challenges to her leadership and vision worried her, but it is obvious from the NACI correspondence and minutes of meetings that her primary goal was to settle on best practices for teaching absolute illiterates. She wanted the Committee on Techniques to "welcome opinions and suggestions from both laymen and educators," and to take into account the opinions and experience of the members of the national committee. She offered a number of compromises, suggesting the committee adopt a 24-lesson, 48-hour course, or even a 36-lesson, 72-hour plan. Either could be "intelligently and enthusiastically taught." Courses of this duration would provide adequate instruction in basic reading and writing at roughly the fourth-grade level and leave further study "as a continuation to be urged" once a student achieved basic literacy. "I am sure that the task will not be thought so formidable but that tens of thousands of teachers and hundreds of thousands of pupils will make a determined effort . . . with success assured."[53] Robertson's support for the longer period of instruction outraged Stewart, who called his support of the manual a "complete desertion." Although Stewart ultimately accepted the manual rather than "disorganize our Committee" and give the Rosenwald organization the impression of dissension at the NACI, she acknowledged to Herbert Houston that it would have been "hard for me to swallow, but for your wise guidance."[54]

Houston urged patience, noting that her handling of the executive committee was a "tour de force" that resulted in "a complete victory to your credit." He counseled against letting the matter trouble her. "You've got too great a vision to be bothered by people who insist on 'looking through a glass darkly.' Personally, I am getting to the philosophical stage . . . where I find there is a good deal of good in everybody and that the best thing to do is to work along in comfort and with a minimum of friction."[55] But Stewart no longer trusted Robertson and feared the two could not work harmoniously toward the same goal. She prevailed upon T. H. Harris to ask that Robertson leave the NACI and return to his home state. Through private arrangement with Harris, she also took personal responsibility for Robertson's salary and expenses for the remainder of his contract with the NACI. Robertson tendered his resignation to Wilbur, and at Stewart's urging the secretary accepted it.[56]

Stewart publicly expressed sympathy and concern for Robertson's professional reputation and happiness, but privately she was glad to be rid of him. He had taken the side of the adult educators whose work she thought threatened her own. "He had a glorious opportunity and lost it here when he might have made a great success by a little team work," said Stewart. Particularly bitter about his final efforts, she observed that in the last weeks of his stay, "he joined deliberately with those who sought to turn our movement from a direct, simple, inexpensive program into a long, tedious one of adult education which would cost the states millions of dollars and would educate only the few comparatively." Interestingly, she also faulted the other side for not coming to his aid. "I think the thing that must be most bitter for Dr. Robertson is that those with whom he aligned himself did nothing for him when he needed them."[57]

Like the NIC, the National Advisory Commission on Illiteracy proved a disappointment as an organization. Although following Robertson's dismissal Stewart regained some control of the NACI, despite her most zealous efforts, the commission did not live up to her expectations. Internecine struggles and financial difficulties weakened the agency and limited its effectiveness. Moreover, the U.S. Census Bureau's announcement that it could no longer provide lists of illiterates undermined the effectiveness of the organization by eliminating an important means of identifying those in need. In addition, the Great Depression had a profoundly negative impact by 1931, and Herbert Hoover's failure to gain reelection in 1932 resulted in the closure of the NACI. The Depression had a similar effect on the NIC, which had continued to supply public information during Stewart's service with the NACI and operated on a limited basis until 1934 when it, too, closed. The crusade, like the NACI, had received aid from the Rosenwald Fund, including $20,000 for 1930, $10,000 for 1931, and $5,000 for 1932.[58] The funds were to have been paid in matching grants, but when it became impossible for Stewart to raise the agency's share, the Rosenwald organization, also strapped by the failing economy, could not continue its support. Although he could no longer assist her, Alfred K. Stern, the fund's director for special activities, encouraged Stewart to keep up her fight against illiteracy: "I hope you will find ways and means of continuing the great work you have been doing," he wrote. "I have felt it a privilege to share with you some of the satisfaction which you have every right to claim for having gone so far in the reduction of illiteracy."[59]

The National Advisory Committee on Illiteracy and the NIC, despite their failure to live up to Stewart's hopes and expectations, actually accomplished a great deal. Through these agencies, Stewart led a vigorous public information campaign, traveling and speaking almost as energetically as she had done in the early days of the Moonlight Schools. She gave five nationally broadcast programs on illiteracy on CBS radio and, along with NACI board members, authored and nearly secured passage of a joint congressional resolution authorizing the census department to continue to release the names of illiterates to state education authorities at no cost.[60] She oversaw the creation of forty-four state advisory committees, which were established as liaisons between the NACI and state authorities, and the agency employed a field secretary, Minnie Jean Nielson, who coordinated the effort in the states. In addition, the NACI and the NIC helped establish literacy programs on Indian reservations in three states and, working with prison authorities, also implemented programs for prisoners in several states.[61]

When the NACI ceased operation on 1 January 1933, Secretary of the Interior Ray Lyman Wilbur, President Hoover's chief adviser on educational matters, wrote to Stewart and other members of the committee, thanking them for their work. He noted that making the public "illiteracy conscious" had been the "main aim" of the NACI. He also praised Stewart and her coworkers for fostering a sense of responsibility in local communities for the education of adult illiterates, a contribution of inestimable importance.[62]

Always a Democrat, Cora Wilson Stewart often reduced complex elements to the common denominator of party politics and philosophies, but by the 1932 presidential election she had distanced herself from party activities and partisan advocacy. Although she thought Franklin Delano Roosevelt "valiant and sincere," she chose not to campaign for him or his opponent. Recruited by Mary Dewson to serve as vice-chairman of the women's division at the Democratic national campaign headquarters in the fall of 1932, a task she would have embraced wholeheartedly in 1920, she declined, mentioning the strenuous nature of her work and the need to stay out of the political fray. Mrs. Ellis Yost, who directed the women's division of the Republican National Committee, asked Stewart to become a member of that organization's board of counselors, a group of twenty-five "nationally known women" chosen for personal achievement, "association with a distinguished husband," or through leadership of outstanding importance. Stewart refused that offer as well, noting that since she took up headquarters in Washington, D.C., she had "consistently declined . . . to ally [herself] publicly with the organization or activities of any party."[63] Accepting either offer might have enabled her to hold on to the federal agency that coordinated the literacy work, but after the NACI officially closed its doors, she refocused her efforts through the NIC.[64]

Cora Wilson Stewart was fifty-eight years old when the mission to which she believed God had called her ended. She was in reasonably good health, and despite an illness that forced her to spend some time in bed in March 1933, still found the strength to work on a book manuscript entitled *His Mark,* which detailed the effects of illiteracy on individuals and related success and inspirational stories. She negotiated publishing terms with the Robert Thomas Hardy Company that winter, although the book never came into print. That summer she explored the possibility of providing literacy training at twenty Civilian Conservation Corps camps across the nation.[65]

The Great Depression had affected not only her work but also her family's financial well-being, and although she had declined to work for Roosevelt's election, at least in part because she still believed in prohibition, the implementation of the New Deal provided an opportunity for paid employment that Stewart never anticipated. She was hired by the Federal Housing Administration as a field representative to women's groups and civic clubs. At an annual salary of $3,000 plus travel expenses, her job was to promote an awareness and understanding of federal housing programs designed to help Americans finance home improvement projects and new housing starts with the ultimate goal of boosting employment in the construction industry. This seemed to her a natural extension of the work she had done in the Moonlight

Schools and the *Country Life Readers,* for she had, she believed, "really been talking about better housing all these years. As the people learned to read and write, they wanted better things and one of the first things they wanted was better homes."[66]

Although Stewart accepted employment with a New Deal agency and embraced the cause she espoused, she bitterly criticized New Deal efforts in adult education. Like many educators, she was shocked at the powerlessness of school systems to deal with the crisis as teacher unemployment climbed to 80 percent. Many local districts simply shut down. In 1933, John Dewey had noted the lack of national leadership in education and criticized the "pathetic . . . lack of social power possessed by the teaching profession."[67] By the summer of 1934, the worsening situation prompted Harry Hopkins, who administered many of the New Deal relief programs, to authorize the hiring of forty thousand teachers to teach unemployed adult illiterates through the Federal Emergency Relief Agency (FERA).[68] His actions were motivated more by teacher unemployment than by concern for illiterates; nevertheless, Stewart might have supported such an initiative had the Roosevelt administration not appointed one of the most outspoken critics of her work, Lewis R. Alderman of Oregon, as the nation's specialist in adult education. Much to her chagrin, Alderman classified as illiterate anyone with less than a sixth-grade education and declared their eligibility to enroll in the program set up by FERA.[69]

Stewart rejected the sixth-grade standard for two reasons. First, it meant that nearly every student who had passed through the Moonlight Schools in the last two decades was still considered illiterate; therefore, all her efforts had been in vain. Just as important, she believed that teachers would focus on students with some skills, and the illiterates would be ignored. In a radio speech, broadcast by NBC radio on 10 December 1933, Stewart attacked this new definition of literacy, noting that the international standard was based on the simple ability to read and write in any language, and Alderman's standard would lower America's statistical ranking, making it appear worse than it really was.[70] Realizing she lacked the power to alter the situation, she gradually distanced herself from the subject, visiting friends and relatives, occasionally working on her book manuscript, and attempting to understand and accept the fact that her mission had ended.[71] Like any number of Progressive Era reformers who witnessed their maternalist policies being reworked in unforeseen ways by New Dealers, Stewart believed that instructional settings that included adults who possessed some literacy skills assured the marginalization of absolute illiterates. Moreover, since FERA literacy classes enrolled anyone with less than a sixth-grade education, the United States would lose ground quickly in statistical terms, and its international education ranking would fall dramatically. Bitter about the new standard that "would make of our fathers and mothers illiterates," Stewart saw its adoption as yet another sign that her public work was over.[72]

Conclusion

In a 1910 letter, Mattie Dalton wrote to her dear friend Cora Wilson Stewart, "Tell me the character of a man's God, and you tell me the character of the man."[1] Certainly Stewart's perception of God and his mission for her on earth shaped her life and work and determined her character as a reformer. It made her an idealist whose faith in education and the symbolic rebirth that it afforded turned her campaign against illiteracy into a crusade and her work into a calling. It also convinced her that she served as an instrument of God's will and was duty-bound to follow her vocation. Stewart's sense of mission profoundly shaped both her personality and her work. Combined with her experiences as a young woman in rural Kentucky, it allowed her to embrace the roles of Southern Lady, Schoolmarm, and Missionary and from them to create for herself the dominant role of Crusading Reformer.

Stewart was strong-willed and determined, well organized and capable, and, above all, charismatic. As a young woman, she was driven by a strong sense of mission that the classroom did not satisfy, and despite an incredibly busy life, she sometimes felt emptiness, frustration, and anger. Unhappy marriages and the death of her infant son left her with no desire for homemaking, and she buried herself in the work she loved. She drove herself at a relentless pace, and although she took joy and pride from her work, negative emotions occasionally surfaced. In their private correspondence she occasionally railed to Mattie Dalton about the sexist interpretation of "God's laws," particularly those regarding marriage, divorce, and the role of women in society. The two shared an intense bond, and Dalton understood her friend's resentment at the narrowness of southern Protestant religious culture, but encouraged her not to blame not God, but those who had so narrowly interpreted his word. "Sooner or later," she told Cora, "you will have to make a religion for yourself."[2]

Although she may have hesitated to call it a religion, Stewart's conversion to the goals of social reform was complete and life-changing, and for her it provided an outlet for the conscience that her upbringing and early life experiences had instilled and that her nearly boundless energy could sustain. Women were barred from the ministry in her denomination, and although she could have entered the foreign mission field, she found her calling in the mountains of eastern Kentucky. The object of her faith was education, around which she built a reform vision based on the desirability of progress and the perfectibility of humankind. In education, she saw the potential for changing the world. Sadly, after more than thirty years of crusading as a prophet for this new faith, Stewart feared that she had allowed her own ambition to subvert God's true calling and cause her to misunderstand his mission for her. When she joined the Oxford Group, she had begun to believe that she had really been called to carry salvation, not learning.

But whether it was God's call or her own, she built her life around a crusade that preached the gospel of progress and economic redemption through education. With the fiery rhetoric of an evangelist, she stigmatized illiteracy, portraying it as an affliction to be cured, a disease to be eradicated, and a curse to be lifted. Stewart cast herself as a saintly figure whose mission in life was to save people from its effects. If they learned to read and write, they could break out of the bondage of illiteracy, become better citizens, more productive workers, and happier, healthier individuals; above all, because they could read the Bible for themselves, they could become more devout Christians.

Stewart's crusading zeal and faith in the gospel of progress with herself as its instrument shaped her work in important ways. Although given to oratory and the dramatic gesture, she was an intensely devout woman who, despite the benevolence rhetoric that characterized her public speeches, still appeared to believe every word she said. Fired by intense, even messianic single-mindedness, she believed her crusade would triumph over illiteracy and brooked opposition from no one. A degree of stubbornness, courage, and confidence was necessary for any woman in public life, and most of the "great-souled southern suffragists" and reformers possessed these traits in abundance.[3]

In Stewart they predominated, but with mixed results. By casting herself as an agent of God's work, she formed alliances with like-minded men in politics. "Honest Bill" Fields, Ollie James, and James B. McCreary had won election supporting moral reforms, especially prohibition, and they intensified their claim to the moral high ground by backing her work. Many reformers of her generation traded on their special virtues as women and mothers, but "Sister Stewart" invoked an even higher virtue: God was on her side. To many journalists and a number of politicians, she was a hero and crusader whose grassroots movement deserved their support. Whether it meant creating a state agency to facilitate her work, stumping on behalf of her cause, or voting appropriations to carry it on, backing her work was good press and good politics. Enormously popular in Kentucky, she inspired reforms that cost her home state very little. She enjoyed the widespread backing of the state's educators and, through her extensive network of clubwomen, possessed the power to bring potential women voters into the Democratic Party.

But her hero status did not ensure the backing of all of Kentucky's political elite, and her allegiance to the Democratic Party guaranteed a measure of partisanship. A tendency already existed among male politicians of both parties to marginalize and underfund reform initiatives led by women, even as they mouthed platitudes of ideological support. Stewart's messianism intensified that marginalization, prompting Kentucky governor Augustus Owsley Stanley to declare that it was more critical for the state to "save" those with physical diseases than to rescue those suffering from the "disease" of illiteracy.[4] To some politicians she became anathema—a demanding, occasionally even unreasonable woman whose requests for commissions, agencies, and financial backing were tiresome but whose cause was difficult to disavow. And when it became apparent to them that the woman vote was not as decisive as women had hoped and men had feared, many, including her old friend William J. Fields, abandoned her entirely.

But Stewart was not alone. As a crusader and as a woman, Stewart participated in a form of activism that reflected a broad national trend. In fact, hundreds of crusaders like her lived out the "special millennialism" that marked southern progressivism. With them she shared a sense of awakening and a dream of progress that combined Protestant social evangelism with the promise of modern efficiency, a "union of missionaries and social engineers."[5] Although she was more missionary than social engineer, an important part of the redemption she preached was economic progress and middle-class mobility. Her vision of progress was hybridized; it grafted the values and traditions of the agrarian past onto modern ideas of economic determinism and social justice. Hers was, to borrow historian Robert M. Crunden's descriptive phrase, "innovative nostalgia."[6] Stewart looked backward to the traditions of neighborliness, Christian charity, the sanctity of the home and family, and the simple life, lived close to the land. But she looked forward to better roads, improved farm productivity, better and more progressive schools, improved sanitary and health conditions—in short, all the benefits of modern, industrialized society with none of its drawbacks. An idealistic, conflicted vision, it was impossible to attain. Although her goal of eliminating illiteracy nationwide by 1930 had a nice ring to it, not surprisingly, she failed to achieve it. In reality, in 1911 when she began the literacy work and in 1934 when she ended it, in Kentucky and much of the Appalachian South, the road to progress was still the road that led out of the mountains.

But guided by their vision of progress and determined to make the state more responsive to the needs of its citizens, hundreds of women like Stewart, whether suffragists, child labor advocates, settlement house workers, or educators, set a maternalist agenda designed to harness the power of the state to the amelioration of social ills. Stewart was part of an older generation of such reformers who based their ideas of social welfare provision on the traditional view of the male breadwinner earning a family wage to support his family. Many of this generation believed that woman's first duty was to home and children, but this did not preclude them from choosing between a family and a public career. Few had both. Their activism stretched from the turn of the century well into the 1920s, changing over time to both facilitate and accommodate woman's move into the public sphere.

Stewart was heavily influenced by this generation of women and by the reform culture they created. She not only adopted their tactics and conformed to the trends they set but also patterned her public identity after three of their greatest achievers, Jane Addams, Ida Tarbell, and Carrie Chapman Catt. Each had a characteristic she admired and sought to emulate. From Addams she took spiritual strength and tried to adopt her saintly and "Christ-like" demeanor. She idealized Tarbell for her ability to present "truth" in such compelling clarity. Catt offered an organizational ability and dynamic public persona that Stewart thought necessary for success. Stewart learned from these women's ideas and methods, and took comfort and confidence from their advice. In fact, she sought to transform herself in the image of her three heroes and to become a southern incarnation of all three. Ultimately, however, their greatness eluded her.

Stewart's life and work document the persistence of a reform ethos that spanned the first two decades of the twentieth century and that still found expression in the New Deal era. It points up some of the complex strands, ideas, and shifting coalitions that have exercised generations of historians in their quest conclusively to delineate the essence of progressivism.[7] Her work is particularly instructive, since in her crusade she represents two opposing strands of progressive reform. On the one hand, she appears to be an agent of upper-class paternalism who sought to impose middle-class values and culture on rural adults living in a poverty-stricken region. On the other, she dispensed the empowering elixir of learning so that adults could become productive agents of change in their own rural communities, thus carrying on the traditions of the Danish folk schools she admired and laying the intellectual groundwork for institutions like the Highlander Folk School established by Myles Horton in the Tennessee mountains in the early 1930s.[8]

At a time when many in her home state and region feared and despised the extension of federal authority, Stewart led a crusade whose success depended on a strong state and federal government role in economic and social welfare. Socialized in a segregated society, she saw all illiterates as equally handicapped and was determined to provide Moonlight Schools for rural blacks as well as whites. She also focused attention on two other powerless and marginalized groups, Native Americans and the prison population. She wanted to improve their lives; therefore, the books she created for adult readers reflect the contemporary affinity for the trappings of middle-class life, upward mobility, and "progress" as Stewart envisioned it. Although her solutions appear simple, she understood the obstacles illiterates encountered. She believed, however, that with the help of thousands of volunteers working with adults in their local communities, those obstacles could be overcome.

Like settlement house work, "muckraking," and agitation for suffrage and world peace, the literacy crusade had a definite goal, but its outcome was not only hard to measure; it was also hard to define. Although Stewart amassed statistics on the link between literacy and various social ills and used them to convince legislators of the practicality of supporting her cause, such figures were imprecise and difficult to document. Thus her measure became the numbers of illiterates taught, and she naturally developed a vested interest in the standard that defined literacy. The record of the illiteracy crusade in Kentucky and across the country reflected phenomenal success when based on her standard of completion of the second *Country Life Reader,* but many educators questioned this as an adequate measure of literacy.

Moonlight Schools, in the twenty-three years of their existence, taught more than 700,000 Americans to read and write. More than 100,000 of these were Kentuckians. Four states whose illiteracy rates led the nation offered impressive numbers taught: Georgia claimed 40,848; Alabama, 41,726; South Carolina, 49,145; and Louisiana, 108,351.[9] Census statistics confirm that significant reduction in illiteracy did take place. For example, Stewart's home state of Kentucky had an illiteracy rate of 12.1 percent in 1910. By 1920, the figure had been reduced to 8.4 percent, and it fell further to 6.6 percent in 1930. Louisiana decreased its percentage from 29 in 1910 to 13.5 in 1930. Arizona, a state where Stewart was very active, reduced its percentage from 15.3 in 1920 to 10.1 in 1930. The nationwide rate fell from 6 percent in 1920 to 4.3 percent in 1930.[10]

Cora Wilson Stewart's illiteracy crusade was a grassroots movement, steeped in the rhetoric of progress and self-improvement and carried out largely by voluntary effort, but its long-term success depended on fundamental structural change in the way educational services were provided and delivered. As Kathryn Kish Sklar and others have shown, women needed "access to the institutional power and positions of public authority" held by men, and men in positions of power and authority needed the grassroots support that women, particularly organized women, could provide.[11] Stewart's network included an army of clubwomen, and she traded on their potential as voters both before and after passage of the Nineteenth Amendment.

Although she did not eliminate illiteracy as she had hoped, or change the world in a single generation as she intended, Stewart shared her "failure" with many other progressive reformers of her day. Reforming women across the country waged campaigns that did not see fruition for decades. Many historians see the New Deal as a culmination of female reform activity that began during the Progressive Era, and the literacy crusade is no exception.[12] In fact, one of the outcomes of Federal Emergency Relief Agency (FERA) and Works Progress Administration (WPA) education programs was remarkably similar to one that Stewart considered important for the Moonlight Schools. The primary goal of the FERA and WPA programs was to employ out-of-work teachers and provide vocational education, but their most striking accomplishment was in the field of "education for avocational and leisure-time activities."[13] Although it was secondary to her emphasis on literacy and progress, Stewart had always stressed the social importance of learning to read and write. It could put people in touch with distant relatives and friends and fill their few leisure hours with "culture" and learning.

Sadly, Stewart saw few similarities between the New Deal work and her own. When she left public work, she did so with the apprehension that she had failed in the larger goal of removing illiteracy because the standard set by the new federal programs meant that the thousands who had passed through the Moonlight Schools did so with a level of skills that fell short of the new criteria for literacy. Moreover, she could perhaps have left the work more content with its potential for future success had she believed it was in good hands, but Cora Wilson Stewart, the crusading reformer, could see little of value in the methods and approaches of the "technique people" who were attempting to institutionalize adult education programs across the country. In her view, they had university degrees and professional training, but they simply lacked the inspiration to do the job. Their formal, and in her view sterile, methods would not facilitate the growth of individual confidence and personal satisfaction instilled by her voluntary, "each one teach one" approach.

Cora Wilson Stewart's faith in humankind was almost as strong as her faith in God. She saw great potential for change in the movement to which she devoted her life, and she loved to quote the old mountaineer who once remarked that the Moonlight Schools had taken his community from moonshine and bullets to lemonade and Bibles. Stewart's "innovative nostalgia" led her to envision a world transformed by full literacy, literacy brought not by trained professionals and precise lists of words memorized but by women volunteers who by nature were better able to inspire and encourage new learners to their task.

Always a devout woman, she prayed intently for guidance and relied on prayer and meditation to help her make the decisions that governed both her public and her private life. In 1933, at the invitation of her friend and consultant to the NIC, Sally Lucas Jean, she attended a meeting of the Oxford Group at the Plaza Hotel in New York. A spiritual organization that called itself "a Christian revolution for remaking the world," the group was founded by Frank Buchman in 1921. The Oxford Group adopted the premise that "national problems begin to straighten out when individuals begin to listen to God—and carry out what they hear." It advocated "world-changing through life-changing" and impressed upon its members the conviction that "God-controlled personalities make God-controlled nationalities. . . . A true patriot gives his life to bring his nation under God's control."[14] Her introduction to the group filled a developing void in her life that her work with the federal housing program could not satisfy.[15]

Stewart's interest in the group drew her to read, study, and meditate and to ask for divine guidance in making a decision about joining. Buchmanism required individuals to begin their spiritual journey by changing themselves rather than seeking to change the "other person." The next step called for complete surrender to God, allowing divine direction of "ambitions, desires, plans, talents, time, and money." Converts also pledged themselves to "four absolutes," absolute honesty, absolute purity, absolute unselfishness, and absolute love. Finally, they had to make restitution to anyone they may have wronged and reconciliation with anyone from whom they had been estranged. The Oxford Group also advocated a quiet time every day in which the individual listened quietly so as to receive God's guidance.[16]

Stewart attended a session on 3 May 1934, and thought her prayers for understanding had been answered. She believed God's "instructions came again" to go to an Oxford Group prayer counselor, Cella Leonard, and pray with her concerning the sacrifices Stewart had to make. The two women talked of Stewart's "sins" and "referred to Olive Jones," the woman who had challenged her leadership of the National Conference on Illiteracy and whom Stewart believed almost single-handedly prevented her election to the NEA presidency. During prayer, she wrote, God asked her to decide whether it was more important that she carry learning or that she carry salvation. If the illiterates "are dear to you are they not dearer to Christ?'" During a three-month period of soul-searching, Stewart felt compelled to write Olive Jones, whom she considered "a stumbling block" to her participation in the Oxford Group. She also distinctly heard a message from God that profoundly changed her life: "You will have to be a humble follower for a while. The role of great leader is not yours."[17]

The Oxford Group appealed to Stewart at a critical time in her life. She had always earnestly believed that God had called her to the illiteracy work, but just as earnestly, she believed God had told her to leave it.[18] Moreover, she believed another equally important task lay before her: "I am shown that because of the present crisis in America I am to be used in a very active way . . . with people of culture and persons in high places." The new calling did not, however, separate her "from the task of seeing that illiterates of the nation and the world are enlightened and brought to Christ."[19]

Although she had fallen a few years short of her goal of ten years service to her state, ten to the nation, and ten to the world, Cora Wilson Stewart had nevertheless contributed to society's understanding and awareness of a major social problem. By joining the Oxford Group, she believed, she now had the opportunity to render even greater service to God and humanity. Buchmanism, as it was sometimes called, did not require an ordained clergy, and accepted the service of lay ministers, including women.[20] This opportunity to serve, combined with the group's plan for changing the world, had great appeal to an aging crusader who had always expected to change the world through literacy.

The Oxford Group offered a vision for a new world, one in which every man, woman, and child could participate and share. The group's leaders believed that global problems, including the world economic crisis, could be solved through "Moral Rearmament." The remedy lay "in a return to those simple home truths that some of us learned at our mother's knee, and which many of us have forgotten and neglected—honesty, purity, unselfishness, and love." The Oxford Group movement offered a new name but an old cause for Stewart, one that she had always espoused but "neglected" because of her literacy work. Frank Buchman's message of Moral Rearmament appealed to millions of Americans, attracting intellectuals and prominent politicians, noted churchmen and ordinary people. Proponents included President Franklin D. Roosevelt, former president Herbert Hoover, Secretary of State Cordell Hull, Speaker of the House William B. Bankhead, and Senate majority leader and fellow Kentuckian, Alben W. Barkley.[21] Its offer of intense spiritual revival resonated with Stewart at a time when her own spirit had flagged, her energy sapped by years of travel and hard work, and her enthusiasm dashed by conflict and disagreement. Stewart's attraction to the movement lay in its striking simplicity. It immediately commanded her devotion, fired her with new energy, and brought spiritual contentment.[22]

Stewart's immersion in the Oxford Group did not cause her to abandon the illiteracy work. Instead, it came at a time of personal uncertainty and insecurity when the work appeared to be ending and her most desperate efforts could not sustain it. The Oxford Group's promise of profound change in individuals and nations perhaps resonated with her own faith in the power of education to change lives and kindled a renewed hope that her work would eventually bring about fundamental change in American society.[23]

If she failed to eradicate illiteracy, Cora Wilson Stewart nevertheless made an important contribution. It has, however, taken decades for that contribution to be recognized by the profession that initially rejected her approach. Although adult education moved in directions that Stewart did not foresee and perhaps would not have approved, she played an important role in its development and is now seen as an important pioneer in the field of literacy training. She saw literacy as a basic human right and dedicated her life to extending its benefits. Confident that children of educated parents stood a better chance of becoming educated adults themselves, she promoted the idea that through the intergenerational transfer of skills and attitudes, parents can influence the subsequent educational achievement of their children, a philosophy that currently drives contemporary family literacy programs in the United States and Canada.[24]

In addition, Stewart pioneered the "kinesthetic" method of learning to write one's name by tracing its imprint in a cardboard template, a magical technique that was passed on through Wil Lou Gray to Septima Poinsette Clark, the civil rights leader and teacher from the Highlander Folk School. Clark noted that "the single greatest thing" this achieves is enabling "a man to raise his head a little higher; knowing how to sign their names, many of those men and women . . . FEEL different. Suddenly they had become a part of the community; they were on their way toward first-class citizenship."[25]

In the years since Cora Wilson's Stewart's first Moonlight School campaign, hundreds of thousands of adults have experienced the empowering gift of literacy, yet millions more have not. Her home state still lags behind the rest of the nation in educational attainment, and thirty-eight of the forty Kentucky counties with the highest illiteracy levels are located in Appalachia. Kentucky's rural inhabitants still have lower high school graduation rates, less access to health care, and lower average incomes than city dwellers despite the efforts of a functioning Department of Adult Education and Literacy located in the Cabinet for Workforce Development. Forty percent of Kentucky's working-age population functions at the two lowest levels of literacy, and "large portions of the state have literacy levels that could only compare with those of developing nations."[26]

Cora Wilson Stewart founded the Moonlight Schools and dedicated her life to teaching the nation's illiterates. In doing so, she inspired a generation of volunteers who pressured politicians to support the cause with legislation and funding and enlisted educational leaders to promote and institutionalize the work. Despite remarkable successes, her crusade was marginalized by professional educators whose faith in university training led them to disavow and even disparage the voluntary effort that won only sporadic government backing. Literacy practitioners now see Stewart's efforts as heroic and seek to achieve her goal of moving adult literacy education from the margins to the mainstream of educational policy and practice. Like her, they recognize the centrality of adult literacy to high educational attainment and call attention to the "multiplier effects" of adult literacy education. Better-educated adults produce better-educated children and demand better schooling for them.[27]

When Cora Wilson Stewart suffered a fatal heart attack on 2 December 1958, she may have believed that because she failed to wipe out illiteracy, her hopes and dreams for a literate nation would die with her. But the educational needs of her state and nation continued to grow, and those who have attempted to understand and meet those needs continue to look to her crusade for both wisdom and example.

Notes

Preface

1. For the most part, Stewart has been portrayed as a hero whose selfless dedication to the Moonlight School movement made her a legend in her own time. See James M. Gifford, "Cora Wilson Stewart and the 'Moonlight School' Movement," in *Appalachia/America: Proceedings of the 1980 Appalachian Studies Conference,* ed. Wilson Somerville (Johnson City, TN: Appalachian Consortium Press, 1981), 169–78; and James McConkey, *Rowan's Progress* (New York: Pantheon, 1992). Willie Nelms was similarly uncritical. Although his work fleshes out the details of Stewart's career and provides important information about the literacy crusade, his analysis does not address the important gender and class aspects of her life and work. Willie Nelms, *Cora Wilson Stewart: Crusader against Illiteracy* (Jefferson, NC: McFarland, 1997), 1–4. His book is an extension of his master's thesis of the same title, University of Kentucky, 1973; see also his two articles "Cora Wilson Stewart and the Crusade against Illiteracy in Kentucky," *Register of the Kentucky Historical Society* 74 (1976): 10–29; and "Cora Wilson Stewart and the Crusade against Illiteracy in Kentucky, 1916–1920, *Register of the Kentucky Historical Society* 82 (Spring 1984): 151–69. Florence Estes's doctoral dissertation critically examined the rhetoric of the crusade and Stewart's motivations as an agent of educational change in a balanced account that exposed some of the contradictions of the literacy campaign and of Stewart herself. See Florence Estes, "Cora Wilson Stewart and the Moonlight Schools of Kentucky: A Case Study in the Rhetorical Uses of Literacy" (Ph.D. diss., University of Kentucky, 1988).

2. In his introduction, McConkey, cited previously, calls for an analysis of Stewart and her work within the context of Progressive Era reform, but it was beyond the scope of his study; Nelms, also cited earlier, correctly characterizes Stewart as a progressive and calls her an "educational entrepreneur" who created a career for herself in educating adults. Estes, cited earlier, established some of the reform context as well. Historians disagree about progressive individual and group identity; thus, characterizing Stewart as a progressive becomes problematic, since she fits few of the traditional descriptions of

the progressive reformer. Hers was clearly a popular movement with middle-class elements, but she was not a privileged white male. In a sense, the literacy movement can be meshed with the "search for order," but it had a rural rather than an urban cast. Thus, neither the older interpretation of Richard Hofstadter, *The Age of Reform: From Bryan to F.D.R.* (New York: Knopf, 1955), nor that of Robert H. Wiebe, *The Search for Order, 1877–1920* (New York: Hill and Wang, 1967), provides an adequate model for analyzing her movement. Certainly the forces of conservatism were at work in the literacy movement, and Gabriel Kolko's influential work, *The Triumph of Conservatism* (New York: Free Press, 1963), and other organizational models shed light on some of the struggles within the education profession. Much more useful, however, are revisionist interpretations that note the diversity of progressivism and the coalitions that afforded momentum for its disparate impulses. Elizabeth Sanders, in *Roots of Reform: Farmers, Workers, and the American State, 1877–1917* (Chicago: University of Chicago Press, 1999), maintains that Populists inspired a great deal of progressive legislation and suggests that agrarianism needs to be reexamined as a catalyst for reform. She argues that historians should focus on what progressives did as opposed to what they thought and move backward from legislation to the ideas that shaped it, rather than from ideas to the legislation progressives managed to pass. Influential interpretations of southern progressivism generally locate reformers in the middle-class urban environment described by Arthur S. Link's seminal article "The Progressive Movement in the South, 1870–1914," *North Carolina Historical Review* 23 (1946): 172–89; and C. Vann Woodward's classic *Origins of the New South, 1877–1913* (Baton Rouge: University of Louisiana Press, 1951), 369–95. Jack Temple Kirby's placement of the progressive impulse in the "frustrations and yearnings of the rural and small town masses" and his articulation of the rural protests of the nineteenth century as a link to those of the twentieth offer one of the least problematic analytical niches for categorizing Stewart and the illiteracy crusade. See *Darkness at the Dawning: Race and Reform in the Progressive South* (Philadelphia: Lippincott, 1972), 1–3, 26–27.

Introduction

1. See, for example, Robyn Muncy, *Creating a Female Dominion in American Reform, 1890–1935* (New York: Oxford University Press, 1991); Noralee Frankel and Nancy S. Dye, eds., *Gender, Class, Race, and Reform in the Progressive Era* (Lexington: University Press of Kentucky, 1991); Barbara Kuhn Campbell, *The "Liberated Woman" of 1914: Prominent Women in the Progressive Era* (Ann Arbor: University of Michigan Research Press, 1979); and Seth Koven and Sonya Michel, eds., *Mothers of a New World: Maternalist Politics and the Origins of Welfare States* (New York: Routledge, 1993).

2. On the personalities of two of the reformers, May Stone and Katherine Pettit, see Jess Stoddart, *Challenge and Change in Appalachia: The Story of the Hindman Settlement School* (Lexington: University Press of Kentucky, 2002); on Alice Lloyd, see P. David Searles, *A College for Appalachia: Alice Lloyd on Caney Creek* (Lexington: University Press of Kentucky, 1995).

3. Stewart approved of the work at Pine Mountain and maintained in a letter to Ethel Zande that she had answered questions about it "not fewer than a thousand times"

as she lectured around the country. She assured Zande of her unfailing support despite Kentucky politicians' unwillingness to fully support education in the state. CWS to Ethel Zande, 9 July 1927, Cora Wilson Stewart Papers, Special Collections, Margaret I. King Library, University of Kentucky, Lexington (hereafter cited as Stewart Papers).

4. Lowell K. Harrison and James C. Klotter, *A New History of Kentucky* (Lexington: University Press of Kentucky, 1997), 383, note that Stewart's "publicity efforts overstated her importance and the results"; James C. Klotter, in *Kentucky: Portrait in Paradox, 1900–1950* (Frankfort, KY: Kentucky Historical Society, 1996), 164, concludes that the illiteracy crusade failed in part because of the personification of the crusade in one person. He also questions the veracity of her statistics.

5. Harrison and Klotter, in *New History of Kentucky*, 383, conclude that the drop in the state's illiteracy rate was roughly the same as in the decade before the schools were founded. David E. Whisnant, in *All That Is Native and Fine: The Politics of Culture in an American Region* (Chapel Hill: University of North Carolina Press, 1983), xvi, 90, opened a long and ongoing debate on the motives and outcomes of Appalachian reformers. He sees the missionaries and social settlement workers as primary agents of the destruction of mountain culture. Identifying them as cultural imperialists, he is especially critical of the motivations of Pettit and Stone. Other authors, including Stoddart and Searles, cited earlier, have argued that historians should examine both the positive and the negative outcomes of mountain uplift work.

6. Although others have done so, it is perhaps inaccurate to describe these as diaries. One set consists of about twenty pieces of loose paper, approximately three inches by two inches. Others are on paper commonly used for making lists, while still others are in small bound pads. Stewart Papers.

7. CWS to Marion McCrea, niece of Cora Wilson Stewart, 7 January 1953, McCrea Collection, in author's possession.

8. CWS to Marion McCrea, 3 May 1955, McCrea Collection.

9. Letters and postcards to Marion McCrea and other family members, McCrea Collection.

10. Diary entry 20 January 1926; diary entry undated (probably later the same month), Stewart Papers.

11. Allen F. Davis, *American Heroine: The Life and Legend of Jane Addams* (New York: Oxford University Press, 1973), x, xi, 103–6; Davis, *Spearheads for Reform: The Social Settlements and the Progressive Movement, 1890–1914* (New York: Oxford University Press, 1967), 81, 104, 148.

12. The Stewart Collection comprises more than sixty boxes and includes correspondence and public documents from presidents, governors, and public officials at all levels. The collection includes official copies of published reports from state and federal agencies, documents and correspondence from and to educational leaders that are not available through either the NEA or the KEA, publications from the KFWC and GFWC not easily found even in large national manuscript collections, and an incredible array of photographs and newspaper clippings.

13. See, for example, McConkey, *Rowan's Progress*. Although many of McConkey's observations of Stewart's life and work are valid, he relied heavily on retrospectives printed

in the *Morehead News,* some of which contained both factual and interpretive errors. I am indebted to Marion McCrea and Noi Doyle, niece and great-niece, and to Bunyan Wilson Jr., whose father was Cora's brother, for their oral history interviews and for the photographs and documents they have lent for this study. Marion McCrea, telephone conversations with author, 17 July 1995 and 9 June 2003; Bunyan Wilson Jr., interview by author, notes, Ashland, Kentucky, 17 July 1995; Noi Doyle, interview by author, notes, Lexington, Kentucky, 19 July 1995.

1. The Making of a Reformer

1. Doyle interview; Annie E. Wilson family Bible, copy furnished to author by Doyle.

2. Doyle interview.

3. "Data furnished by Public Library, Morehead, Kentucky"; "The Founder of the Illiteracy Movement"; entry in "autograph book" by Bunyan Wilson, Stewart Papers.

4. Doyle interview; Bunyan Wilson interview; Ann Halley Diary; CWS to Homer Wilson, 12 February 1940, Stewart Papers.

5. Annie Wilson family Bible; CWS to Homer Wilson, 12 February 1940.

6. Census data list the entire Wilson family and their birth dates. They lived on Main Street. Bunyan is listed as a lawyer, Homer a clerk, Cora a teacher. The eldest brother, Clefford, is listed as a physician, boarding at the home of James Hurley. 1900 Census of the United States, microfilm, Kentucky Department of Libraries and Archives, Frankfort, Kentucky.

7. Bunyan Wilson interview.

8. Quotations are from CWS to Homer Wilson, 12 February 1940.

9. "The Founder of the Illiteracy Movement"; CWS to Homer Wilson, 12 February 1940; Bunyan Wilson, Doyle interviews.

10. John Kleber, ed., *The Kentucky Encyclopedia* (Lexington: University Press of Kentucky, 1992), 783–84.

11. Stuart Sprague's *A Pictorial History of Eastern Kentucky* (Norfolk/Virginia Beach: Donning, 1986), 59, shows a panoramic view of the town. The Main Street area, listed in the 1900 and 1910 census records as home to the Wilsons, is dotted with neat, white frame single- and two-story dwellings; see also Rowan County Historical Society, *Rowan County, Kentucky: A Pictorial History* (Paducah, KY: Turner, 2001), frontispiece. The Wilsons built a house on what is now known as Wilson Avenue, at Fifth Street. Jack D. Ellis, *Morehead Memories: True Stories from Eastern Kentucky* (Ashland, KY: Jesse Stuart Foundation, 2001), 23; and Photo Archives, Stewart Papers.

12. Klotter, *Portrait in Paradox,* 15–34.

13. CWS to Homer Wilson, 12 February 1940; Ellis, *Morehead Memories,* 239–46.

14. Quotation is from Samuel Johnson, "Life in the Kentucky Mountains. By a Mountaineer," reprinted in *Appalachian Images in Folk and Popular Culture,* 2nd ed., ed. W. K. McNeil (Knoxville: University of Tennessee Press, 1995), 176. Some reasons that many Appalachian families chose to avoid schooling are explored by Una Mae Lange Reck and Gregory C. Reck in "Living Is More Important Than Schooling: Schools and Self Concept in Appalachia," *Appalachian Journal* 27 (Winter 2000): 152–59. Also see

Klotter, *Portrait in Paradox*, 48, 49, for a description of rural sensibilities at the turn of the twentieth century.

15. Diary entry in Stewart's hand, 14 January 1926, Stewart Papers. For a brief overview of the various ties that bind people in this region, see Loyal Jones, *Appalachian Values* (Ashland, KY: Jesse Stuart Foundation, 1994), 39–52.

16. Ida Clyde Clarke, "The Moonlight-School Lady," *Pictorial Review,* January 1926.

17. Diary entry in Stewart's hand, 14 January 1926, Stewart Papers. Anne Firor Scott, *The Southern Lady: From Pedestal to Politics, 1830–1930* (Chicago: University of Chicago Press, 1970), 122–23. Many have used the term "southern lady," and the literature on southern women is vast. Margaret Ripley Wolfe has drawn conclusions that allow the extension of this term to the highlands of the upper South and has also accurately noted the pitfalls in *Daughters of Canaan: A Saga of Southern Women* (Lexington: University Press of Kentucky, 1995), 7. Although most historical figures do not perfectly fit the garments historians construct for them, this classification allows a fuller understanding of the impulses that drove Cora Wilson Stewart to undertake a crusade that occupied most of her adult life and provides useful insights into the public willingness to accept her ministrations.

18. Maxine Schwartz Seller, ed., *Women Educators in the United States, 1820–1993: A Bio-bibliographical Sourcebook* (Westport, CT: Greenwood Press, 1994), xv; Margaret Smith Crocco, Petra Munro, and Kathleen Weiler, *Pedagogies of Resistance: Women Educator Activists, 1880–1960* (New York: Teachers College Press, 1999), 1, 2.

19. Dewey W. Grantham, *Southern Progressivism: The Reconciliation of Progress and Tradition* (Knoxville: University of Tennessee Press, 1983), 208; Campbell, *"Liberated Woman" of 1914*, 2, 3.

20. Marjorie Julian Spruill, *New Women of the New South: The Leaders of the Woman Suffrage Movement in the Southern States* (New York: Oxford University Press, 1993), 39, 40–45; Wolfe, *Daughters of Canaan*, 141.

21. Nancy Hewitt, *Women's Activism and Social Change: Rochester, New York, 1822–1872* (Ithaca, NY: Cornell University Press, 1984), 44.

22. Bunyan Wilson interview; interview with Virginia Williams, Morehead, KY, 12 October 1990, in "Cora Wilson Stewart and the Moonlight School Oral History Project," Camden Carroll Library Special Collections, Morehead State University (hereafter cited as MSU/CWS Oral Histories). For a discussion of the medical profession in Appalachia at this time, see Sandra Lee Barney, *Authorized to Heal: Gender, Class, and the Transformation of Medicine in Appalachia, 1880–1930* (Chapel Hill: University of North Carolina Press, 2000), 4–8.

23. Bunyan Wilson interview; Cyrus Blaud, a fifty-year-old black, is listed as a "servant" in the household of Homer Wilson in the 1910 Census of the United States, microfilm, Kentucky Department of Libraries and Archives, Frankfort, Kentucky. On blacks in Kentucky at this time, see Klotter, *Portrait in Paradox*, 37, 38; William H. Turner, "The Demography of Black Appalachia: Past and Present," in *Blacks in Appalachia*, ed. William H. Turner and Edward J. Cabbell (Lexington: University Press of Kentucky, 1985), 237–43.

24. "The Founder of the Illiteracy Movement," Stewart Papers. For a history of the Disciples, including information on the Morehead church, see Alonzo W. Fortune, *The*

Disciples in Kentucky (Lexington, KY: Convention of the Christian Churches in Kentucky, 1932), 228, 356–61. Cora and her sisters, neither of whom pursued a career, were very active in church and civic organizations, according to Stewart's niece Noi Doyle. Doyle's adoptive mother, Cora's sister Flora, was "active in every club, and president of several." Doyle interview. See also *Huntington Herald Dispatch*, 13 August 1938.

25. Note in Stewart's hand, 17 January 1924; undated note in Stewart's hand, Stewart Papers.

26. Robert M. Crunden, *Ministers of Reform: The Progressives' Achievement in American Civilization, 1889–1920* (New York: Basic Books, 1982), 4, 5, 17, 18, 99–102.

27. Ibid., 17.

28. All the quotations are taken from her memoir and history of the Moonlight movement, Cora Wilson Stewart, *Moonlight Schools for the Emancipation of Adult Illiterates* (New York: Dutton, 1922), 11, 12, 13. The "young mountain balladeer" reference in the stories is particularly interesting and timely, given the emphasis placed on mountain music at the Hindman Settlement School, where Katherine Pettit had begun to collect lyrics as early as 1900. See Stoddart, *Challenge and Change in Appalachia*, 87. Kentucky was home to the first folk music society, organized in 1912. See Benjamin Filene, *Romancing the Folk: Public Memory and American Roots Music* (Chapel Hill: University of North Carolina Press, 2000), 4–8.

29. Ellis, *Morehead Memories*, 245–46. The former director of Morehead State University's Camden Carroll Library, Dr. Jack Ellis has a large collection of Stewart papers and documents, cited herein as Ellis Collection. He learned a great deal about Stewart from his father and grandfather, who were both active in school affairs in Rowan County and were acquainted with her. Dr. Jack Ellis, interview by author, notes, Morehead, Kentucky, 19 November 1993.

30. The term "contemporary ancestors" was used by William Goodell Frost, one of the most active purveyors of the Anglo-Saxon worthiness myth. His intent was to dispel negative stereotypes, but instead the term furthered the image of the region as backward. William G. Frost, "Berea College," *Berea Quarterly* 1 (May 1895): 24. On Frost and his efforts in the mountains, see Shannon H. Wilson, "Window on the Mountains: Berea's Appalachia, 1870–1930," *Filson Club History Quarterly* 64 (July 1990): 384–99.

31. The head of the Southern Highlands Division of the Russell Sage Foundation, John C. Campbell, wrote that more things were known that were not true about Appalachia than about any other American place. John C. Campbell, *The Southern Highlander and His Homeland* (1921; reprint, with a foreword by Rupert Vance and an introduction by Henry D. Shapiro, Lexington: University Press of Kentucky, 1969), 3.

32. Gordon B. McKinney, *Southern Mountain Republicans, 1865–1900: Politics and the Appalachian Community* (1978; reprint, with a foreword by Durwood Dunn and a new preface, Knoxville: University of Tennessee Press, 1998), xii.

33. Henry Shapiro, *Appalachia on Our Mind: The Southern Mountains and Mountaineers in American Consciousness, 1870–1920* (Chapel Hill: University of North Carolina Press, 1978), 32–50; Hambleton Tapp and James C. Klotter, *Kentucky: Decades of Discord, 1865–1900* (Frankfort, KY: Kentucky Historical Society, 1977); and Klotter, *Portrait in Paradox*, 51–72.

34. Ellen Church Semple, "The Anglo-Saxons of the Kentucky Mountains," *Bulletin*

of the American Geographical Society 42 (August 1910), 565–93; Horace Kephart, *Our Southern Highlanders: A Narrative of Adventure in the Southern Appalachians and a Study of Life among the Mountaineers* (1913 and 1924; reprint, Knoxville: University of Tennessee Press, 1984). On the "myth," see Shapiro, *Appalachia on Our Mind,* 32–50, 113–115; see also Altina Waller, *Feud: Hatfields, McCoys, and Social Change in Appalachia, 1860–1900* (Chapel Hill: University of North Carolina Press, 1988); and Whisnant, · *All That Is Native and Fine.*

35. James C. Klotter, "The Black South and White Appalachia," in Turner and Cabbell, *Blacks in Appalachia,* 52–67.

36. Karen Tice, "School-Work and Mother-Work," *Journal of Appalachian Studies* 4 (Fall 1998): 191.

37. This theme is especially prominent in two articles on the Moonlight Schools that reached national audiences. See David Rankin Barbee, "Freeing America Is Her Huge Job, *Washington Post,* 26 January 1930; and Clarke, "Moonlight-School Lady."

38. Stewart, *Moonlight Schools for the Emancipation of Adult Illiterates,* 53.

39. Tice, "School-Work and Mother-Work," 202, 203. The quotation is from Mary Swain Routzhan, "Presenting Mountain Work to the Public," *Mountain Life and Work,* July 1928, 27–31.

40. Copies of both these stories can be found in Box 37, Stewart Papers. Stewart's casting of the conflict in political and familial terms anticipates more recent interpretations of the political origins of the feuds. See Waller, *Feud.* For an interesting look at how Appalachia appeared to the rest of the nation, see Tommy R. Thompson, "The Image of Appalachian Kentucky in American Popular Magazines," *Register of the Kentucky Historical Society* 91 (Spring 1993): 176–202.

41. "Biographical Notes," Stewart Papers; Bunyan Wilson interview; Ellis interview.

42. Morehead Rowan County Centennial, "Within This Valley," Commemorative Booklet, May 1956; Fannie Madden-Grider and Alvin Madden-Grider, "The Feud That Produced a College," *Rural Kentuckian* 38 (December 1984): 9–12, 18; both in "Rowan County Histories," Special Collections, Camden-Carroll Library, Morehead State University. See also *Days of Anger, Days of Tears,* a popular history of the feud written by two local residents, Juanita Blair and Fred Brown (Morehead, KY: Pioneer Print Service, 1984). On mountain feuding in general, see James C. Klotter, "Feuds in Appalachia: An Overview," *Filson Club Historical Quarterly* 56 (July 1982): 290–317; and Waller, *Feud.* Stories of feuding in the popular press defined a violent Appalachia that became a negative stereotype. See also Allen W. Batteau, *The Invention of Appalachia* (Tucson: University of Arizona Press, 1990), 111–12.

43. John Ed Pearce, *Days of Darkness: The Feuds of Eastern Kentucky* (Lexington: University Press of Kentucky, 1994), 106.

44. Fortune, *Disciples in Kentucky,* 228, 356–61.

45. *Morehead Rowan County News,* 10 May 1956.

46. For a summary of the impact of the feud on the founding of Morehead Normal School, see Donald F. Flatt, *A Light to the Mountains: Morehead State University, 1887–1997* (Ashland, KY: Jesse Stuart Foundation, 1997), 1–12. See also Madden-Grider and Madden-Grider, "The Feud That Produced a College."

47. Klotter, *Portrait in Paradox,* 51–72.

48. Anastasia Sims, *The Power of Femininity in the New South: Women's Organizations and Politics in North Carolina, 1880–1930* (Columbia: University of South Carolina Press, 1997), 80–127; Paula Baker, "The Domestication of Politics: Women and American Political Society, 1780–1920," *American Historical Review* 89 (June 1984): 640–42; Carl N. Degler, *At Odds: Women and the Family in America from the Revolution to Present* (New York: Oxford University Press, 1980), 319–27; Molly Ladd-Taylor, *Mother-Work: Women, Child Welfare, and the State, 1890–1930* (Urbana: University of Illinois Press, 1994), 3–7; Muncy, *Creating a Female Dominion,* 30–31.

49. Scott, *Southern Lady,* 138–42; Fortune, *Disciples in Kentucky,* 360; Doyle interview, 340–65; Lester G. McAllister and William E. Tucker, *Journey in Faith: A History of the Christian Church* (St. Louis, MO: Disciples of Christ, 1975), 175–200. Stewart's involvement with this group is mentioned in numerous articles in scrapbook, Stewart Papers. Both Marion McCrea and Noi Doyle stressed the importance of churchwomen's groups to their family. McCrea, Doyle interviews.

50. "Mountain Work," pamphlet published by the Christian Woman's Board of Missions, Indianapolis, 1908, Stewart Papers.

51. Nancy K. Forderhase, "'The Clear Call of Thoroughbred Women': The Kentucky Federation of Women's Clubs and the Crusade for Education Reform, 1903–1909," *Register of the Kentucky Historical Society* 83 (Winter 1985): 19–35; Forderhase, "Eve Returns to the Garden: Women Reformers in Appalachian Kentucky in the Early Twentieth Century," *Register of the Kentucky Historical Society* 85 (Summer 1987): 237–61; Tice, "School-Work and Mother-Work," 197.

52. Grantham, *Southern Progressivism,* 258; Klotter, *Portrait in Paradox,* 145–47; William A. Link, *The Paradox of Southern Progressivism, 1880–1930* (Chapel Hill: University of North Carolina Press, 1992), 267–74.

53. Woodward, *Origins of the New South,* 397; Grantham, *Southern Progressivism,* 246–58; Klotter, *Portrait in Paradox,* 145–47; Link, *Paradox of Southern Progressivism,* 267–74; McKinney, *Southern Mountain Republicans,* 206, 207. McKinney maintains that prior to 1900, this was the result of Democratic state governments' determination to retain low taxes. McKinney's statistics do not include Rowan but do include neighboring Carter, Elliot, Menifee, and Morgan counties.

54. Klotter, *Portrait in Paradox,* 147–48.

55. Link, *Paradox of Southern Progressivism,* 273, 274.

56. Harrison and Klotter, *New History of Kentucky,* 377–79. Information on the physical condition of the rural schools of the state is also available in the quarterly reports of Frank C. Button, state agent for rural schools. General Education Board, Early Southern Program, Kentucky (microfilm, University of Kentucky Education Library). Rolls 62, 63, 64 (hereafter cited as GEB Microfilm).

57. Nancy Woloch, *Women and the American Experience,* 2nd ed. (New York: McGraw-Hill, 1994), 246–48.

58. Jurgen Herbst, *And Sadly Teach: Teacher Education and Professionalization in American Culture* (Madison: University of Wisconsin Press, 1989), 185–86.

59. Link, *Paradox of Southern Progressivism,* 18, 19.

60. Campbell, *Southern Highlander and His Homeland,* 264–65. "Cousined" is the mountain equivalent of nepotism.

61. Diary entry in Stewart's hand, 17 January 1923, notebook, Stewart Papers.

62. Jackie M. Blount, *Destined to Rule the Schools: Women and the Superintendency, 1873–1995* (Albany: State University of New York Press, 1998), 1, 2; Blount, "Ella Flagg Young and the Chicago Schools," in *Founding Mothers and Others: Women Educational Leaders during the Progressive Era,* ed. Alan R. Sadovnik and Susan F. Semel (New York: Palgrave, 2002), 163–76.

63. Sadovnik, *Founding Mothers,* 3. For a discussion of feminist analyses of gender and schooling, see Kathleen Weiler, *Women Teaching for Change: Gender, Class and Power* (South Hadley, MA: Bergin and Garvey, 1988), 27–56.

64. Jessie O. Yancey to CWS, 11 July 1911; Mattie Dalton to CWS, June [indistinct] 1908, Stewart Papers; Ellis, *Morehead Memories,* 46.

65. Ellis interview; "The Founder of the Illiteracy Movement"; and undated, untitled newspaper clippings, especially from *Advance Kentuckian,* scrapbook, Stewart Papers.

66. Neither Stewart's biographical information sheets nor her diaries mention this marriage or the subsequent divorce. The *Rowan County, Kentucky, Marriage Records 1881–1933* say the marriage bond and record of this marriage is listed on page 94 of *Rowan County Marriage Records,* Book 3. The actual record is not there. It may have been destroyed in a fire that swept through the courthouse at the turn of the century. Although some relatives insist that Cora never married Grant Carey, the divorce is recorded as "Cora Carey vs. U. G. Carey," *Rowan Circuit Court Book #9,* 9 June 1898, 345–46.

67. "The Founder of the Illiteracy Movement," Stewart Papers.

68. "In Memory of Mrs. Annie E. Wilson," eulogy, Stewart Papers; Noi Doyle interview; Marion McCrea interview.

69. McCrea, Doyle, and Wilson interviews.

70. "B. S. Wilson, 1st Mayor of Morehead, Dies at Residence in Ashland," newspaper clipping, 18 August 1938, scrapbook, Stewart Papers; Wilson interview. Interestingly, Stewart does not mention her brother or his term as mayor when she writes about the election.

71. Newspaper clipping, *Mount Sterling Advocate,* 13 August 1901; undated, untitled newspaper clipping; diary entry in Stewart's hand, 17 January 1923, Stewart Papers.

72. Edward Moses Ligon, *A History of Public Education in Kentucky* (Frankfort, KY: Bureau of School Service, 1942), 150.

73. Link, *Paradox of Southern Progressivism,* 13; "Annual Report of the County Superintendent, Rowan County, for the Year Ending June 30, 1910," Box 64, Stewart Papers.

74. Woodward, *Origins of the New South,* 400; Annual Report, Stewart Papers.

75. Paul E. Fuller, "Women's Suffrage," in Kleber, *Encyclopedia of Kentucky,* 965–66; Klotter, *Portrait in Paradox,* 146; "Illiteracy and the Rural School," *Survey* 30 (19 April 1913): 100; Harrison and Klotter, *New History of Kentucky,* 288.

76. David B. Tyack and Elisabeth Hansot, *Managers of Virtue: Public School Lead-*

ership in America, 1820–1980 (New York: Basic Books, 1982), 180–83; see also Joan K. Smith's *Ella Flagg Young: Portrait of a Leader* (Ames, IA: Educational Studies Press, 1977); and Smith, "Progressive School Administration: Ella Flagg Young and the Chicago Schools, 1905–1915," *Journal of the Illinois State Historical Society* 73 (Spring 1980): 27–44.

77. Blount, *Destined to Rule the Schools*, 8, 39–60.

78. Correspondence from Mattie Dalton is extensive. For examples, see especially her letters in April, May, and June 1910, Stewart Papers. For an example of Stewart's column, see "Department of County Superintendents," *Southern School Journal*, GEB Microfilm, Roll 62.

79. D. F. Gray to CWS, 12 August 1910; "Kentucky Woman Mentioned as Probable Candidate for Membership in Blue Grass Delegation"; "Cora Wilson Stewart—Shall Kentucky Be Longer Deprived of Her Services"; "Champions Mrs. Stewart"; and numerous other mostly undated newspaper clippings, scrapbook, Stewart Papers.

80. CWS to Frank Button, undated, GEB Microfilm, Roll 62.

81. Correspondence from McCreary is frequent from 1914 through 1916. Most of his letters are handwritten, and all express his keen admiration, political support, and personal warmth for Stewart. For pertinent examples, see James B. McCreary to CWS, 16 June, 7 and 9 September, and 15 October 1914, Stewart Papers. Although a great deal of correspondence from McCreary can be found in the Stewart Papers, I found no correspondence between the two in the McCreary Papers.

82. Diary entry in Stewart's hand, 17 January 1923, notebook, Stewart Papers.

83. Stewart, *Moonlight Schools*, 1–7.

84. "Our Mountain Jewels," 2, Stewart Papers.

85. Ibid., 3, 4, 9.

86. For an overview of the role of the schoolmarm, see Kathryn Kish Sklar, *Catharine Beecher: A Study in American Domesticity* (New Haven, CT: Yale University Press, 1973).

87. See autograph book from her days at the National Normal, Stewart Papers. On Stewart's taste in clothes, physical appearance, and so forth, see correspondence with Mattie Dalton, who wrote several letters a week. The descriptions of Stewart's dress and demeanor were made in author's interview with Norma Powers, a (now deceased) relative, Morehead, Kentucky, 17 November 1993. Miss Powers, who taught school all her life, was related to Stewart, and as a teenager her job was to pick her up at the train station when she arrived in Morehead for a visit; interview with Norma Powers, 23 November 1990, in MSU/CWS Oral Histories.

88. Campbell, *"Liberated Woman" of 1914,* 80.

89. Ellis, Wilson, McCrea interviews. Documentation of the first marriage to Stewart was probably also lost in the courthouse fire. Their subsequent remarriage is recorded, however, and indicates that the bride, Miss Cora Wilson, was twenty-nine years old and embarking upon her third marriage. This same bond notes that it is the second marriage for Stewart, age twenty-six. Rowan County, Kentucky, Marriage Book 5, 1904–1906, 87; Bunyan Wilson interview; "Wilson Family History," genealogy provided by Noi Doyle.

90. "Affidavit of the Plaintiff," Cora Wilson Stewart, Rowan Circuit Court, 24 March 1910, biographical folder, Box 1; "Deposition of C. C. Nichols," 23 March 1910; "Depo-

sition of Mrs. E. B. McGlone [Stella McGlone, Cora's sister]," 23 March 1910; Stewart Papers.

91. "Petition in Equity," Cora Wilson Stewart vs. Alexander Stewart, Rowan Circuit Court, 23 March 1910, biographical folder, Box 1, Stewart Papers. A. T. Stewart later remarried, but the children of his second marriage knew nothing of his marriage to Cora Wilson until he confided to one son during a visit to Morehead that he had fathered a baby who was buried in a local cemetery. The children of the second marriage said they never knew their father to drink and could not imagine that he had engaged in violence against his first wife. Author's interview with Stewart family, Morehead, Kentucky, 24 November 1999.

92. Ellis interview; Ellis, *Morehead Memories,* 254; Bunyan Wilson in his interview recalled that some in the community claimed the baby was small and unhealthy from birth, a condition they attributed to the tight corsets Cora wore.

93. "The Founder of the Illiteracy Movement"; diary entry in Stewart's hand, 17 January 1923, Stewart Papers.

94. "Judgment against A. T. Stewart," Rowan Circuit Court Books, no. 13, 8 June 1910, 16–17.

95. For many southern women, the fear of being an old maid was intense. Scott, *Southern Lady,* 24.

96. Ellis and Powers interviews.

97. Undated, untitled newspaper clipping, biographical folder, Stewart Papers.

98. Recommendation letters from Nannie E. Fields, 25 September 1908; E. L. McDougle, 30 July 1908; and C. C. Adams, 7 October 1908, Stewart Papers.

99. Numerous letters and newspaper clippings attest to this relationship. See especially correspondence from June through September 1908 and July through August 1914; untitled newspaper clipping, 23 March 1914, scrapbook, Stewart Papers.

100. Barksdale Hamlett, *History of Education in Kentucky,* Bulletin 17:4 (Frankfort, KY: Kentucky Department of Education, July 1914), 195.

101. Ibid.; Thomas D. Clark, *A History of Kentucky* (Lexington, KY: John Bradford Press, 1960), 366–67.

102. Hamlett, *History of Education in Kentucky,* 197–98.

103. Diary entry in Stewart's hand, 30 December 1922; diary entry in Stewart's hand, 17 January 1923; untitled newspaper clipping, 30 October 1909, scrapbook, Stewart Papers.

104. Jessie O. Yancey to CWS, 11 July 1911, Stewart Papers.

105. W. J. Vaughan to CWS, 5 January 1911, Stewart Papers.

106. Mattie Dalton to CWS, 12 October 1910, Stewart Papers.

107. Mattie Dalton to CWS, 12 April 1911, Stewart Papers.

108. Mattie Dalton to CWS, 8 April 1911, Stewart Papers.

109. Quoted in Tyack and Hansot, *Managers of Virtue,* 180; Dalton to CWS, 8 April 1911, Stewart Papers.

110. J. H. Boothe to CWS, 1 July 1911; D. M. Holbrook to CWS, 1 July 1911; Coates's remark is from undated newspaper clipping, scrapbook; J. G. Crabbe to CWS, 6 July 1911, Stewart Papers.

111. Undated newspaper clipping, scrapbook, Stewart Papers.

112. Woodward, *Origins*, 410–13; Roy V. Scott, *The Reluctant Farmer: The Rise of Agricultural Extension to 1914* (Urbana: University of Illinois Press, 1970), 26, 27.

113. Geo. Roberts to CWS, 7 April 1911; Thomas J. Bigstaff to CWS, 21 December 1911, Stewart Papers.

114. Edward H. Reisner to CWS, undated, 1911, Stewart Papers; presidential address to the Kentucky Educational Association's 1912 meeting, Box 22, Cora Wilson Stewart Collection, Special Collections, Camden-Carroll Library, Morehead State University, Morehead, Kentucky (hereafter cited as Stewart Collection, Morehead).

115. Presidential address, KEA.

116. Lawrence A. Cremin, *The Transformation of the School: Progressivism in American Education, 1876–1957* (New York: Knopf, 1961), viii, vix.

117. Link, *Paradox of Southern Progressivism*, 207.

118. For an account of the KFWC's involvement in Kentucky education reform, see Forderhase, "'Clear Call of Thoroughbred Women,'" 19–35. On clubwomen and education, see Karen J. Blair, *The Clubwoman as Feminist: True Womanhood Redefined, 1868–1914* (New York: Holmes and Meier, 1980), 57–92. On the founding and growth of the Louisville club, see Nancy K. Forderhase, "'Limited Only by Earth and Sky': The Louisville Woman's Club and Progressive Reform, 1900–1910," *Filson Club History Quarterly* 59 (July 1985): 327–43. On the traveling libraries in Kentucky, see Mrs. Desha Breckinridge, "The Educational Awakening in Kentucky," *Federation Bulletin*, October 1908, 5, 6; "Shakespeare Club," undated newspaper clipping, scrapbook, Stewart Papers.

119. GFWC women were socialized through their interactions via printed articles and readings, and the federation served as an intermediate institution between the family and the state. Anne Ruggles Gere, *Intimate Practices: Literacy and Cultural Work in U.S. Women's Clubs, 1880–1920* (Urbana: University of Illinois Press, 1997), 13.

120. Caroline Luck to CWS, 8 October 1910, Stewart Papers.

121. The number of letters and notes soliciting Stewart's support, responding to a request from her, or relating some matter of common concern is huge. For numerous examples, see correspondence folders in Box 2, especially Mrs. Desha Breckinridge to CWS, 20 December 1911; Frank C. Button to CWS, 25 January 1910; Caroline A. Luck, 6 October 1910; Mrs. M. E. Harlan to CWS, 2 February 1910, Stewart Papers; Harrison and Klotter, *New History of Kentucky*, 288.

122. Paula Baker, *The Moral Frameworks of Public Life: Gender, Politics, and the State in Rural New York, 1870–1930* (New York: Oxford University Press, 1991), xvi; on Madeline McDowell Breckinridge, see Sophonisba P. Breckinridge, *Madeline McDowell Breckinridge: A Leader in the New South* (Chicago: University of Chicago Press, 1921); Melba Porter Hay, "Madeline McDowell Breckinridge: Her Role in the Kentucky Woman Suffrage Movement, 1908–1920," *Register of the Kentucky Historical Society* 72 (1974): 342–63; and Hay, "Madeline McDowell Breckinridge: Kentucky Suffragist and Progressive Reformer" (Ph.D. diss., University of Kentucky, 1980).

123. This speech appears in both handwritten and typed versions, with some variations in wording but none in theme. This one is in a notepad marked "notes for address." This version was given to a church circle in Louisville, Box 46, Stewart Papers.

124. G. F. Friel to CWS, 21 July 1910; "The Founder of the Illiteracy Movement," Stewart Papers.

125. See 1911 correspondence from Mattie Dalton, G. F. Friel, and numerous others, Stewart Papers.

126. *Louisville Courier Journal,* 18 February 1912.

127. Frank L. McVey, *The Gates Open Slowly: A History of Education in Kentucky* (Lexington: University of Kentucky Press, 1949), 202–3; Porter H. Hopkins, *KEA: The First 100 Years: The History of an Organization, 1857–1957* (Louisville: Kentucky Education Association, 1957), 54.

128. Presidential address, KEA, 1912.

129. *Louisville Courier Journal,* undated, untitled clipping, scrapbook, Stewart Papers.

130. Barbee, "Freeing America Is Her Huge Job."

2. The Moonlight Campaign

1. Stewart, *Moonlight Schools,* 1, 2, 5–7. An excerpt from Roosevelt appears in note form. In it he defines the "backwoodsman" as distinct and vastly different from the rest of America and from Europe.

2. Both Estes and Nelms treat Stewart as a social feminist. The term "social feminism" gained widespread use following William L. O'Neill's articulation of a dichotomy between "social" and "hard-core" feminist activity. His best-known work on the subject is *Everyone Was Brave: A History of Feminism in America* (Chicago: University of Illinois Press, 1971).

3. Nancy F. Cott, "What's in a Name? The Limits of 'Social Feminism'; or, Expanding the Vocabulary of Women's History," *Journal of American History* 76 (December 1989): 800–829.

4. See particularly Ladd-Taylor, *Mother-Work;* and Theda Skocpol, *Protecting Soldiers and Mothers: The Political Origins of Social Policy in the United States* (Cambridge, MA: Belknap Press of Harvard University Press, 1992).

5. Katherine C. Reynolds and Susan L. Schramm, *A Separate Sisterhood: Women Who Shaped Southern Education in the Progressive Era* (New York: Peter Lang, 2002), 127–38.

6. Crocco, Munro, and Weiler, *Pedagogies of Resistance,* 2–3.

7. Robert Disch, *The Future Of Literacy* (Englewood Cliffs, NJ: Prentice-Hall, 1973), 4–5.

8. Harvey J. Graff, *The Literacy Myth: Literacy and Social Structure in the Nineteenth-Century City* (New York: Academic Press, 1979).

9. Carl F. Kaestle, "Studying the History of Literacy," in *Literacy in the United States: Readers and Reading since 1880,* ed. Carl F. Kaestle, Helen Damon-Moore, L. C. Stedman, K. Tinsley, and W. V. Trollinger Jr. (New Haven, CT: Yale University Press, 1991), 3–32.

10. Suzanne de Castell, Allen Luke, and David MacLennan, "On Defining Literacy," in *Literacy, Society, and Schooling: A Reader,* ed. Suzanne de Castell, Allen Luke, and Kieran Egan (Cambridge: Cambridge University Press, 1986), 11.

11. U.S. Department of the Interior, Bureau of Education, "Illiteracy in the United States and an Experiment for Its Elimination," Bulletin 20:530 (Washington, DC: Government Printing Office, 1913), 28, 29.

12. Ibid., 29. Adults, like children, learned at different rates. Some could write a legible letter after seven nights of study.

13. Clarence J. Karier, "Business Values and the Educational State," in *Roots of Crisis: American Education in the Twentieth Century,* ed. Clarence J. Karier, Paul C. Violas, and Joel Spring (Chicago: Rand McNally, 1973), 7.

14. Stewart, presidential address, KEA.; Stewart, *Moonlight Schools,* 17.

15. Stewart, *Moonlight Schools,* 18; emphasis added.

16. Ellis interview.

17. Stewart, *Moonlight Schools,* vii.

18. Ibid., 16; "No Illiteracy Sunday," scrapbook, Stewart Papers.

19. "Facts Every Teacher Should Know: Interesting and Significant Statistics of State School Systems which show the big facts of educational Progress," *Journal of the National Education Association* 10, no. 3 (March 1921): 55. These statistics were compiled by the NEA from figures provided by the U.S. Bureau of Education.

20. Jerrie A. Weaver to CWS, 10 July 1911; on Louisville clubwomen, see Forderhase, "'Limited Only by Earth and Sky,'" 327–43; Ellis, *Mountain Memories,* 254–55.

21. Stewart, *Moonlight Schools,* 21, 22.

22. Clarke, "Moonlight-School Lady."

23. Stewart, *Moonlight Schools,* 27.

24. James Watt Raine, *The Land of Saddle-bags: A Study of the Mountain People of Appalachia* (New York: Published jointly by the Council of Women for Home Missions and Missionary Education Movement of the United States and Canada, 1924), 95–106. Raine concludes a chapter entitled "The Mountains Go to School" with a description of the Moonlight Schools in which he notes the "remarkable loyalty in the teachers and an equally remarkable loyalty in the people to follow such unanimous leadership" (185–88).

25. "The Cora Wilson Stewart Moonlight Schoolhouse," pamphlet published by Morehead State University to commemorate the fiftieth anniversary of Morehead Normal School, Stewart Collection, Morehead; Stewart, *Moonlight Schools,* 21, 22.

26. Cora Wilson Stewart, "Moonlight School Course of Study: War Number" (Frankfort, KY: Kentucky Illiteracy Commission, 1917), 5, 6.

27. U.S. Department of the Interior, Bureau of Education, "Illiteracy in the United States," 34.

28. Stewart, *Moonlight Schools,* 52, 53.

29. Ibid., letters follow page 80. She also backed her official stationery with sample letters, so most correspondence files contain numerous examples.

30. "Illiteracy in the United States," 37; "The Moonlight Schools of Rowan County," *Lexington Herald,* 18 February 1912.

31. U.S. Department of the Interior, Bureau of Education, "Illiteracy in the United States," 34.

32. Teachers who filed their reports and letters from pupils with the Kentucky Illiteracy Commission were, after 1915, given "credit on one branch for one ten weeks' term" by both the Eastern and the Western State Normals and the Berea Normal School.

"Moonlight School Bulletin for 1919" (Frankfort, KY: Kentucky Illiteracy Commission, 1919), 3.

33. M. A. Cassidy to CWS, 17 August 1911, Stewart Papers.

34. "Address delivered before the S.E.A., The Education of the Mountain Child," Box 46, Stewart Papers.

35. Stewart, *Moonlight Schools,* 31–32, 28–29.

36. U.S. Department of the Interior, Bureau of Education, "Illiteracy in the United States." This report used extracts from an article that appeared in the *Louisville Courier-Journal* on 29 December 1912. There are no reliable statistics on the actual numbers of illiterates taught. The data that exist are often unspecific as to numbers and the actual status of students in terms of ability.

37. These statistics are repeated in virtually all the accounts of the Moonlight Schools for 1912. It is, of course, extremely unlikely that the success rate was that high; however, no documents exist to refute them. The key lies in Mrs. Stewart's definition of success—which was simply that the student be able to write his or her name and a simple letter. The level of function no doubt varied considerably.

38. The *Lexington Herald,* although often reflecting its editor's Democratic politics, was frequently at odds with both parties over such causes as the regulation of business, child labor laws, improvements in education, prison reform, and woman suffrage. Its editor, Desha Breckinridge, and his wife, Madeline McDowell, were both leaders of the progressive movement in Kentucky. See James C. Klotter, *The Breckinridges of Kentucky, 1760–1981* (Lexington: University Press of Kentucky, 1986).

39. *Lexington Herald,* 18 February 1912.

40. Crunden, *Ministers of Reform,* 16.

41. Grantham, *Southern Progressivism,* 21–25.

42. Link, *Paradox of Southern Progressivism,* 27.

43. Grantham, *Southern Progressivism,* 16.

44. Harrison and Klotter, *New History of Kentucky,* 278.

45. This description is taken from Ida Clyde Clarke's "Moonlight-School Lady," *Pictorial Review,* January 1926, because it is representative of the flowery and sentimental descriptions of the Moonlighters and of their portrayal as pitiful victims.

46. Klotter, "Black South and White Appalachia," 52–67. Klotter's article describes how the "discovery" of Appalachian whites as a new mission field allowed benevolent workers to turn with a clear conscience away from blacks.

47. CWS to Frank C. Button, 26 May 1915, GEB Microfilm, Roll 62.

48. "Organizing a County for Moonlight Schools," "other materials" folder, Box 45, Stewart Papers.

49. "Facts of Illiteracy in Kentucky Told to Lexington Audience," *Lexington Herald,* 25 November 1914, 1.

50. "Census of Illiterates," Box 65; and "Census of Illiterates," Box 64, Stewart Papers.

51. "Facts of Illiteracy in Kentucky," 1.

52. U.S. Department of the Interior, Bureau of Education, "Illiteracy in the United States," 5.

53. Ibid., 7–23. This kind of language was common throughout the nineteenth and most of the twentieth centuries, but in recent years literacy workers have begun to talk about literacy and degrees of literacy rather than using the term "illiteracy" and the phrase "stamping out illiteracy." See Thomas G. Sticht, "The Rise of the Adult Education and Literacy System in the United States: 1600–2000," in *Annual Review of Adult Learning and Literacy*, vol. 3, ed. J. Comings, B. Garner, and C. Smith (San Francisco: Jossey-Bass, 2002), 10–43.

54. Grantham, *Southern Progressivism*, 301, 302.

55. This is particularly evident in CWS to Frank C. Button, undated letter in GEB Microfilm, roll 62. Also, one of the most powerful local politicians was Judge Albert W. (Allie) Young, whose support Stewart won for her friend Rice Eubanks in his unsuccessful 1911 bid for state superintendent of public instruction. Eubanks wrote to thank her for the support she had won for his candidacy, and mentions his dinner with the judge: "I am glad to know that you have so many friends in your county and I hope I may serve them and the state." Stewart's friendly relationship with Judge Young is interesting because her brother Bun Wilson was frequently at odds with him. In fact, the family credits the judge with Bun's decision to leave Morehead for Ashland. Rice Eubank to CWS, 19 April 1911; Wilson interview.

56. "List of Prizes in Moonlight Schools," in GEB Microfilm, roll 62.

57. State of Kentucky, Kentucky Illiteracy Commission, "First Biennial Report, 1915–1916" (Louisville, KY, 1916), 2–9; State of Kentucky, Kentucky Illiteracy Commission, "Report of the Kentucky Illiteracy Commission, 1916–1920" (Louisville, KY, 1920), 6–7.

58. Numerous newspaper clippings, most untitled, esp. *Jackson Times*, 24 April 1914; *Corbin Times*, 17 July 1914, scrapbook, Stewart Papers. See also *Lexington Herald*, 26 April 1914.

59. "Mrs. Stewart Makes Eloquent Speech," undated newspaper clipping, scrapbook, Stewart Papers.

60. Theda Skocpol makes the point that certain categories of needy citizens were willingly surrendered to women in *Protecting Soldiers and Mothers*, 371–72.

61. Numerous newspaper clippings; see *Lexington Herald*, 12 February 1914; William F. DeMoss, "Wiping Out Illiteracy in Kentucky," *Illustrated World*, 828–32, undated copy in Dr. Jack Ellis's Cora Wilson Stewart Collection.

62. *Lexington Herald*, 12 February 1914.

63. "Adult Illiteracy in the United States," *Congressional Record*, 3 March 1914, 6–24.

64. Klotter, *Breckinridges of Kentucky*, 227.

65. *Lexington Leader*, 28 November 1914, 2; *Lexington Herald*, 23 November 1914, 1.

66. *Lexington Leader*, 21 November 1914, 2; *Lexington Leader*, 23 November 1914, 5.

67. *Lexington Leader*, 24 November 1914, 1.

68. State University, Lexington, became the University of Kentucky in 1916. Harrison and Klotter, *New History of Kentucky*, 153; Kleber, *Kentucky Encyclopedia*, 911; "Facts of Illiteracy," *Lexington Herald*, 25 November 1914, 1.

69. "Illiteracy Must Be Eradicated Here," *Lexington Leader,* 25 November 1914, 3.

70. "Kentucky's War on Illiteracy," p. 6, address before Kentucky Federation of Women's Clubs, Box 45, Stewart Papers.

71. "Illiteracy Meeting to Be Announced from Pulpits," *Lexington Herald,* 21 November 1914, 1.

72. *Lexington Leader,* 25 November 1914, 3.

73. "Illiteracy," pamphlet published by Kentucky State Federation of Women's Clubs' Education Department, scrapbook, Stewart Papers.

74. Kentucky affiliated with the GFWC in 1894, becoming the fifth state to do so. Francis Simrall Riker, "Historical Sketches of Kentucky Federation of Women's Clubs: From Organization, 1894, through Administration Ending June, 1909," unpublished manuscript, Kentucky Federation of Women's Clubs, Louisville, Kentucky.

75. Baker, "Domestication of Politics," 620–47.

76. Blair, *Clubwoman as Feminist,* 93–115.

77. Skocpol, *Protecting Soldiers and Mothers,* 363–65. On the origins of the purity crusades and women's earlier efforts at moral reform, see David J. Pivar, *Purity Crusade: Sexual Morality and Social Control, 1868–1900* (Westport, CT: Greenwood Press, 1973).

78. Following the lead of the GFWC, the KFWC sent libraries to areas where even schools did not exist. Janice Theriot, *Tradition of Service: A History of the Kentucky Federation of Women's Clubs* (Louisville, KY: Kentucky Federation of Women's Clubs, 1994), 41–45. It also supported Katherine Pettit's Camp Industrial for mountain children with no other access to schooling. Forderhase, "'Clear Call of Thoroughbred Women,'" 20, 21.

79. In the letterhead margin were printed the words "No Illiteracy in Kentucky in 1920. Use your school house all the time. Vocational Education fits the child for life. Do all you can for peace." Francis C. Simpson to Mrs. W. J. Fowler, January 1915, Ila Earle Fowler Papers, Special Collections, Margaret I. King Library, University of Kentucky, Lexington; "Illiteracy," pamphlet, 1, 2.

80. General Federation of Women's Clubs Magazine, undated clipping, scrapbook, 130; see also numerous notes and letters in 1911–14 correspondence folders, and numerous undated, generally untitled newspaper clippings in scrapbook, Stewart Papers.

81. Blair, *Clubwoman as Feminist,* 57–71.

82. Kentucky Department of Education, "Report of the Kentucky Illiteracy Commission," in *Report of the Superintendent of Public Instruction of Kentucky Department of Education for the Two Years Ending December 31, 1919* (Frankfort, KY, 1919), 424; Theriot, *Tradition of Service,* 58.

83. "Illiteracy," pamphlet, 5.

84. "Campaign Will Open in Lexington Sunday," *Lexington Herald,* 18 November 1914, 6.

85. *Ashland Independent,* 4 October 1915, scrapbook, Stewart Papers.

86. "Movement in Close Touch with People," *Louisville Times,* 19 November 1915, scrapbook, Stewart Papers.

87. Ibid.

88. *Ashland Independent,* 4 October 1915.

89. Ibid.

90. Mary S. Hoffschwelle, *Rebuilding the Rural Southern Community: Reformers, Schools, and Homes in Tennessee, 1900–1930* (Knoxville: University of Tennessee Press, 1998), 14–33. Tennessee's efforts paralleled those in Kentucky and other southern states during the first ten years of the twentieth century.

91. General Federation of Women's Club Magazine, Box 55, Stewart Papers.

92. "Commonwealth of Kentucky Executive Department Proclamation by the Governor on the Subject of Adult Illiteracy," August–November 1914 Folder, McCreary Papers, Kentucky Department of Libraries and Archives.

93. Ibid.

94. See especially James B. McCreary to CWS, 23 January 1916; 1 February 1916; and 18 February 1916, Stewart Papers.

95. "Mrs. Stewart Hits Illiteracy Move Smashing Blows," *Lexington Leader,* 29 November 1914, 2.

96. Ibid.

97. "Proclamation," 5 July 1915, scrapbook, Stewart Papers.

98. Barksdale Hamlett, "Biennial Report of the Superintendent of Public Instruction," 30 June 1915, 246, 250, 251, 261, 299.

99. Letters from Mattie Dalton are the best source of evidence of who supported Stewart's work. Fiercely protective of Stewart's efforts and extremely outspoken, Dalton blasted many of the state's educators in her letters over the years. See 1912–16 correspondence folders, Stewart Papers.

100. "Broadsides" folder, Box 1, Stewart Papers.

101. "Illiteracy," *Shelby Record,* 29 January 1915, scrapbook, Stewart Papers.

102. *Lexington Herald,* 22 November 1914, 4.

103. Ibid.

104. As the Moonlight Schools grew, the name *Rowan County Messenger* was no longer appropriate. The newspaper grew into a regional publication, the *Mountaineer.* John S. Lawrence to CWS, 23 February 1914, Stewart Papers.

105. "Editor of Morehead Mountaineer Points Out What Editors Owe Community," newspaper clipping bearing handwritten date of 30 December 1913; "Able Paper by Woman Editor of Kentucky on Mission of the Press to Public," undated newspaper clipping, both in scrapbook, Stewart Papers.

106. "Literacy and Illiteracy in Alabama," pamphlet issued by Alabama Department of Education, 30 September 1914, 5–6, Alabama folder, Box 66, Stewart Papers.

107. "Illiteracy in the United States and an Experiment for Its Elimination," 10, 11.

108. Grantham, *Southern Progressivism,* 260–61; J. Morgan Kousser, "Progressivism—For Middle-Class Whites Only: North Carolina Education, 1880–1910," *Journal of Southern History* 46 (May 1980): 169–94; Hoffschwelle, *Rebuilding the Rural Southern Community,* 89.

109. "K.N.E.A. Report Urges Better Negro Education," *Proceedings of the Kentucky Negro Educational Association,* Kentuckiana Digital Library, http://kdl.kyvl.org/cgi/t/text, accessed 26 November 2003.

110. R. H. Williams to CWS, 13 March 1921, Box 4, Stewart Papers.

111. Henry J. Allen to CWS, 20 June 1922; see also various newspaper clippings in scrapbook, Stewart Papers.

112. "Illiteracy Campaign Proposed for State," undated newspaper clipping, scrapbook, Stewart Papers.

113. "Moonlight School Idea Is Applauded," undated newspaper clipping, scrapbook, Stewart Papers.

114. Margaret Woodrow Wilson, "The School House as a Community Center," series II, no. 9 (Washington, DC: American Civic Association: March 1916), pamphlet in Box 2, Madeline McDowell Breckinridge Papers, Special Collections, Margaret I. King Library, University of Kentucky, Lexington; "Mrs. Stewart and Miss Wilson Guests of Honor," undated newspaper clipping, scrapbook, Stewart Papers.

115. George M. Smith, "The Opportunity Schools and the Founder Wil Lou Gray," (booklet published by Wil Lou Gray Opportunity School, August 2000, 3, 12; DaMaris E. Ayres, *Let My People Learn: The Biography of Wil Lou Gray* (Grenwood, SC: Attic Press, 1988), 50–72; Leon Fink, *Progressive Intellectuals and the Dilemmas of Democratic Commitment* (Cambridge, MA: Harvard University Press, 1997), chap. 8, "Teaching the People: Wil Lou Gray and the Siren of Educational Opportunity," 242–74; author's interview with Pat Smith, director of Wil Lou Gray Opportunity School, West Columbia, South Carolina, 6 October 2003.

116. David L. Carlton, *Mill and Town in South Carolina, 1880–1920* (Baton Rouge: Louisiana State University Press, 1982), 263.

117. Fink, *Progressive Intellectuals*, 243.

118. South Carolina Educational Television Network, Wil Lou Gray TV Interview, 1973; interview with Dr. Wil Lou Gray, June 1974, Special Collections, South Caroliniana Library, Columbia, South Carolina.

119. Smith, "Opportunity Schools," 23–27; Smith interview; historical reprint in author's possession.

120. Cora Wilson Stewart, "The Elimination of Illiteracy," *Journal of the National Education Association*, 3 July, 1916, 56–58.

3. Moonlight Schools and Progressivism

1. Used by J. Stanley Lemons in *The Woman Citizen* (Urbana: University of Illinois Press, 1973) as a chapter title, this phrase comes from Winifred Starr Dobyns, "The Lady and the Tiger, Or, the Woman Voter and the Political Machine," *Woman Citizen* 11 (January 1927): 20. Dobyns, who chaired the Republican Women's Committee of Illinois, uses the following poem as an illustration of her point that women were the losers: "There was a young lady of Niger, Who smiled as she rode on a tiger—They returned from the ride, With the lady inside, And the smile on the face of the tiger."

2. Skocpol, *Protecting Soldiers and Mothers,* 319; and her response in "The Enactment of Mothers' Pensions: Civic Mobilization and Agenda Setting or Benefits of the Ballot," *American Political Science Review* 89 (1995): 710–30.

3. Nancy Cott, "Across the Great Divide: Women in Politics before and after 1920," in *Women, Politics, and Change,* ed. Louise A. Tilley and Patricia Gurin (New York: Russell Sage Foundation, 1990), 153, 167.

4. Arthur S. Link and Richard L. McCormick, *Progressivism* (Arlington Heights, IL: Harlan Davidson, 1983), 8, 9.

5. Steven A. Channing, *Kentucky: A Bicentennial History* (New York: Norton, 1977), 183.

6. Skocpol, *Protecting Soldiers and Mothers,* 319, 361.

7. Grantham, *Southern Progressivism,* 226, 227.

8. Task Force on Adult Education, "Adult Education and Literacy in Kentucky," Research Report No. 296 (Frankfort, KY: Legislative Research Commission, 2000), x.

9. "An Important Bill," undated newspaper clipping, Box 55, Stewart Papers.

10. "Campaign to Wipe Out Illiteracy Being Pushed," undated newspaper clipping, Box 60, Stewart Papers.

11. "Criticizes Use of State's Money," undated newspaper clipping, Box 55, Stewart Papers.

12. "Illiteracy Commission Censured by Attorney General Opinion," undated newspaper clipping, Box 55, Stewart Papers.

13. "Mrs. Cora W. Stewart Replies to Critics," 12 January 1916, newspaper clipping, Box 55, Stewart Papers.

14. *Owensboro Daily Messenger,* 15 January 1916.

15. "Mrs. Cora W. Stewart Replies to Critics."

16. "Turning on the Light," editorial, *Lexington Herald,* 11 January 1916.

17. "Defend Record of Mrs. Stewart," undated newspaper clipping, Box 55, Stewart Papers.

18. "Unfair Attack upon Mrs. Stewart Denounced by State Papers," *Owensboro Messenger,* 9 January 1916.

19. William A. Young to Prof. Henry Lloyd, 25 April 1916, Stewart Papers; Harrison and Klotter, *New History of Kentucky,* 275.

20. James B. McCreary to CWS, 23 February 1916, and 11 April 1916, Stewart Papers.

21. "Champions Mrs. Stewart," newspaper clipping with handwritten date, 1–29–16, Box 55, Stewart Papers.

22. Mattie Dalton to CWS, 12 January 1915, Stewart Papers.

23. J. G. Crabbe to CWS, 14 January 1916, Stewart Papers.

24. "Report on the Kentucky Illiteracy Commission," 24 December 1918, Box 60, Stewart Papers.

25. Harrison and Klotter, *New History of Kentucky,* 283–86; Nicholas C. Burckel, "A. O. Stanley and Progressive Reform, 1902–1919," *Register of the Kentucky Historical Society* 79 (Spring 1981): 158. See also Robert Fenimore Sexton, "Kentucky Politics and Society: 1919–1932" (Ph.D. diss., University of Washington, 1970), 19–21.

26. Amanda O. Stanley to CWS, 8 May 1921, Stewart Papers.

27. This is obvious in an introduction Stewart made of the governor to a group of literacy workers. In her address, she noted his continuing support for the illiteracy work and his dedication to the Moonlight Schools. Box 4, A. O. Stanley Papers, Margaret I. King Library, University of Kentucky, Lexington.

28. "Governor to Oppose New Appropriations," 18 February 1916, newspaper clipping, Box 55, Stewart Papers.

29. Undated clipping, Box 60, Stewart Papers.

30. "Illiteracy Commission Bill Gets Aid," undated newspaper clipping, Box 55, Stewart Papers.

31. "Mrs. Cora Wilson Stewart Is Victor over Her Critics," *Lexington Herald,* Box 55, Stewart Papers.

32. Editorial, *Lexington Herald,* 27 June 1915.

33. "An Important Bill," undated newspaper clipping, Box 55, Stewart Papers.

34. Wm. A. Young to Senator Charles D. Arnett, 5 February 1916, Stewart Papers.

35. James B. McCreary to CWS, 23 January 1916; and 1 February 1916, Stewart Papers.

36. Cora Wilson Stewart, "Address to Kentucky General Assembly," 19 February 1916, 20–21, Box 45, Stewart Papers.

37. Ibid., 21.

38. Ibid., 22, 23.

39. Most of the major newspapers covered Stewart's address and the legislative reaction to it. See particularly *Lexington Herald,* 18 February 1916; *Louisville Courier-Journal,* 18 February 1916.

40. "State Has No Money for Its Illiterates Now," 19 February 1916, newspaper clipping, Box 55, Stewart Papers.

41. "The Kentucky Illiteracy Commission," in Report, 31 December 1917, 304.

42. Sticht, "Rise of the Adult Education and Literary System," 17. Large institutional education providers, mainly public systems supported by tax dollars, typically provide adult education in the broadest sense, while the least educated and most needy adults tend to be served by community-based organizations relying on charitable donations and volunteer teachers.

43. Lemons, *Woman Citizen,* 30.

44. Stewart, presidential address, KEA. The desire of professional educators to broaden the role of the school in society is especially evident in the NEA Bulletins. For relevant examples, see H. R. Pattengill, "The School Stands by the Flag," and Katherine Devereux Blake, "The Opportunities of the War," in *NEA Bulletin* 6, no. 28 (April 1917): 27, 28. An NEA department called "Wider Use of the School House" worked on ways to use schools as centers for community activity.

45. Crocco, Munro, and Weiler, *Pedagogies of Resistance,* 3–4; see also Paulo Freire, *Pedagogy of the Oppressed* (1970; reprint, New York: Continuum, 1993).

46. Cremin, in *Transformation of the School,* 179–81, shows that progressive reformers concentrated primarily on public education, applying scientific management techniques to school administration, reforming curriculum, and creating vocational programs that were "child centered."

47. Crocco, Munro, and Weiler, *Pedagogies of Resistance,* 20–23.

48. William L. Bowers, *The Country Life Movement in America, 1900–1920* (Port Washington, NY: Kennikat Press, 1974), 2–8, 137, 138. For a concise discussion of Country Life reform in the South, see also Grantham, *Southern Progressivism,* chap. 10.

49. Grantham, *Southern Progressivism,* 348; David B. Danbom, *The Resisted Revolution: Urban America and the Industrialization of Agriculture, 1900–1930* (Ames: Iowa State University Press, 1979), vii, viii.

50. Joseph Kett, *The Pursuit of Knowledge under Difficulties: From Self-Improvement to Adult Education in America, 1750–1900* (Stanford, CA: Stanford University Press, 1994), 292–330; Harold W. Stubblefield and Patrick Keane, *Adult Education in the American Experience: From the Colonial Period to the Present* (San Francisco: Jossey-Bass, 1994), 153–74.

51. Cora Wilson Stewart, *Country Life Readers, First Book* (Richmond, VA: B. F. Johnson, 1915), 3; B. F. Johnson Publishers to CWS, 3 July 1915; F. J. Norvel to CWS, 3 January 1917, Stewart Papers.

52. "Country Life Readers, by Cora Wilson Stewart," advertising pamphlet, scrapbook, Stewart Papers.

53. "Country Life Readers, by Cora Wilson Stewart," advertising pamphlet for second edition, scrapbook, Stewart Papers.

54. Cora Wilson Stewart, *Country Life Readers, Second Book* (Richmond, VA: B. F. Johnson, 1916), 3.

55. Michael W. Apple and Linda K. Christian-Smith, eds., *The Politics of the Textbook* (New York: Routledge, 1991), 3.

56. Fred Inglis, *The Management of Ignorance: A Political Theory of the Curriculum* (New York: Basil Blackwell, 1985), 22–23.

57. For a discussion of potential responses to text, see Apple and Christian-Smith, *Politics of the Textbook*, 14.

58. For a discussion of American textbooks of the nineteenth century, including McGuffey, see David B. Tyack, ed., *Turning Points in American Educational History* (Waltham, MA: Blaisdell, 1967), 178–227.

59. Stewart, *First Book*, 9.

60. Everett L. Dix, "Textbooks Suitable to Adult Beginners," 1, Box 51, Stewart Papers.

61. Ibid., 2. Despite the gendered language, modern readers assume women were included.

62. Ibid.

63. Ruth Miller Elson, *Guardians of Tradition: American Schoolbooks of the Nineteenth Century* (Lincoln: University of Nebraska Press, 1964), vii.

64. Link and McCormick, *Progressivism*, 114–15. The authors' synthesis points out that most progressives "fundamentally accepted" an industrial society and sought mainly to control and ameliorate its worst effects.

65. For an account of industrial Americanization and its impact on West Virginia during the Great War, see John C. Hennen, *The Americanization of West Virginia: Creating a Modern Industrial State, 1916–1925* (Lexington: University Press of Kentucky, 1996).

66. Tyack, *Turning Points in American Educational History*, 182–83.

67. Stewart, *First Book*, 46.

68. Grantham, *Southern Progressivism;* see particularly his table on southern school statistics, 1900–1920, 258.

69. Stewart, *First Book*, 18, 19.

70. Stewart, *Moonlight Schools*, 72–73.

71. Stewart, KEA presidential address.

72. Harrison and Klotter, *New History of Kentucky*, 314–15.

73. Thomas Warren Ramage, "Augustus Owsley Stanley: Early Twentieth Century Kentucky Democrat" (Ph.D. diss., University of Kentucky, 1968), 203, 214. Quoted in Ibid., 315.

74. *Clay City (Kentucky) Times*, 26 September [1914], untitled newspaper clipping, scrapbook, Stewart Papers.

75. "Speeches of Hon. William J. Fields, of Kentucky, in the House of Representatives, Friday, February 6, 1914," Box 2, Madeline McDowell Breckinridge Papers.

76. "Facts Concerning the Moonlight School Work," pamphlet issued by the Kentucky Illiteracy Commission, undated, probably 1920, Stewart Collection, Morehead.

77. Stewart, *First Book*, 52, 53.

78. "Weeding Out Illiteracy," *Woman Citizen*, 30 August 1919, 306.

79. Not all women supported woman suffrage, and many publicly active women actually rejected it for themselves and advocated narrower access to the electoral process. Manuela Thurner, "'Better Citizens without the Ballot': American Antisuffrage Women and Their Rationale during the Progressive Era," *Journal of Women's History* 5 (Spring 1993): 33–57.

80. Link and McCormick, *Progressivism*, 53–56.

81. Harrison and Klotter, *New History of Kentucky*, 250–51.

82. Grantham, *Southern Progressivism*, 310–18; Link, *Paradox of Southern Progressivism*, 159.

83. This is a common theme. See, for example, "Report of the Commission on Country Life," quoted in Hoffschwelle, *Rebuilding the Rural Southern Community*, 18.

84. Stewart, *First Book*, 45.

85. Ibid., 46, 47.

86. Stewart, *Second Book*, 53, 72, 25.

87. Ibid., 90.

88. Ibid., 80, 81.

89. Ibid., 82, 85.

90. Hoffschwelle, *Rebuilding the Rural Southern Community*, 110, 111.

91. Stewart, *Second Book*, 26, 27.

92. Ibid., 38, 39, 4,5.

93. Stewart, *Second Book*, 9.

94. CWS to James Lane Allen, 20 December 1915, Stewart Papers.

95. Stewart, *Second Book*, 52.

96. Ibid., 98.

97. Stewart, *First Book*, 82–86; Stewart, *Second Book*, 158–59.

98. Grantham, *Southern Progressivism*, 348.

99. Quoted in Stewart, *Moonlight Schools*, 30, 31.

100. CWS to J. D. Crump,18 May 1916; reply, 24 May, Box 2, Stewart Papers.

101. CWS to J. D. Crump, 18 May 1916.

102. It is impossible to estimate total sales. See M. M. Guhin to B. F. Johnson Publishing Co., 16 April 1921; G. Ramsey Bancroft to CWS, 16 June 1921; royalty statements, 10 December 1919; 25 January 1919; 31 December 1920; 31 December 1922. An undated newspaper clipping claims Stewart's books were adopted by Russian educa-

tors, who ordered fifty thousand copies, and that several European countries ordered "large shipments" as well, although I found nothing in Stewart's financial records to substantiate the claim. In fact, correspondence shows that Johnson refused to translate and print the books for sale in Russia due to an uncertain political climate and copyright issues. B. F. Johnson to CWS, 17 September and 18 October 1918, and CWS to B. F. Johnson, 25 October 1918. Royalty records and correspondence indicate that as late as 1930, she earned $865.45 on the sale of 28,741 books. B. F. Johnson to CWS, 7 May 1930 and 15 October 1930, Stewart Papers.

 103. Hoffschwelle, *Rebuilding the Rural Southern Community,* 149.

4. Nationalizing the Illiteracy Campaign

 1. "The Kentucky Illiteracy Commission," Report, 31 December 1917, 305.

 2. Harrison and Klotter, *New History of Kentucky,* 290; Klotter, *Portrait in Paradox,* 237. Census figures placed the percentage of illiteracy in 1910 at 7.7, and in 1920 at 6.0. Educational authorities disputed these figures, however, and testing by the army indicated that illiteracy was much higher. Despite later criticism of the tests used to determine literacy, the census figures, the army figures, and the relationship between the two are explained in Winthrop Talbot, "Illiteracy of Adults," *Bulletin of the Woman's Department National Civic Federation,* March 1924, Box 51, Stewart Papers.

 3. On the training camps and Kentucky's role in preparing soldiers, see Klotter, *Portrait in Paradox,* 236, 237; Cora Wilson Stewart, "Illiteracy and the War," 11, Box 56, Stewart Papers.

 4. Stewart, "Illiteracy and the War," 1–2.

 5. Ibid., 3.

 6. Stewart, "Moonlight School Course of Study, War Number," 10.

 7. Ibid., 12.

 8. Cora Wilson Stewart, "Moonlight School Course of Study, 1918" (Frankfort, KY: Kentucky Illiteracy Commission, 1918), 5.

 9. See royalty statements from B. F. Johnson Publishing Company, 1917–1918, Box 2, Stewart Papers.

 10. Stewart, "Moonlight School Course of Study," 1918, 7; "Moonlight School an Aid in the War," undated newspaper clipping in Box 60, Stewart Papers.

 11. Stewart, *Moonlight Schools,* 82, 83.

 12. Stewart, "Moonlight School Course of Study," 1918, 67.

 13. Ibid., 69.

 14. Cora Wilson Stewart, *Soldier's First Book* (New York: Association Press, 1918), 11–12.

 15. Ibid., 14, 30, 37.

 16. NEA president Mary C. C. Bradford created a "Commission on the National Emergency in Education and the Program for Readjustment during and after the War." The commission's goal was "to enlist the services of all the educators of the country and to cooperate with all the agencies related to educational readjustment in outlining a progressive program of education." *NEA Bulletin* 6, no. 5 (April 1918): 16–17.

 17. Grantham, *Southern Progressivism,* 397; Lemons, *Woman Citizen,* 14–33.

18. A. E. Winship to CWS, [indistinct] September 1918 and 8 September 1918, Stewart Papers.

19. A. N. Farmer to CWS, 5 September 1918, Stewart Papers.

20. "Mrs. Stewart Is Drafted by Government"; "To Head Fight on Illiteracy"; and "More Honors for Mrs. Cora Wilson Stewart," undated newspaper clippings, Box 60, Stewart Papers.

21. *NEA Bulletin* 6, no. 5 (April 1918): 17, 18.

22. Cora Wilson Stewart, "Illiteracy and the War," 1–5, Box 56, Stewart Papers.

23. Stewart, *Moonlight Schools*, 85.

24. Klotter, in *Portrait in Paradox*, 236, notes that the majority of Kentuckians "wholeheartedly" supported the war effort, and that to some, it represented the "transference of the Progressive Crusade to the world."

25. A hundred or so of these letters survive, carbon copies in 1917 correspondence file, Box 2; *Glasgow Times*, 13 August 1917, untitled newspaper clipping, Box 55, Stewart Papers.

26. "Critics Complain of Posters Concerning Illiterate Soldiers," *Hazard Herald*, 13 October 1917.

27. Ibid.

28. "Illiteracy Statistics Questioned," undated, *Louisville Courier-Journal,* Box 60; "Illiteracy in the State," undated, *Louisville Courier-Journal,* Box 55, Stewart Papers.

29. CWS to the Editor of the *Courier-Journal,* 24 August 1917, Box 2, Stewart Papers.

30. "More Honors for Mrs. Cora Wilson Stewart," undated newspaper clipping, Box 60, Stewart Papers.

31. "Illiteracy in the State," undated, *Louisville Courier-Journal,* Box 55, Stewart Papers.

32. Diary entry in Stewart's hand, 4 January 1918, Box 29, Stewart Papers.

33. Several letters to and from colleagues indicate the stress she was under. See especially A. E. Winship to CWS, 11 July 1918; J. G. Crabbe to CWS, 13 July 1918; CWS to A. J. Gray Jr., 5 February 1919; and CWS to J. D. Crump, 5 February 1919, Stewart Papers.

34. Sarah Smithers to CWS, 25 January 1919; CWS to A. J. Gray Jr., 5 February 1919, Stewart Papers.

35. CWS to Woodrow Wilson, 23 August 1917; CWS to J. C. W. Beckham, 25 August 1917, Stewart Papers.

36. Stewart, *Moonlight Schools*, 158, 159.

37. *Calhoun Star,* 20 July 1917; *Nashville Southern Agriculturalist,* 1 July 1917, newspaper clippings, Box 55, Stewart Papers.

38. Thomas Cromwell, "Education Said to Be Needed," *Cincinnati Enquirer,* 16 November 1919.

39. "Illiteracy in the United States Army," 11, Box 60, Stewart Papers.

40. "The Kentucky Illiteracy Commission," in Report, 31 December 1917, 304.

41. Acts of the Kentucky General Assembly, 28 March 1918, 154–56.

42. Cora Wilson Stewart, "Moonlight School Course of Study, War Number"; "Moonlight School Course of Study, 1918," both in Stewart Collection, Morehead; for other printed materials, see Boxes 66, 67, and 68, Stewart Papers.

43. "County School News"; "Kentucky Illiteracy Commission's Plans," undated newspaper clippings, Box 60, Stewart Papers; "Report of the Kentucky Illiteracy Commission," Report of the Superintendent of Public Instruction of Kentucky Department of Education for the Two Years Ending December 31, 1919 (Frankfort, KY, 1920).

44. "Kentucky Hero Will Make Plea for Education," undated newspaper clipping, Box 60, Stewart Papers.

45. Zilpha Roberts to CWS, 13 March 1923; Sandlin's story is a sad one. He was nearly destitute, and Stewart later arranged for a group of friends to raise enough money to purchase a farm for him. Although it is impossible to piece together exactly how it happened, the money was placed in a bank, but the bank failed and the money was lost. Stewart wrote many letters on his behalf, trying to recoup the loss. The correspondence on this issue is handwritten, mostly by Mrs. Sandlin, and is difficult to decipher. Numerous letters in correspondence files, Boxes 4, 5, and 6, Stewart Papers.

46. "Orators Will Be Invoked to Aid Education," 10 January 1919; "Women to War on Illiteracy," 16 January 1919, both in *Louisville Courier-Journal;* "Illiteracy Drive Starts in State," *Lexington Leader,* 25 August 1919.

47. "Illiteracy Campaign Will Open June 18," *Lexington Herald,* 19 May 1919; "Illiteracy Campaign," *Louisville Courier-Journal,* 19 May 1919; and "Boyce Is Best School Taught by Moonlight," *Louisville Courier-Journal,* 23 October 1919.

48. Untitled biographical sketch, Box 1; individual state folders, Box 63, Stewart Papers.

49. "Says Key to Democracy Is Education," *Louisville Courier-Journal,* 16 January 1917.

50. "To Wipe Out Illiteracy," undated, *Danville Daily Messenger,* Box 60, Stewart Papers.

51. Grantham, *Southern Progressivism,* 178–99. This is more prevalent in industrial towns, particularly in the textile industry in the Deep South. See Carlton, *Mill and Town in South Carolina.*

52. "Address delivered by Hon. L. E. Foster, at Princeton, Kentucky, on 30 August 1919," manuscript, Box 51, Stewart Papers; "School Needs Arouse State," *Louisville Courier-Journal,* 31 August 1919.

53. "School Needs Arouse State."

54. "Says Key to Democracy Is Education."

55. Ibid.

56. "County School News"; "The Times' Weekly Moonlight School News," undated newspaper clippings, Box 60, Stewart Papers.

57. Although all reports contain some positive information, those that contain negative comments include report of Sallie Ford, 17 August 1919; report of May McEllister, 18 September 1919; and report of J. C. Williams, 10 October 1919. Reports with highly positive information include report of Ora Pruden, 22 July 1919; report of Mary Norris, 18 August 1919; and Joseph B. Ross, 25 August 1919, Box 2a, Stewart Papers.

58. Report of Ora Pruden, 22 July 1919; report of Elizabeth Baker 2 August 1919; report of Joseph B. Ross, 25 August 1919, Stewart Papers.

59. McVey, *Gates Open Slowly,* 238–43; Clark, *History of Kentucky,* 476–78.

60. Harrison and Klotter, *New History of Kentucky,* 383, 384.

61. "Weeding Out Illiteracy," *Woman Citizen,* 30 August 1919, 306; "Great War Biennial of Clubwomen Ends," and "Education Said to Be Needed," undated newspaper clippings, Box 60, Stewart Papers.

62. Madeline McDowell Breckinridge, "Kentucky," in *The History of Woman Suffrage,* 6 vols., ed. Elizabeth Cady Stanton, Susan B. Anthony, Mathilda Gage, and Ida Husted Harper (Rochester, NY: Arno Press, 1881–1922), 6:210–11; Paul E. Fuller, *Laura Clay and the Woman's Rights Movement* (Lexington: University Press of Kentucky, 1975), 150, 199; Harrison and Klotter, *New History of Kentucky,* 277–79. On the woman vote in Kentucky, see Claudia Knott, "The Woman Suffrage Movement in Kentucky, 1879–1920" (Ph.D. diss, University of Kentucky, 1989); see also Carol Crowe-Carraco, "Women's Quest for Reform," in *Our Kentucky: A Study of the Bluegrass State,* ed. James C. Klotter (Frankfort, KY: Kentucky Historical Society, 1992).

63. "Squad of Airplanes," *Louisville Courier-Journal,* 30 October 1919.

64. Geo. S. Lehman to CWS, 30 September 1919, Stewart Papers.

65. S. E. Knarris to CWS, 30 September 1919, Stewart Papers.

66. Samuel B. Scaggs to CWS, 30 September 1919; *Nashville Tennessean,* 5 October 1919, and *Lexington Herald,* 19 March 1920, both clippings in Box 55, Stewart Papers.

67. Clark, *History of Kentucky,* 443; Kleber, *Kentucky Encyclopedia,* 655; Harrison and Klotter, *New History of Kentucky,* 349–51; Channing, *Kentucky,* 185–86.

68. Klotter, *Portrait in Paradox,* 265.

69. "Colvin Record Bars Claim as Illiteracy Foe," undated newspaper clipping, Box 68, Stewart Papers.

70. George Colvin to M. L. Brittain, 23 June 1922, Stewart Papers.

71. "Official Reports of County Superintendents to Kentucky Illiteracy Commission," 1.

72. Ibid., 2.

73. Ibid., 10.

74. Ibid., 5.

75. "Report of the Superintendent of Public Instruction of Kentucky, June 20, 1921" (Frankfort, KY: Department of Education), 7–9; Kleber, *Kentucky Encyclopedia,* 217; Ligon, *History of Public Education in Kentucky,* 180.

76. George Colvin to M. L. Brittain, 23 June 1922, Stewart Papers. Colvin was known for his frankness and is said to have once summoned staff members to his office and said, "Well, boys, its right, but not legal; in a form letter to superintendents last week, I made demands I can't enforce. Now, I want you to help me back up as gracefully as possible." H. W. Peters, *History of Education in Kentucky, 1915–1940* (Frankfort, KY: Department of Education, 1940), 30. Colvin commanded respect in the Kentucky Republican Party, a fact that earned his appointment in 1923 as president of the University of Louisville, where he promptly alienated several key faculty and became embroiled in a controversial academic freedom court case. See Duane Cox, "The Gottschalk-Colvin Case: A Study in Academic Purpose and Command," *Register of the Kentucky Historical Society* 85 (Winter 1987): 46–68.

77. *Lexington Herald,* 10 March 1920.

78. *Lexington Herald*, 13 March 1920.

79. *Lexington Herald*, 11 and 12 March 1920.

80. Stewart, "Report of the Kentucky Illiteracy Commission," 1919.

81. "Colvin Record," Box 68, Stewart Papers.

82. Zilpha Roberts to CWS, 3 May 1920, Stewart Papers. Colvin lost his bid for the Republican nomination to Charles I. Dawson. Klotter, *Portrait in Paradox*, 275.

83. Zilpha Roberts to CWS, 3 May 1920, Stewart Papers.

84. Undated newspaper clipping, Box 60, Stewart Papers.

85. "Cora Wilson Stewart, Shall Kentucky Be Longer Deprived of Her Services," *Lexington Herald*, 13 February 1914.

86. CWS to Robert G. Higdon, 16 November 1920; Mary Bronaugh to CWS, 21 January 1921, Stewart Papers.

87. Dorothy M. Brown, *Setting a Course: American Women in the 1920s* (Boston: Twayne, 1987), 50.

88. For a discussion of the fight for passage of this bill, see Lynn Dumenil, "'The Insatiable Maw of Bureaucracy': Antistatism and Education Reform in the 1920s," *Journal of American History* 77 (September 1990): 499–524; and Edgar Bruce Wesley, *NEA: The First Hundred Years: The Building of the Teaching Profession* (New York: Harper, 1957), 243–49.

89. Stewart makes this clear in her untitled speech on woman suffrage given at the Democratic National Convention in July 1920, "Speeches on Women's Suffrage" folder, Box 46, Stewart Papers.

90. Cott, "Across the Great Divide," 172.

91. CSW to Robert G. Higdon, 16 November 1920, Stewart Papers.

92. H. M. McChesney to CWS, 7 September 1920, Stewart Papers.

93. Ibid.

94. Lemons, *Woman Citizen*, 87.

95. Telegram from Charl O. Williams to CWS, Sunday, 9 P.M., [June 1920], Box 3, Stewart Papers.

96. Cora Wilson Stewart, speech to Kentucky delegation, "Speeches on Women's Suffrage" folder, Box 46, Stewart Papers.

97. Telegram from Desha Breckinridge to CWS, 17 July 1920, Stewart Papers.

98. Ibid.

99. Brainard Platt to CWS, 14 July 1920, Stewart Papers.

100. CWS to Sarah E. Luther, 5 January 192[1], Stewart Papers.

101. Telegram from J. W. Crabtree to CWS, 25 June 1920, Stewart Papers.

102. Charl Williams to CWS, 4 August 1920, Stewart Papers.

103. Josephine Preston to James Cox, 7 July 1920, Stewart Papers.

104. *Lexington Herald*, 19 July 1920; Fuller, *Laura Clay*, 159, 160.

105. Franklin D. Roosevelt to CWS, 20 August 1920, Stewart Papers.

106. James B. Cox to CWS, 8 September 1920, Stewart Papers.

107. CWS to Sarah Luther, 5 January 1920, Stewart Papers.

108. James B. Cox to CWS, 21 July 1920, Stewart Papers.

109. CWS to Sarah Luther, 5 January 1920, Stewart Papers.

110. W. J. Fields to CWS, 8 November 1920, Stewart Papers.

111. Stewart's secretary, Lela Mae Stiles, reported this to Mrs. Stewart. Calling Colvin a "modern Judas Iscariot," she noted that he was "up to his old tricks," sending out questionnaires to all the county superintendents "asking how much money we spent in each county." Lela Mae Stiles to CWS, 17 October 1920, Stewart Papers.

112. Ibid.

113. Kleber, *Kentucky Encyclopedia,* s.v. "William Purcell Dennis Haly," by Thomas H. Appleton, Jr.

114. Lela Mae Stiles to CWS, 20 July 1922, Stewart Papers.

115. Woodson May to CWS, 24 August 1922, Stewart Papers.

116. Lela Mae Stiles to CWS, undated, 1922 correspondence folder, Box 5, Stewart Papers.

117. J. W. Riley to CWS, 29 September 1923, Stewart Papers.

118. CWS to Judge John W. Riley, 27 September 1923, Stewart Papers.

119. "Pete" to CWS [Cody], 23 November 1923, Stewart Papers.

120. CWS to Governor Fields, 6 December 1923, Stewart Papers.

121. CWS to Lela Mae Stiles, 23 November 1923, Stewart Papers.

122. Quoted in Lemons, *Woman Citizen,* 90.

123. Quoted in Kristi Andersen, "Women and Citizenship in the 1920s," in Tilley and Gurin, *Women, Politics, and Change,* 185.

124. Quoted in Lemons, *Woman Citizen,* 109.

125. Nancy F. Cott, *The Grounding of Modern Feminism* (New Haven, CT: Yale University Press, 1987), 85–114.

126. Dobyns, "The Lady and the Tiger," 20.

5. The National Crusade against Illiteracy

1. Anne Firor Scott, "After Suffrage: Southern Women in the Twenties," *Journal of Southern History* 30 (August 1964): 298–315. Scott emphasizes women reformers' conceptualization of the role of the state in its responsibility for public welfare less in the custodial sense and more in the ameliorative sense. See also Patrick Gerster and Nicholas Cords, eds., *Myth and Southern History,* vol. 2, *The New South,* 2nd ed. (Urbana: University of Illinois Press, 1989), 99–100.

2. Ibid.

3. Allen W. Batteau, ed., *Appalachia and America: Autonomy and Regional Dependence* (Lexington: University Press of Kentucky, 1983), 4. In Appalachia, argues Batteau, professionalization ultimately created an alienating and dependent relationship between the client and the professional. See also Burton Bledstein, *The Culture of Professionalism: The Middle Class and the Development of Higher Education in America* (New York: Norton, 1976), 98. Bledstein notes that working-class Americans tended to deny the status sought by professionals.

4. Sanfor Winston, *Illiteracy in the United States* (Chapel Hill: University of North Carolina Press, 1930), 9, 17. Winston uses 1910 and 1920 census data for his tables, which show comparative illiteracy rates for the nation.

5. "The Crusade against Illiteracy and Its Founder," biographical folder, Box 1, Stewart Papers. It is difficult to measure the actual outcome of the Moonlight Schools, but the two leading historians who have examined the literacy campaign conclude that it had a positive effect on the statistics. Grantham, *Southern Progressivism,* 253; Link, *Paradox of Southern Progressivism,* 139–41.

6. "Committee Reports Education Bill," *Journal of the National Education Association* 10 (March 1921): 42.

7. Winston, *Illiteracy in the United States,* 58; high school attendance percentages from "Illiteracy a Major American Problem," Pierce and Hedrick, Inc., 1930, Box 52, Stewart Papers.

8. Cora Wilson Stewart, "Report of Illiteracy Commission," *NEA Proceedings,* 1926; "The Menace of Illiteracy," *Journal of the National Education Association* 11 (October 1922): 344

9. Fred M. Hunter to CWS, 14 January 1921, Stewart Papers.

10. "Committees of the National Education Association—1921–1922," *Journal of the National Education Association* 11 (May 1922): 203.

11. "Events in Mrs. Stewart's Career," biographical folder, Box 1, Stewart Papers.

12. 1922 correspondence folders, Stewart Papers.

13. Details are from CWS to Governor Henry J. Allen of Kansas, 15 July 1922, although numerous nearly identical letters are in the 1922 correspondence folders, Stewart Papers.

14. CWS to Hon. Will C. Wood, 25 November 1921, Stewart Papers.

15. "Illiteracy Commission," typed summary, Box 1, Stewart Papers.

16. Cora Wilson Stewart, "Report of the Illiteracy Committee of the National Council of Education," NEA *Proceedings* 66 (1928): 251, copy in Stewart Papers.

17. "Illiteracy Report of the Illiteracy Commission of the National Education Association," July 1924, 9, Box 35, Stewart Papers.

18. Information concerning the national campaign can be pieced together from correspondence with Josephine Corliss Preston, who helped organize the western tour, and Lela Mae Stiles, who coordinated the campaign from Frankfort. For examples, see CWS to Lela Mae, 27 and 29 July 1921; Fannie B. Williams to CWS, 31 August; G. W. Nash to Josephine Corliss Preston, 23 July; Josephine Corliss Preston to State Superintendents and Presidents of State Normal Schools, 22 July, Stewart Papers.

19. N. E. Kendall to CWS, 9 November 1921, Stewart Papers.

20. Henry J. Allen to CWS, 22 November 1920 and 15 July 1922; John Conway to CWS, 13 November 1920, Stewart Papers.

21. Elsie Toles to CWS, 15 May 1922, Stewart Papers.

22. CWS to Henry J. Allen, 15 July 1922, Stewart Papers.

23. CWS to Hon. A. H. McClure, 11 May 1922, Stewart Papers.

24. CWS to Mrs. Pearl Heckel, 25 August 1922, Stewart Papers.

25. Stewart, *Moonlight Schools,* viii.

26. CWS to Lela Mae Stiles, 27 July 1922, Stewart Papers.

27. CWS to Lela Mae Stiles, 18 November 1923, Stewart Papers.

28. Lela Mae Stiles to CWS, 11 July 1923, Stewart Papers.

29. Lela Mae Stiles to CWS, 14 July 1923, Stewart Papers.

30. Lela Mae Stiles to CWS, 26 June 1923, Stewart Papers.

31. Lela Mae Stiles to CWS, 29 June 1923, Stewart Papers.

32. CWS to Lela Mae Stiles, 12 October 1923, Stewart Papers.

33. CWS to Lela Mae Stiles, 29 July 1922, Stewart Papers.

34. CWS to Lela Mae Stiles, 16 July and 9 July 1923; and diary entry in small notebook, 30 December 1922, Stewart Papers.

35. CWS to Lela Mae Stiles, 23 December 1918, Stewart Papers.

36. Linda Gordon, "Black and White Visions of Welfare: Women's Welfare Activism, 1890–1945," in *Unequal Sisters: A Multicultural Reader in U.S. Women's History,* 2nd ed., ed. Ellen Carol DuBois and Vicki Ruiz (New York: Routledge, 1990), 164–66.

37. CWS to Mrs. J. J. Puhl, 5 December 1921, Stewart Papers.

38. Mrs. Alfred Zuger to CWS, 19 December 1921, Stewart Papers.

39. Mrs. Alfred Zuger to CWS, 28 December 1921, Stewart Papers.

40. Mrs. Alfred Zuger to CWS, 28 November 1921, Stewart Papers.

41. The language of intimacy among female friends has caused many to speculate on the reality of the relationships. A good example is Eleanor Roosevelt's letters to and from Lorena Kickok. Geoffrey C. Ward, *A First-Class Temperament: The Emergence of Franklin Roosevelt* (New York: Harper and Row, 1989), 737.

42. *Journal of the National Educational Association* 13 (September–October 1924): 248. Mrs. John B. Sherman, the president of the GFWC, lobbied for the education bill and various other education initiatives.

43. "Administrative Women in Education," *Journal of the National Education Association* 12 (January 1923): 9.

44. NEA officers and committees are listed in every issue of the *Journal of the National Education Association.* Correspondence from this group of women is extensive and documents their interactions within the various organizations. For representative examples, see Katherine Devereux Blake to CWS, 12 April 1924 and 21 April 1925; Alice M. Winter to CWS, 7 February 1924; CWS to Mrs. John D. Sherman, 19 March 1925; CWS to Katherine Devereux Blake, 28 March 1925; Caroline Woodruff to CWS, 12 January 1926; Sally Lucas Jean to CWS, 2 March 1926; CWS to Josephine Preston, 8 September 1927, Stewart Papers.

45. CWS to Lela Mae Stiles, 27 July 1922, Stewart Papers.

46. Fannie B. Williams to CWS, 31 August 1922, Stewart Papers.

47. CWS to Lela Mae Stiles, 9 July 1923, Stewart Papers.

48. CWS to Agnes W. Winn, 15 July 1922; CWS to Josephine Preston, 8 September 1927, Stewart Papers.

49. CWS to Miss Lida Hafford, 30 August 1920, Stewart Papers.

50. Wesley, *NEA,* 145–47; Dumenil, "'Insatiable Maw,'" 499, 518, 523.

51. The measure was introduced and reported out of committee several times in different versions and under different names, including Smith-Towner, Towner-Sterling, Sterling-Reed, Curtis-Reed, and Capper-Robinson. Dumenil, "'Insatiable Maw,'" 501. Mary Bronaugh to CWS, 24 January 1921; CWS to Laura B. Summers, 7 December 1920, Stewart Papers.

52. Minutes of the Meeting of the Board of Directors, Kentucky Federation of Women's Clubs, 15 October 1924, Ida Earle Fowler Papers.

53. Dumenil, "'Insatiable Maw,'" 501, 502.

54. Program, Illiteracy Conference of the Eastern States, Box 4, Stewart Papers.

55. "Illiteracy Report," 1924, 20, 21.

56. Ibid., 20–23.

57. David Nasaw, *Schooled to Order: A Social History of Public Schooling in the United States* (New York: Oxford University Press, 1979), 144. This fairly constant theme is reflected in the NEA journal. See specifically M. Catherine Sexauer, "Americanizing Illiterates," and Charl Ormond Williams, "The Democratic Awakening and Professional Organization," *Journal of the National Education Association* 11 (June 1922): 233, 261.

58. "Illiteracy Report," 1924, 29.

59. Ibid., 25, 26.

60. Charles H. Williams, "Europe and the World Conference on Education," *Journal of the National Education Association* 12 (March 1923): 98–99; "World Conference on Education, *Journal of the National Education Association* 12 (June 1923): 98–99.

61. "Illiteracy Report," 1924, 30–33.

62. Dumenil, "'Insatiable Maw,'" 505. For a text of the Smith-Towner Bill, see *Congressional Record*, 66th Cong., 1st sess., July 28, 1919, 3239–40. Both houses reported the bill favorably in 1921, but the bill did not come to a vote. Reported again as Towner-Sterling (1921), Sterling-Reed (1924), Curtis-Reed (1925), and without funding as Capper-Robinson (1929), the measure failed. See also Frank J. Munger and Richard F. Fenno Jr., *National Politics and Federal Aid to Education* (Syracuse: New York University Press, 1962), 5.

63. George D. Strayer, "The Education Bill," *Journal of the National Education Association* 12 (October 1923): 308.

64. Note in Stewart's hand, 17 January 1924; undated note in Stewart's hand, Stewart Papers.

65. CWS to Mrs. John D. Sherman, 1 June 1923, Stewart Papers.

66. Garland Powell to CWS, 21 June 1923, Stewart Papers.

67. CWS to Garland Powell, 26 September 1923, Stewart Papers.

68. CWS to Governor William E. Sweet, 9 October 1923 (note in margin lists governors to whom letter was also sent); and Lela Mae Stiles to CWS, undated, listing agencies and individuals to whom letters had been mailed, October–November 1923 correspondence folder, Stewart Papers.

69. CWS telegram to Mrs. Thomas G. Winter, 8 November 1923, Stewart Papers.

70. Mrs. Thomas G. Winter to CWS and Dr. Tigert, 8 November 1923, Stewart Papers.

71. CWS to Lela Mae Stiles, 13, 14, and 15 November 1923, Stewart Papers.

72. Ibid.; Lela Mae Stiles to CWS, 15 November 1923, Stewart Papers.

73. Lela Mae Stiles to CWS, 16 November 1923, Stewart Papers.

74. Garland Powell to Calvin Coolidge, 1 October 1923, copy with note: "send to Mrs. Stewart," Stewart Papers.

75. Augustus O. Thomas to CWS, and Florence M. Hale to CWS, both 17 November 1923, Stewart Papers.

76. CWS to Lela Mae Stiles, 19 November 1923, Stewart Papers.

77. "State Groups to Co-operate with Campaign on Illiteracy," *Christian Science Monitor,* 14 January 1923; "The National Illiteracy Conference," *Journal of the National Education Association* 13 (March 1924): 107.

78. CWS to Mrs. John D. Sherman, 19 and 21 March 1925; CWS to J. W. Crabtree, 19 March 1925, Stewart Papers.

79. CWS to Charl O. Williams, 28 February 1925, Stewart Papers.

80. "Education Bill Hearings," *Journal of the National Education Association* 13 (April 1924): 150.

81. "Progress on the Education Bill," *Journal of the National Education Association* 13 (May 1924): 188, 189.

82. Link and McCormick, *Progressivism,* 69–70, 102–3; Stewart distinguishes her work from that of Americanizers in CWS to A. R. Nestos, 28 May 1923, Stewart Papers.

83. John Higham, *Strangers in the Land: Patterns of American Nativism, 1860–1925* (New Brunswick, NJ: Rutgers University Press, 1955), 194–262.

84. Stubblefield and Keane, *Adult Education,* 180–83.

85. Higham, *Strangers in the Land,* 199, 224, 244.

86. S. K. Mardis to CWS, 15 March and 19 May 1923; CWS to Miss Sarah E. Luther, 13 December 1921, Stewart Papers.

87. Clipping, *School Journal,* 18 May 1916, scrapbook, 122, Stewart Papers.

88. "The Education Bill Advances," *Journal of the National Education Association* 13 (March 1924): 112.

89. Robert A. Luke, *The NEA and Adult Education: A Historical Review: 1921–1972* (Sarasota, FL: by the author, 1992), 5–45; Roy Lubove, *The Professional Altruist: The Emergence of Social Work as a Career, 1880–1930* (Cambridge, MA: Harvard University Press, 1965), 19, 23.

90. For an examination of this phenomenon and its result, see Oscar Handlin, "Education and the European Immigrant, 1820–1920," and John F. McClymer, "The Americanization Movement and the Education of the Foreign-Born Adult, 1914–1925," in *American Education and the European Immigrant: 1840–1940,* ed. Bernard J. Weiss (Urbana: University of Illinois Press, 1982), 3–16, 96–116.

91. Luke, *NEA and Adult Education,* 52.

92. CWS to A. E. Winship, 14 December 1925, Stewart Papers.

93. Robert C. Deming to CWS, 29 November 1925, Stewart Papers.

94. CWS to Robert Deming, 14 December 1925, Stewart Papers.

95. Robert C. Deming to CWS, 18 December 1925, Stewart Papers.

96. CWS to A. E. Winship, 14 December 1925, Stewart Papers.

97. NEA *Proceedings* 65 (1927): 295, copy in Stewart Papers.

98. Cora Wilson Stewart, "Report of the Illiteracy Committee of the National Council of Education," NEA *Proceedings* 66 (1928): 246, copy in Stewart Papers.

99. Lubove, *Professional Altruist,* 52–53.

100. CWS, "Report of the Illiteracy Committee," 248.

101. Ibid.

102. Ibid., 249.

103. Ibid., 250.

6. A New Vision

1. CWS to Sally Lucas Jean, 8 March 1926, Stewart Papers.

2. Willie Lawson, "State and Local Support and Leadership for Adult Education," NEA *Proceedings* 63 (1925): 348–52, copy in Stewart Papers.

3. *Pictorial Review,* reprint edition, 11 February 1925, biographical folder, Box 1; diary entry in Stewart's hand, 1 January 1926, Box 1, Stewart Papers.

4. Diary entry in Stewart's hand, 1 January 1925, biographical folder, Box 1, Stewart Papers.

5. Diary entry, 1 January 1925.

6. Cora Wilson Stewart, "My Experience in Forming the National Illiteracy Association," handwritten notes, biographical folder, Box 1, Stewart Papers.

7. Ibid., 3, 4.

8. Ibid., 11.

9. Davis, *Spearheads for Reform,* 57–58.

10. Ibid., 5, 6, 11, 12; diary entry in Stewart's hand, 10 January 1925, biographical file, Box 1, Stewart Papers.

11. On White, see *The Autobiography of William Allen White* (New York: Macmillan, 1946); and David Hinshaw, *A Man from Kansas: The Story of William Allen White* (New York: Putnam's, 1945).

12. CWS to Jane Addams, 19 June 1925; CWS, "My Experience," 1, 2, Stewart Papers.

13. CWS, "My Experience," 4, Stewart Papers.

14. Linda Gordon, *Pitied but Not Entitled: Single Mothers and the History of Welfare, 1890–1935* (New York: Free Press, 1994), 84.

15. Higham, *Strangers in the Land,* 236–37, 244.

16. Jean Bethke Elshtain, *Jane Addams and the Dream of American Democracy* (New York: Basic Books, 2002), 245.

17. CWS to William Allen White, 15 June 1926, Stewart Papers.

18. William Allen White to CWS, 21 June 1926, Stewart Papers.

19. The correspondence on this issue is extensive. See particularly CWS to Mrs. Phelps, 24 April 1928; CWS to William Allen White, 3 April 1928; and CWS to Sally Lucas Jean, 11 April 1928, Stewart Papers.

20. Cora Wilson Stewart, *Mother's First Book: A First Reader for Home Women* (Washington, DC: National Illiteracy Crusade, 1929), 6.

21. Ibid., 40.

22. Ibid., 43.

23. CWS to W. J. Rice, 17 March 1928; undated newspaper clipping, Stewart Papers; "Wipe Out Illiteracy and Lift the Nation from Tenth Place," *Woman's Journal,* May 1929, 48.

24. Stewart, *Mother's First Book*, 56–68.

25. CWS to Henry J. Allen, 31 May 1928; Stewart, *Mother's First Book*, 6; CWS to Roscoe Edlund, 3 March 1927; CWS to William Allen White, 2 December 1926, Stewart Papers. The amount of the donation is not specified but was probably $2,000.

26. "Metropolitan Life Insurance Project," small pamphlet [1929]; CWS to "Dear Friend," 10 September 1931, Stewart Papers. In this letter she wrote, "It takes a hero to start school when he is crippled as you are," and encouraged the adult student to pursue his dream of education.

27. CWS to William Allen White, 27 February 1926, Stewart Papers.

28. CWS to William Allen White, 12 May 1926, Stewart Papers.

29. Calvin Coolidge to CWS, 6 March 1926, Stewart Papers.

30. CWS to Sally Lucas Jean, 8 March 1926, Stewart Papers.

31. Program, "Celebration, Northwest Indian Congress," 30–31 October 1925, Stewart Papers.

32. CWS to Governor Nestos, 3 February 1931; mimeographed copy of *Indian's First Book*, Stewart Papers.

33. CWS to Josephine Preston, 1 December 1926, Stewart Papers.

34. CWS to Sally Lucas Jean, 16 June 1927; CWS to Henry G. Leach, 8 September 1927; M. C. Turner to CWS, 21 August 1928; Alkahest to CWS, 24 August 1928; CWS to William Allen White, 3 October 1928, Stewart Papers.

35. Hoover, who was once regarded by historians as a conservative or reactionary, is now generally seen as one of the most active and innovative men in government in the twenties and throughout his presidency. Ellis W. Hawley, ed., *Herbert Hoover as Secretary of Commerce: Studies in New Era Thought and Practice* (West Branch, IA: Herbert Hoover Presidential Library Association, 1974); James Stuart Olson, *Herbert Hoover and the Reconstruction Finance Corporation, 1931–1933* (Ames: Iowa State University Press, 1977); Joan Hoff Wilson, *Herbert Hoover: Forgotten Progressive* (Boston: Little, Brown, 1975).

36. CWS to Governor Allen, 31 May 1928, Stewart Papers. Allen and Hoover were close friends, and Stewart noted in this letter that she expected Allen to be named to Hoover's cabinet.

37. CWS to Senator Allen, 17 October 1929, Stewart Papers.

38. CWS to Herbert Houston, 28 October 1929, Stewart Papers.

39. On Huey Long and the crusade, see T. Harry Williams, *Huey Long* (New York: Knopf, 1960), 253. Interestingly, Stewart received no credit for the Louisiana literacy crusade, although her participation is fully documented. Huey B. Long, *Early Innovators in Adult Education* (London: Routledge, 1991). On Stewart's role in the Louisiana campaign, see, for example, CWS to Roscoe Edlund, 29 April 1929; T. H. Harris to Josephine Preston, 13 May 1929; CWS to John Finley, 6 May 1929; CWS to John Finley, 15 May 1929; and CWS to May W. Harding, 15 May 1929, Stewart Papers.

40. Notes in Stewart's hand, biographical file, Box 1, Stewart Papers.

41. *New York Times*, 10 May 1930.

42. Evelyn Williams to Belmont Farley, 18 July 1929; CWS to Evelyn Williams, 14 July 1929; undated newspaper clipping, Box 1, Stewart Papers.

43. French Strother to CWS, 21 October 1929, Stewart Papers.

44. CWS to Herbert Houston, 13 November 1929; CWS to Col. Andrew Gray, 29 November 1929, Stewart Papers.

45. CWS to Herbert Houston, 23 September 1930, Stewart Papers.

46. Herbert Houston to French Strother, 13 November 1929, appended to Herbert Houston to CWS, 13 November 1929, Stewart Papers.

47. Herbert Houston to Ray Lyman Wilbur, 7 November 1929, appended to Herbert Houston to CWS, 8 November 1929, Stewart Papers.

48. CWS to Governor Nestos, 1 March 1930, Stewart Papers. By this time, Americans had become less concerned about private power and increasingly suspicious of growing federal bureaucracies, which they had earlier embraced to checkmate the former. This reversal profoundly affected the professionalization of education. Dumenil, "'Insatiable Maw,'" 523.

49. CWS to T. H. Harris, 1 March 1930, Stewart Papers.

50. Herbert Houston to CWS, 2 May 1930; CWS to R. A. Nestos, 8 May 1930; CWS to Herbert Houston, 23 May 1930, Stewart Papers.

51. CWS to Miss Ellen M. Kelly, 31 July 1930; Ellen M. Kelly to CWS, 31 July 1930, Stewart Papers.

52. CWS to T. H. Harris, 20 August 1930, Stewart Papers.

53. "Memo for Conference with Dr. Gray"; CWS to T. H. Harris, 26 August 1930; CWS to Governor Nestos, 11 September 1930; R. A. Nestos to CWS, 15 September 1930, Stewart Papers.

54. CWS to Herbert Houston, 16 September 1930, Stewart Papers.

55. Herbert Houston to CWS, 17 September 1930, Stewart Papers.

56. CWS telegram to Mrs. Blanche Nagel, 29 September; CWS telegrams to T. H. Harris, 30 September and 2 October; CWS to T. H. Harris, 3 and 4 October; and T. H. Harris to CWS, 6 October 1930, Stewart Papers.

57. CWS to T. H. Harris, 28 October 1930, Stewart Papers.

58. National Illiteracy Crusade, "Minutes," 21 November 1929, Box 35, Stewart Papers.

59. Alfred K. Stern to CWS, 8 November 1932, Stewart Papers.

60. CWS to Ray Lyman Wilbur, 12 December 1932; 71st Cong., 3rd sess., Joint Resolution 219; CWS to Governor Nestos, 8 October 1930, and R. A.. Nestos to CWS, 6 November 1930, Stewart Papers.

61. CWS to Governor Nestos, 8 October 1930; "Summary of Activities of the Field Secretary—Minnie Jean Nielson," 31 January–30 September; CWS to Senator Allen, 3 December 1930, Stewart Papers.

62. Ray Lyman Wilbur to Board Members of the NACI, 12 December 1932, Stewart Papers.

63. CWS telegram to Mary W. Dewson, 10 October 1932; Mrs. Ellis Yost to CWS, 2 September 1932; CWS to Mrs. Ellis Yost, 7 September 1932, Stewart Papers.

64. CWS to Frank C. Button, 6 March 1933; Ray Lyman Wilbur to Board Members of the NACI, 12 December 1932; Alfred K. Stern, director for special activities of the Julius Rosenwald Fund, told her the new administration would "find a way" to continue

her services and urged Stewart to seek an extension of the NACI through her friend Ruth Bryan Owen, assuring her that "some definite set-up can be provided for your program in the Department of the Interior under the new administration." Alfred K. Stern to CWS, 8 November and 29 November 1932, Stewart Papers.

65. Ruth Bryan Owen to CWS, 2 February 1933 and 1 March 1933; CWS to Robert Thomas Hardy, Inc., 16 December 1933; Major F. R. Garcin to CWS, 3 August 1933, Stewart Papers.

66. Dr. Homer Wilson to CWS, 23 January 1933; quotation is from an undated newspaper clipping from the *Memphis Press Scimitar,* scrapbook; CWS to Governor Pearson, 24 April 1935; CWS to Ruth Bryan Owen, 25 April 1935, Stewart Papers.

67. Quoted in Dominic W. Moreo, *Schools in the Great Depression* (New York: Garland, 1996), 4.

68. *New York Times,* 16 August 1934, 1.

69. Arthur E. Bestor, "The A.B.C. of Federal Emergency Education," *Journal of Adult Education* 6 (April 1934): 150, 151.

70. Cora Wilson Stewart, "Radio Address," 10 December 1933, Stewart Papers.

71. CWS to J. Herbert Killey, 14 December 1933; CWS to Ida B. Nance, 16 December 1933, Stewart Papers. The manuscript remained unfinished.

72. Stewart, "Radio Address"; Skocpol, *Protecting Soldiers and Mothers,* 319, 320. Skocpol argues that many of the maternalist policies surviving from the Progressive Era became "subordinate and marginal parts" of national social welfare provision.

Conclusion

1. Mattie Dalton to CWS, 19 October 1910, Stewart Papers.

2. Ibid.

3. The term was used by Carrie Chapman Catt and Nellie Rogers Shuler in *Woman Suffrage and Politics: The Inner Story of the Suffrage Movement* (1923), quoted in Spruill, *New Women of the New South,* xiii.

4. "State Has No Money for Its Illiterates Now," 19 February 1916, newspaper clipping, Box 55, Stewart Papers.

5. Crunden makes this clear in *Ministers of Reform,* 3–15. Quotations are from Tyack and Hansot, *Managers of Virtue,* 93.

6. Crunden, *Ministers of Reform,* 3–15. Although Crunden does not include a category of "innovative nostalgia" in education (possibly because the very nomenclature smacks of academic schizophrenia), Stewart embodies his descriptive phrase. Crunden identifies commonalities in upbringing, religious conviction, education, and "conversion" experiences that molded a generation of progressives, including Jane Addams, Theodore Roosevelt, Ida Tarbell, and others.

7. See particularly Peter Filene, "An Obituary for 'The Progressive Movement,'" *American Quarterly* 22 (Spring 1970): 20–34; and David M. Kennedy, "Overview: The Progressive Era," *Historian* 37 (May 1975): 453–68. Also, Daniel T. Rodgers, "In Search of Progressivism," *Reviews in American History* 10 (December 1982): 113–32; John C. Burnham, "Essay," in *Progressivism,* ed. John D. Buenker, John C. Burnham, and Rob-

ert M. Crunden (Cambridge, MA: Harvard University Press, 1977), 3–29; Arthur S. Link, "What Happened to the Progressive Movement in the 1920s?" *American Historical Review* 64 (July 1959): 833–51; and Lemons, *Woman Citizen.*

8. Stewart, like Philander P. Claxton, John C. Campbell, and other educational leaders, was intrigued by the possibilities the Danish model offered for schooling in the mountains. Transportation of the folk high schools was never fully successful, however. See Campbell, *Southern Highlander and His Homeland;* Olive Dame Campbell, *The Danish Folk School: Its Influence in the Life of Denmark and the North* (New York: Macmillan, 1928); Whisnant, *All That Is Native and Fine;* Harold W. Stubblefield, *Towards a History of Adult Education in America* (London: Croom Helm, 1988); and Harold W. Stubblefield, "The Danish Folk High School and Its Reception in the United States: 1870s–1930s," at http://www.distance.syr.edu/stubblefield.html. See also Fink, *Progressive Intellectuals,* especially chap. 8, "Teaching the People: Wil Lou Gray and the Siren of Educational Opportunity." On the Highlander Folk School, see Myles Horton with Judith Kohl and Herbert Kohl, *The Long Haul: An Autobiography* (New York: Teachers College Press, 1998).

9. Cora Wilson Stewart, "The Challenge to Home Missions," *World Call* 13, no. 9 (September 1931): 11–14, in Morehead State University Papers, Special Collections, Morehead; "Moonlight Trysts for Education," *Literary Digest,* January 10, 1931, 19, 20.

10. U.S. Census Bureau, Fourteenth Census of the United States, 1920, vol. 3; Winston, *Illiteracy in the United States,* 16–18; "Rank of States," National Advisory Committee on Illiteracy, 11–12, statistics folder, Box 63, Stewart Papers.

11. Kathryn Kish Sklar, "The Historical Foundations of Women's Power in the Creation of the American Welfare State, 1830–1930," in *Mothers of a New World: Maternalist Politics and the Origins of Welfare States,* ed. Seth Koven and Sonya Michel (New York: Routledge, 1993), 69.

12. Susan Ware, *Beyond Suffrage: Women in the New Deal* (Cambridge, MA: Harvard University Press, 1981); and Ware, *Partner and I: Molly Dewson, Feminism, and New Deal Politics* (New Haven, CT: Yale University Press, 1987).

13. Kett, *Pursuit of Knowledge,* 396–97.

14. Oxford Group National Assembly "Programme," Box 41, Stewart Papers.

15. CWS to Ruth Bryan Owen, 25 April 1935, Stewart Papers.

16. "The Oxford Group, a Way of Life," Box 41, Stewart Papers.

17. Untitled notes in Stewart's hand, 3 May 1934, religious writings folder, Box 38, Stewart Papers. There is no evidence in Stewart's correspondence that Jones acknowledged the letter.

18. Untitled notes in Stewart's hand, 3 May 1934, religious writings folder, Box 38, Stewart Papers.

19. Ibid.

20. For thorough and critical contemporary analyses of Buchman and his movement, see Henry P. Van Dusen, "Apostle to the Twentieth Century," *Atlantic Monthly,* July 1934, 1–24; and Van Dusen, "The Oxford Group Movement, an Appraisal," *Atlantic Monthly,* August 1934, 240–252.

21. Messages from these men and others, sent from all parts of the world to the

meetings for Moral Rearmament in New York and Washington, D.C., in May and June 1938, were reprinted in a pamphlet entitled "Moral Re-Armament," Box 41, Stewart Papers.

22. Untitled note in Stewart's hand, [May] 1934, religious writings folder, Box 38, Stewart Papers.

23. Ibid.

24. Thomas G. Sticht, "Mother's First Book and Family Literacy Day in Canada," online at: http://www.nald.ca/WHATNEW/hnews/2002/mother.htm, accessed 3 September 2004.

25. Septima P. Clark, *Echo in My Soul* (New York: Dutton, 1962), 149; Thomas G. Sticht, "A String of Pearls: Three Leading Ladies of Adult Literacy in the 20th Century" (paper presented at the meeting of the History of Reading Special Interest Group of the International Reading Association in Reno, Nevada, 4 May 2004).

26. Elgin Mannion, "Education, Longevity, Income: Measuring Kentucky's Human Development Index" (Lexington: University of Kentucky Appalachian Center, 2003), 4, 5; "Adult Education and Literacy in Kentucky," Research Report No. 296 (Frankfort, KY: Legislative Research Commission, 2000), 17. Quotation is from page 7 of this report.

27. Thomas G. Sticht, "Moving Adult Literacy Education from the Margins to the Mainstream of Educational Policy and Practice" (Washington, DC: Division of Adult Education and Literacy, 1998), 2–4.

Bibliography

Primary Sources

MANUSCRIPTS

Mary Elliott Flannery Papers. Special Collections. Margaret I. King Library, University of Kentucky, Lexington.

Ila Earle Fowler Papers. Special Collections. Margaret I. King Library, University of Kentucky, Lexington.

General Education Board. Early Southern Program, Kentucky. Microfilm. University of Kentucky Education Library, Lexington.

Wil Lou Gray Papers. South Caroliniana Library, University of South Carolina, Columbia.

James B. McCreary Papers. Kentucky Department of Libraries and Archives, Frankfort.

Southern Education Board Records. Southern Historical Collection, Library of the University of North Carolina, Chapel Hill.

Augustus O. Stanley Papers. Special Collections, Margaret I. King Library, University of Kentucky, Lexington.

Cora Wilson Stewart Collection. Special Collections, Camden-Carroll Library, Morehead State University, Morehead, Kentucky.

Cora Wilson Stewart Papers. Special Collections, Margaret I. King Library, University of Kentucky, Lexington.

INTERVIEWS

Noi Doyle. Lexington, Kentucky, 28 July 1995.

Dr. Jack Ellis. Morehead, Kentucky, 19 November 1993.

Marion McCrea. Houston, Texas, 17 July 1995 and 9 June 2003.

Norma Powers. Morehead, Kentucky, 17 November 1993.

Patrick Smith. Director, Wil Lou Gray Opportunity School, West Columbia, South Carolina, 6 October 2003.

Descendants of A. T. Stewart. Morehead, Kentucky, 24 November 1999.
Bunyan Wilson Jr. Ashland, Kentucky, 17 July 1995.

PUBLISHED REPORTS, PROCEEDINGS

Kentucky Department of Education. Bulletin 17:4. Barksdale Hamlett. *History of Education in Kentucky,* Frankfort: July 1914.
———. "Report of the Kentucky Illiteracy Commission." In *Report of the Superintendent of Public Instruction of Kentucky Department of Education for the Two Years Ending December 31, 1919.* Frankfort, KY, 1919.
National Education Association. Addresses and Proceedings, 1917–28. Washington, DC: National Education Association.
State of Kentucky, Kentucky Illiteracy Commission. "First Biennial Report, 1915–1916." Frankfort, KY, 1916.
———. "Report of the Kentucky Illiteracy Commission, 1916–1920." Frankfort, KY, 1920.
U.S. Bureau of the Census. 1900. Rowan County, Kentucky. Magisterial District No. 1. Kentucky Department of Libraries and Archives. Microfilm
———. 1910. Rowan County, Kentucky. Magisterial District No. 1. Kentucky Department of Libraries and Archives. Microfilm
U.S. Department of the Interior. Bureau of Education. "Education in the Southern Mountains." Washington, DC, 1937.
———. "Illiteracy in the United States and an Experiment for Its Elimination." Bulletin 20:530. Washington, DC: Government Printing Office, 1913.

Primary Sources by Cora Wilson Stewart

Country Life Readers, First Book. Richmond, VA: B. F. Johnson, 1915.
Country Life Readers, Second Book. Richmond, VA: B. F. Johnson, 1916.
"Facts Concerning the Moonlight School Work." Frankfort, KY: Kentucky Illiteracy Commission, n.d. [1920].
"Illiteracy and the War." Washington, DC: National Illiteracy Committee, 1918.
"Moonlight School Course of Study, 1918." Frankfort, KY: Kentucky Illiteracy Commission, 1918.
"Moonlight School Course of Study, War Number." Frankfort, KY: Kentucky Illiteracy Commission, 1917.
"Moonlight Schools Bulletin." Frankfort, KY: Kentucky Illiteracy Commission, 1919.
Moonlight Schools for the Emancipation of Adult Illiterates. New York: Dutton, 1922.
Mother's First Book: A First Reader for Home Women. Washington, DC: National Illiteracy Crusade, 1929.
Soldier's First Book. New York: Association Press, 1918.
Cora Wilson Stewart and the Moonlight Schools, photographic archive online at http://kdl.kyvl.org/cgi/f/findaid/findaid-idx?xc=1;c=kukead;idno=kukavpa58m25.

Secondary Sources

Apple, Michael W., and Linda K. Christian-Smith, eds. *The Politics of the Textbook*. New York: Routledge, 1991.

Ayres, DaMaris E. *Let My People Learn: The Biography of Wil Lou Gray*. Grenwood, SC: Attic Press, 1988.

Baker, Paula. "The Domestication of Politics: Women and American Political Society, 1780–1920." *American Historical Review* 89 (June 1984): 620–47.

———. *The Moral Frameworks of Public Life: Gender, Politics, and the State in Rural New York, 1870–1930*. New York: Oxford University Press, 1991.

Barney, Sandra Lee. *Authorized to Heal: Gender, Class, and the Transformation of Medicine in Appalachia, 1880–1930*. Chapel Hill: University of North Carolina Press, 2000.

Batteau, Allen W., ed. *Appalachia and America: Autonomy and Regional Dependence*. Lexington: University Press of Kentucky, 1983.

———. *The Invention of Appalachia*. Tucson: University of Arizona Press, 1990.

Beard, Mary Ritter. *Woman's Work in Municipalities*. Reprint, New York: Arno Press, 1972.

Bernier, Normand R., and Jack E. Williams. *Beyond Beliefs: Ideological Foundations of American Education*. Englewood Cliffs, NJ: Prentice-Hall, 1973.

Bestor, Arthur E. "The A.B.C. of Federal Emergency Education." *Journal of Adult Education* 6 (April 1934): 150–54.

Birdwhistell, Terry L., and Susan E. Allen. "The Appalachian Image Re-examined: An Oral History View of Eastern Kentucky." *Register of the Kentucky Historical Society* 81 (Spring 1983): 287–302.

Blair, Juanita, and Fred Brown. *Days of Anger, Days of Tears*. Morehead, KY: Pioneer Print Service, 1984.

Blair, Karen J. *The Clubwoman as Feminist: True Womanhood Redefined, 1868–1914*. New York: Holmes and Meier, 1980.

Bledstein, Burton. *The Culture of Professionalism: The Middle Class and the Development of Higher Education in America*. New York: Norton, 1976.

Blount, Jackie M. *Destined to Rule the Schools: Women and the Superintendency, 1873–1995*. Albany: State University of New York Press, 1998.

Bowers, William L. *The Country Life Movement in America, 1900–1920*. Port Washington, NY: Kennikat Press, 1974.

Breckinridge, Sophonisba P. *Madeline McDowell Breckinridge: A Leader in the New South*. Chicago: University of Chicago Press, 1921.

———. *New Homes for Old*. Reprinted in series *Americanization Studies: The Acculturation of Immigrant Groups into American Society*. Vol. 6. Edited by William S. Bernard. Montclair, NJ: Patterson Smith, 1971.

Brown, Dorothy M. *Setting a Course: American Women in the 1920s*. Boston: Twayne, 1987.

Brumberg, Joan Jacobs, and Nancy Tomes. "Women in the Professions: A Research Agenda for American Historians." *Reviews in American History* 10 (June 1982): 275.

Buenker, John D., John C. Burnham, and Robert M. Crunden, eds. *Progressivism*. Cambridge, MA: Harvard University Press, 1977.

Burckel, Nicholas C. "A. O. Stanley and Progressive Reform, 1902–1919." *Register of the Kentucky Historical Society* 79 (Spring 1981): 158.

———. "From Beckham to McCreary: The Progressive Record of Kentucky Governors." *Register of the Kentucky Historical Society* 76 (October 1978): 299–303.

Campbell, Barbara Kuhn. *The "Liberated Woman" of 1914: Prominent Women in the Progressive Era*. Ann Arbor: University of Michigan Research Press, 1979.

Campbell, John C. *The Southern Highlander and His Homeland*. 1921. Reprint, with a foreword by Rupert Vance and an introduction by Henry D. Shapiro. Lexington: University Press of Kentucky, 1969.

Campbell, Olive Dame. *The Danish Folk School: Its Influence in the Life of Denmark and the North*. New York: Macmillan, 1928.

Carlton David L. *Mill and Town in South Carolina, 1880–1920*. Baton Rouge: Louisiana State University Press, 1982.

Chambers, Clarke A. *Seedtime of Reform: American Social Service and Social Action, 1918–1933*. Minneapolis: University of Minnesota Press, 1963.

Channing, Steven A. *Kentucky: A Bicentennial History*. New York: Norton, 1977.

Clark, Thomas D. *A History of Kentucky*. Lexington, KY: John Bradford Press, 1960.

Cott, Nancy. "Across the Great Divide: Women in Politics before and after 1920." In *Women, Politics, and Change*, edited by Louise A. Tilley and Patricia Gurin, 153–76. New York: Russell Sage Foundation, 1990.

———. *The Grounding of Modern Feminism*. New Haven, CT: Yale University Press, 1987.

———. "What's in a Name? The Limits of 'Social Feminism'; or, Expanding the Vocabulary of Women's History." *Journal of American History* 76 (December 1989): 800–829.

Counts, George. *The Selective Character of American Secondary Education*. Chicago: University of Chicago Press, 1922.

Cox, Duane. "The Gottschalk-Colvin Case: A Study in Academic Purpose and Command." *Register of the Kentucky Historical Society* 85 (Winter 1987): 46–68.

Cremin, Lawrence A. *The Transformation of the School: Progressivism in American Education, 1876–1957*. New York: Knopf, 1961.

Crocco, Margaret Smith, Petra Munro, and Kathleen Weiler. *Pedagogies of Resistance: Women Educator Activists, 1880–1960*. New York: Teachers College Press, 1999.

Crunden, Robert M. *Ministers of Reform: The Progressives' Achievement in American Civilization, 1889–1920*. New York: Basic Books, 1982.

Curti, Merle. *The Social Ideas of American Educators*. Paterson, NJ: Littlefield, Adams, 1935.

Dabney, Charles W. *Universal Education in the South*. Chapel Hill: University of North Carolina Press, 1936.

Danbom, David B. *The Resisted Revolution: Urban America and the Industrialization of Agriculture, 1900–1930*. Ames: Iowa State University Press, 1979.

———. *The World of Hope: Progressives and the Struggle for an Ethical Public Life*. Philadelphia: Temple University Press, 1987.

Davis, Allen F. *American Heroine: The Life and Legend of Jane Addams.* New York: Oxford University Press, 1973.

———. *Spearheads for Reform: The Social Settlements and the Progressive Movement, 1890–1914.* New York: Oxford University Press, 1967.

Dawley, Alan. *Struggles for Justice: Social Responsibility and the Liberal State.* Cambridge, MA: Belknap Press of Harvard University Press, 1991.

de Castell, Suzanne, Allen Luke, and Kieran Egan, eds. *Literacy, Society, and Schooling: A Reader.* Cambridge: Cambridge University Press, 1986.

Degler, Carl N. *At Odds: Women and the Family in America from the Revolution to Present.* New York: Oxford University Press, 1980.

Disch, Robert. *Future of Literacy.* Englewood Cliffs, NJ: Prentice-Hall, 1973.

DuBois, Ellen Carol, and Vicki Ruiz, eds. *Unequal Sisters: A Multicultural Reader in U.S. Women's History.* 2nd ed. New York: Routledge, 1990.

Dumenil, Lynn. "'The Insatiable Maw of Bureaucracy': Antistatism and Education Reform in the 1920s." *Journal of American History* 77 (September 1990): 499–524.

Eldred, Janet Carey, and Peter Mortensen. "Reading Literacy Narratives." *College English* 54 (September 1992): 512–39.

Eller, Ronald. *Miners, Millhands, and Mountaineers: Industrialization of the Appalachian South, 1880–1930.* Knoxville: University of Tennessee Press, 1982.

Ellis, Jack D. *Morehead Memories: True Stories from Eastern Kentucky.* Ashland, KY: Jesse Stuart Foundation, 2001.

Elshtain, Jean Bethke. *Jane Addams and the Dream of American Democracy.* New York: Basic Books, 2002.

Elson, Ruth Miller. *Guardians of Tradition: American Schoolbooks of the Nineteenth Century.* Lincoln: University of Nebraska Press, 1964.

Estes, Florence. "Cora Wilson Stewart and the Moonlight Schools of Kentucky: A Case Study in the Rhetorical Uses of Literacy." Ph.D. diss., University of Kentucky, 1988.

Filene, Benjamin. *Romancing the Folk: Public Memory and American Roots Music.* Chapel Hill: University of North Carolina Press, 2000.

Filene, Peter. "An Obituary for 'The Progressive Movement.'" *American Quarterly* 22 (Spring 1970): 20–34.

Fink, Leon. *Progressive Intellectuals and the Dilemmas of Democratic Commitment.* Cambridge, MA: Harvard University Press, 1997.

Flatt, Donald F. *A Light to the Mountains: Morehead State University, 1887–1997.* Ashland, KY: Jesse Stuart Foundation, 1997.

Forderhase, Nancy K. "'The Clear Call of Thoroughbred Women': The Kentucky Federation of Women's Clubs and the Crusade for Educational Reform, 1903–1909." *Register of the Kentucky Historical Society* 83 (Winter 1985): 19–35.

———. "Eve Returns to the Garden: Women Reformers in Appalachian Kentucky in the Early Twentieth Century." *Register of the Kentucky Historical Society* 85 (Summer 1987): 237–61.

———. "'Limited Only by Earth and Sky': The Louisville Woman's Club and Progressive Reform, 1900–1910." *Filson Club History Quarterly* 59 (July 1985): 327–43.

Fortune, Alonzo W. *The Disciples in Kentucky.* Lexington, KY: Convention of the Christian Churches in Kentucky, 1932.

Frankel, Noralee, and Nancy S. Dye, eds. *Gender, Class, Race, and Reform in the Progressive Era.* Lexington: University Press of Kentucky, 1991.

Fraser, Walter, Jr., ed. *The Web of Southern Social Relations.* Athens: University of Georgia Press, 1985.

Freedman, Estelle. "Separatism as Strategy: Female Institution Building and American Feminism, 1870–1930." *Feminist Studies* 5 (Fall 1979): 512–29.

Freire, Paulo. *Pedagogy of the Oppressed.* 1970. Reprint, New York: Continuum, 1993.

Frost, William G. "Berea College." *Berea Quarterly* 1 (May 1895): 24.

Fuller, Paul E. *Laura Clay and the Woman's Rights Movement.* Lexington: University Press of Kentucky, 1975.

Gere, Anne Ruggles. *Intimate Practices: Literacy and Cultural Work in U.S. Women's Clubs, 1880–1920.* Urbana: University of Illinois Press, 1997.

Gerster, Patrick, and Nicholas Cords, eds. *Myth and Southern History.* Vol. 2, *The New South.* 2nd ed. Urbana: University of Illinois Press, 1989.

Gifford, James M. "Cora Wilson Stewart and the 'Moonlight School' Movement." In *Appalachia/America: Proceedings of the 1980 Appalachian Studies Conference,* edited by Wilson Somerville, 169–78. Johnson City, TN: Appalachian Consortium Press, 1981.

Gordon, Linda. *Pitied but Not Entitled: Single Mothers and the History of Welfare 1890–1935.* New York: Free Press, 1994.

———. "Putting Children First: Women, Maternalism, and Welfare in the Early Twentieth Century." In *U.S. History as Women's History: New Feminist Essays,* edited by Linda K. Kerber, Alice Kessler-Harris, and Kathryn Kish Sklar, 63–86. Chapel Hill: University of North Carolina Press, 1995.

Graff, Harvey J. *The Literacy Myth: Literacy and Social Structure in the Nineteenth-Century City.* New York: Academic Press, 1979.

Grantham, Dewey W. "The Contours of Southern Progressivism." *American Historical Review* 86 (December 1981): 1035–59.

———. *Southern Progressivism: The Reconciliation of Progress and Tradition.* Knoxville: University of Tennessee Press, 1983.

Harrison, Lowell K., and James C. Klotter. *A New History of Kentucky.* Lexington: University Press of Kentucky, 1997.

Hawley, Ellis W., ed. *Herbert Hoover as Secretary of Commerce: Studies in New Era Thought and Practice.* West Branch, IA: Herbert Hoover Presidential Library Association, 1974.

Hay, Melba Porter. "Madeline McDowell Breckinridge: Her Role in the Kentucky Woman Suffrage Movement, 1908–1920." *Register of the Kentucky Historical Society* 72 (1974): 342–63.

———. "Madeline McDowell Breckinridge: Kentucky Suffragist and Progressive Reformer." Ph.D. diss., University of Kentucky, 1980.

Hays, Samuel P. *The Response to Industrialism, 1885–1914.* Chicago: University of Chicago Press, 1955.

Hennen, John C. *The Americanization of West Virginia: Creating a Modern Industrial State, 1916–1925.* Lexington: University Press of Kentucky, 1996.

Herbst, Jurgen. *And Sadly Teach: Teacher Education and Professionalization in American Culture.* Madison: University of Wisconsin Press, 1989.

Hewitt, Nancy. *Women's Activism and Social Change: Rochester, New York, 1822–1872.* Ithaca, NY: Cornell University Press, 1984.

Higham, John. *Strangers in the Land: Patterns of American Nativism, 1860–1925.* New Brunswick, NJ: Rutgers University Press, 1955.

Hinshaw, David. *A Man from Kansas: The Story of William Allen White.* New York: Putnam's, 1945.

Hoffschwelle, Mary S. *Rebuilding the Rural Southern Community: Reformers, Schools, and Homes in Tennessee, 1900–1930.* Knoxville: University of Tennessee Press, 1998.

Hofstadter, Richard. *The Age of Reform: From Bryan to F.D.R.* New York: Knopf, 1955.

Hopkins, Porter H. *KEA: The First 100 Years: The History of an Organization, 1857–1957.* Louisville, KY: Kentucky Education Association, 1957.

Horton, Myles, with Judith Kohl and Herbert Kohl. *The Long Haul: An Autobiography.* New York: Teachers College Press, 1998.

Hunter, Carman St. John, and David Harman. *Adult Illiteracy in the United States: A Report to the Ford Foundation.* New York: McGraw-Hill, 1979.

Inglis, Fred. *The Management of Ignorance: A Political Theory of the Curriculum.* New York: Basil Blackwell, 1985.

Johnson, Samuel. "Life in the Kentucky Mountains. By a Mountaineer." Reprinted in *Appalachian Images in Folk and Popular Culture,* 2nd ed., edited by W. K. McNeil, 175–85. Knoxville: University of Tennessee Press, 1995.

Jones, Loyal. *Appalachian Values.* Ashland, KY: Jesse Stuart Foundation, 1994.

Kaestle, Carl F., Helen Damon-Moore, L. C. Stedman, K. Tinsley, and W. V. Trollinger Jr., eds. *Literacy in the United States: Readers and Reading since 1880.* New Haven, CT: Yale University Press, 1991.

Karier, Clarence J., Paul C. Violas, and Joel Spring, eds. *Roots of Crisis: American Education in the Twentieth Century.* Chicago: Rand McNally, 1973.

Katz, Michael B. *The Irony of Early School Reform: Educational Innovation in Mid-Nineteenth Century Massachusetts.* Cambridge, MA: Harvard University Press, 1968.

Kennedy, David M. "Overview: The Progressive Era." *Historian* 37 (May 1975): 453–68.

Kephart, Horace. *Our Southern Highlanders: A Narrative of Adventure in the Southern Appalachians and a Study of Life among the Mountaineers.* 1913 and 1924. Reprint, Knoxville: University of Tennessee Press, 1984.

Kett, Joseph. *The Pursuit of Knowledge under Difficulties: From Self-Improvement to Adult Education in America, 1750–1990.* Stanford, CA: Stanford University Press, 1994.

Kirby, Jack Temple. *Darkness at the Dawning: Race and Reform in the Progressive South.* Philadelphia: Lippincott, 1972.

———. *Rural Worlds Lost: The American South, 1920–1960.* Baton Rouge: Louisiana State University Press, 1987.

Kleber, John, ed. *The Kentucky Encyclopedia.* Lexington: University Press of Kentucky, 1992.

Klotter, James C. "The Black South and White Appalachia." *Journal of American History* 66 (March 1980): 832–49.

————. *The Breckinridges of Kentucky, 1760–1981.* Lexington: University Press of Kentucky, 1986.

————. "Feuds in Appalachia: An Overview." *Filson Club Historical Quarterly* 56 (July 1982): 290–317.

————. *Kentucky: Portrait in Paradox, 1900–1950.* Frankfort, KY: Kentucky Historical Society, 1996.

————, ed. *Our Kentucky: A Study of the Bluegrass State.* Frankfort, KY: Kentucky Historical Society, 1992.

Klotter, James C., and Peter J. Sehlinger, eds. *Kentucky Profiles: Biographical Essays in Honor of Holman Hamilton.* Frankfort, KY: Kentucky Historical Society, 1982.

Knott, Claudia. "The Woman Suffrage Movement in Kentucky, 1879–1920." Ph.D. diss., University of Kentucky, 1989.

Kolko, Gabriel. *The Triumph of Conservatism.* New York: Free Press, 1963.

Kousser, J. Morgan. "Progressivism—For Middle-Class Whites Only: North Carolina Education, 1880–1910." *Journal of Southern History* 46 (May 1980): 169–94.

Koven, Seth, and Sonya Michel, eds. *Mothers of a New World: Maternalist Politics and the Origins of Welfare States.* New York: Routledge, 1993.

Ladd-Taylor, Molly. *Mother-Work: Women, Child Welfare, and the State, 1890–1930.* Urbana: University of Illinois Press, 1994.

————. "Toward Defining Maternalism in U.S. History." *Journal of Women's History* 5 (Fall 1993): 110–13.

Lemons, J. Stanley. *The Woman Citizen.* Urbana: University of Illinois Press, 1973.

Ligon, Edward Moses. *A History of Public Education in Kentucky.* Frankfort, KY: Bureau of School Service, 1942.

Link, Arthur S. "The Progressive Movement in the South, 1870–1914." *North Carolina Historical Review* 23 (1946): 172–89.

————. "What Happened to the Progressive Movement in the 1920s?" *American Historical Review* 64 (July 1959): 833–51.

Link, Arthur S., and Richard L. McCormick. *Progressivism.* Arlington Heights, IL: Harlan Davidson, 1983.

Link, William A. *The Paradox of Southern Progressivism, 1880–1930.* Chapel Hill: University of North Carolina Press, 1992.

Long, Huey B. *Early Innovators in Adult Education.* London: Routledge, 1991.

Lubove, Roy. *The Professional Altruist: The Emergence of Social Work as a Career, 1880–1930.* Cambridge, MA: Harvard University Press, 1965.

Luke, Robert A. *The NEA and Adult Education: A Historical Review: 1921–1972.* Sarasota, FL: By the author, 1992.

McAllister, Lester G., and William E. Tucker. *Journey in Faith: A History of the Christian Church.* St. Louis, MO: Disciples of Christ, 1975.

McConkey, James. *Rowan's Progress.* New York: Pantheon, 1992.

McKinney, Gordon B. *Southern Mountain Republicans, 1865–1900: Politics and the Appalachian Community.* 1978. Reprint, with a foreword by Durwood Dunn and a new preface. Knoxville: University of Tennessee Press, 1998.

McNeil, W. K., ed. *Appalachian Images in Folk and Popular Culture.* 2nd ed. Knoxville: University of Tennessee Press, 1995.

McVey, Frank L. *The Gates Open Slowly: A History of Education in Kentucky.* Lexington: University Press of Kentucky, 1949.

Moreo, Dominic W. *Schools in the Great Depression.* New York: Garland, 1996.

Muncy, Robyn. *Creating a Female Dominion in American Reform, 1890–1935.* New York: Oxford University Press, 1991.

Munger, Frank J., and Richard F. Fenno Jr. *National Politics and Federal Aid to Education.* Syracuse: New York University Press, 1962.

Nasaw, David. *Schooled to Order: A Social History of Public Schooling in the United States.* New York: Oxford University Press, 1979.

Nelms, Willie Everette, Jr. "Cora Wilson Stewart: Crusader against Illiteracy." Master's thesis, University of Kentucky, 1973.

———. *Cora Wilson Stewart: Crusader against Illiteracy.* Jefferson, NC: McFarland, 1997.

———. "Cora Wilson Stewart and the Crusade against Illiteracy in Kentucky." *Register of the Kentucky Historical Society* 74 (1976): 10–29.

———. "Cora Wilson Stewart and the Crusade against Illiteracy in Kentucky, 1916–1920." *Register of the Kentucky Historical Society* 82 (Spring 1984): 151–69.

Olson, James Stuart. *Herbert Hoover and the Reconstruction Finance Corporation, 1931–1933.* Ames: Iowa State University Press, 1977.

O'Neill, William L. *Everyone Was Brave: A History of Feminism in America.* Chicago: University of Illinois Press, 1971.

Pearce, John Ed. *Days of Darkness: The Feuds of Eastern Kentucky.* Lexington: University Press of Kentucky, 1994.

Peters, H. W. *History of Education in Kentucky, 1915–1940.* Frankfort, KY: Department of Education, 1940.

Pivar, David J. *Purity Crusade: Sexual Morality and Social Control, 1868–1900.* Westport, CT: Greenwood Press, 1973.

Raine, James Watt. *The Land of Saddle-bags: A Study of the Mountain People of Appalachia.* New York: Published jointly by the Council of Women for Home Missions and Missionary Education Movement of the United States and Canada, 1924.

Ramage, Thomas Warren. "Augustus Owsley Stanley: Early Twentieth Century Kentucky Democrat." Ph.D. diss., University of Kentucky, 1968.

Reck, Una Mae Lange, and Gregory C. Reck. "Living Is More Important Than Schooling: Schools and Self Concept in Appalachia." *Appalachian Journal* 27 (Winter 2000): 152–59.

Reynolds, Katherine C., and Susan L. Schramm. *A Separate Sisterhood: Women Who Shaped Southern Education in the Progressive Era.* New York: Peter Lang, 2002.

Riker, Francis Simrall. "Historical Sketches of Kentucky Federation of Women's Clubs: From Organization, 1894, through Administration Ending June, 1909." Unpublished manuscript. Louisville, KY: Kentucky Federation of Women's Clubs.

Rodgers, Daniel T. "In Search of Progressivism." *Reviews in American History* 10 (December 1982): 113–32.

Rowan County Historical Society. *Rowan County, Kentucky: A Pictorial History.* Paducah, KY: Turner, 2001.

Russell, Harvey C. *The Kentucky Negro Education Association, 1877–1946.* Norfolk, VA: Guide Quality Press, 1946.

Sadovnik, Alan R., and Susan F. Semel, eds. *Founding Mothers and Others: Women Educational Leaders during the Progressive Era.* New York: Palgrave, 2002.

Sanders, Elizabeth. *Roots of Reform: Farmers, Workers, and the American State, 1877–1917.* Chicago: University of Chicago Press, 1999.

Scott, Anne Firor. "After Suffrage: Southern Women in the Twenties." *Journal of Southern History* 30 (August 1964): 298–315.

———. *The Southern Lady: From Pedestal to Politics, 1830–1930.* Chicago: University of Chicago Press, 1970.

Scott, Roy V. *The Reluctant Farmer: The Rise of Agricultural Extension to 1914.* Urbana: University of Illinois Press, 1970.

Searles, P. David. *A College for Appalachia: Alice Lloyd on Caney Creek.* Lexington: University Press of Kentucky, 1995.

Seller, Maxine Schwartz, ed. *Women Educators in the United States, 1820–1993: A Bio-bibliographical Sourcebook.* Westport, CT: Greenwood Press, 1994.

Semple, Ellen Church. "The Anglo-Saxons of the Kentucky Mountains." *Bulletin of the American Geographical Society* 42 (August 1910): 565–93.

Sexton, Robert Fenimore. "Kentucky Politics and Society: 1919–1932." Ph.D. diss., University of Washington, 1970.

Shapiro, Henry. *Appalachia on Our Mind: The Southern Mountains and Mountaineers in American Consciousness, 1870–1920.* Chapel Hill: University of North Carolina Press, 1978.

Sims, Anastasia. *The Power of Femininity in the New South: Women's Organizations and Politics in North Carolina, 1880–1930.* Columbia: University of South Carolina Press, 1997.

Sklar, Kathryn Kish. *Catharine Beecher: A Study in American Domesticity.* New Haven, CT: Yale University Press, 1973.

———. "Two Political Cultures in the Progressive Era: The National Consumers' League and the American Association for Labor Legislation." In *U.S. History as Women's History: New Feminist Essays,* edited by Linda K. Kerber, Alice Kessler-Harris, and Kathryn Kish Sklar, 36–86. Chapel Hill: University of North Carolina Press, 1995.

Skocpol, Theda. "The Enactment of Mother's Pensions: Civic Mobilization and Agenda Setting or Benefits of the Ballot." *American Political Science Review* 89 (1995): 710–30.

———. *Protecting Soldiers and Mothers: The Political Origins of Social Policy in the United States.* Cambridge, MA: Belknap Press of Harvard University Press, 1992.

Skocpol, Theda, Marjorie Abend-Wein, Christopher Howard, and Susan Goodrich Lehman. "Women's Associations and the Enactment of Mothers' Pensions in the United States." *American Political Science Review* 87 (September 1993): 686–701.

Smith, George M. "The Opportunity Schools and Their Founder Wil Lou Gray." Booklet. Wil Lou Gray Opportunity School, August 2000.

Smith, Joan K. *Ella Flagg Young: Portrait of a Leader.* Ames, IA: Educational Studies Press, 1977.

———. "Progressive School Administration: Ella Flagg Young and the Chicago Schools, 1905–1915." *Journal of the Illinois State Historical Society* 73 (Spring 1980): 27–44.

Sprague, Stuart. *A Pictorial History of Eastern Kentucky.* Norfolk/Virginia Beach: Donning, 1986.

———. "The Rowan County Trouble: Anatomy of a Mountain Feud." *Mountain Review* 2, no. 4 (July 1976): 5–9.

Spruill, Marjorie Julian. *New Women of the New South: The Leaders of the Woman Suffrage Movement in the Southern States.* New York: Oxford University Press, 1993.

Stanton, Elizabeth Cady, Susan B. Anthony, Matilda Gage, and Ida Husted Harper, eds. *The History of Woman Suffrage.* 1881. Reprint, Rochester, NY: Arno Press, 1969.

Sticht, Thomas G. "The Rise of the Adult Education and Literacy System in the United States: 1600–2000." In *Annual Review of Adult Learning and Literacy.* Vol. 3. Edited by J. Comings, B. Garner, and C. Smith, 10–43. San Francisco: Jossey-Bass, 2002.

Stoddart, Jess. *Challenge and Change in Appalachia: The Story of the Hindman Settlement School.* Lexington: University Press of Kentucky, 2002.

Stubblefield, Harold W. "The Danish Folk High School and Its Reception in the United States: 1970s–1930s." Http://www.distance.syr.edu/stubblefield.html.

———. *Towards a History of Adult Education in America.* London: Croom Helm, 1988.

Stubblefield, Harold W., and Patrick Keane. *Adult Education in the American Experience: From the Colonial Period to the Present.* San Francisco: Jossey-Bass, 1994.

Tapp, Hambleton, and James C. Klotter. *Kentucky: Decades of Discord, 1865–1900.* Frankfort, KY: Kentucky Historical Society, 1977.

Theriot, Janice. *Tradition of Service: A History of the Kentucky Federation of Women's Clubs.* Louisville, KY: Kentucky Federation of Women's Clubs, 1994.

Thompson, Tommy R. "The Image of Appalachian Kentucky in American Popular Magazines." *Register of the Kentucky Historical Society* 91 (Spring 1993): 176–202.

Thurner, Manuela. "'Better Citizens without the Ballot': American Antisuffrage Women and Their Rationale during the Progressive Era." *Journal of Women's History* 5 (Spring 1993): 33–57.

Tice, Karen. "School-Work and Mother-Work: The Interplay of Maternalism and Cultural Politics in the Educational Narratives of Kentucky Settlement Workers, 1910–1930." *Journal of Appalachian Studies* 4 (Fall 1998): 191–224.

Tilley, Louise A., and Patricia Gurin, eds. *Women, Politics, and Change.* New York: Russell Sage Foundation, 1990.

Tindall, George Brown. *The Emergence of the New South, 1913–1945.* Baton Rouge: Louisiana State University Press, 1967.

Turner, William H., and Edward J. Cabbell, eds. *Blacks in Appalachia.* Lexington: University Press of Kentucky, 1985.

Tyack, David B. "Pilgrim's Progress: Toward a Social History of the School Superintendency, 1860–1960." *History of Education Quarterly* 16 (1976): 295–300.

———, ed. *Turning Points in American Educational History.* Waltham, MA: Blaisdell, 1967.

Tyack, David B., and Elisabeth Hansot. *Managers of Virtue: Public School Leadership in America, 1820–1980.* New York: Basic Books, 1982.

Van Dusen, Henry P. "Apostle to the Twentieth Century." *Atlantic Monthly,* July 1934, 1–24.

————. "The Oxford Group Movement: An Appraisal." *Atlantic Monthly,* August 1934, 240–52.

Waller, Altina. *Feud: Hatfields, McCoys, and Social Change in Appalachia, 1860–1900.* Chapel Hill: University of North Carolina Press, 1988.

Ward, Geoffrey C. *A First-Class Temperament: The Emergence of Franklin Roosevelt.* New York: Harper and Row, 1989.

Ward, William S. *A Literary History of Kentucky.* Knoxville: University of Tennessee Press, 1988.

Ware, Susan. *Beyond Suffrage: Women in the New Deal.* Cambridge, MA: Harvard University Press, 1981.

————. *Partner and I: Molly Dewson, Feminism, and New Deal Politics.* New Haven, CT: Yale University Press, 1987.

Weiler, Kathleen. *Women Teaching for Change: Gender, Class and Power.* Edited by Paulo Freire and Henry A. Giroux. South Hadley, MA: Bergin and Garvey, 1988.

Weiss, Bernard J., ed. *American Education and the European Immigrant: 1840–1940.* Urbana: University of Illinois Press, 1982.

Wesley, Edgar Bruce. *NEA: The First Hundred Years: The Building of the Teaching Profession.* New York: Harper and Row, 1957.

Whisnant, David E. *All That Is Native and Fine: The Politics of Culture in an American Region.* Chapel Hill: University of North Carolina Press, 1983.

White, William Allen. *The Autobiography of William Allen White.* New York: Macmillan, 1946.

Wiebe, Robert H. *The Search for Order, 1877–1920.* New York: Hill and Wang, 1967.

Williams, T. Harry. *Huey Long.* New York: Knopf, 1960.

Wilson, Joan Hoff. *Herbert Hoover: Forgotten Progressive.* Boston: Little, Brown, 1975.

Wilson, Shannon H. "Window on the Mountains: Berea's Appalachia, 1870–1930." *Filson Club History Quarterly* 64 (July 1990): 384–99.

Winston, Sanfor. *Illiteracy in the United States.* Chapel Hill: University of North Carolina Press, 1930.

Wolfe, Margaret Ripley. *Daughters of Canaan: A Saga of Southern Women.* Lexington: University Press of Kentucky, 1995.

Woloch, Nancy. *Women and the American Experience.* 2nd ed. New York: McGraw-Hill, 1994.

Woodward, C. Vann. *Origins of the New South, 1877–1913.* Baton Rouge: Louisiana State University Press, 1951.

Index